THE VARIETIES OF ATHEISM

The Varieties of Atheism

Connecting Religion and Its Critics

EDITED BY

David Newheiser

THE UNIVERSITY OF CHICAGO PRESS
CHICAGO AND LONDON

The University of Chicago Press, Chicago 60637
The University of Chicago Press, Ltd., London
© 2022 by The University of Chicago
All rights reserved. No part of this book may be used or
reproduced in any manner whatsoever without written
permission, except in the case of brief quotations in critical
articles and reviews. For more information, contact the
University of Chicago Press, 1427 E. 60th St., Chicago, IL 60637.
Published 2022
Printed in the United States of America

31 30 29 28 27 26 25 24 23 22   1 2 3 4 5

ISBN-13: 978-0-226-82267-9 (cloth)
ISBN-13: 978-0-226-82269-3 (paper)
ISBN-13: 978-0-226-82268-6 (e-book)
DOI: https://doi.org/10.7208/chicago/9780226822686.001.0001

LCCN: 2022017521

♾ This paper meets the requirements of ANSI/NISO Z39.48-1992
(Permanence of Paper).

CONTENTS

INTRODUCTION
The Genealogy of Atheism
David Newheiser
1

1
ATHEISM AND SCIENCE
On Einstein's "Cosmic Religious Sense"
Mary-Jane Rubenstein
19

2
ATHEISM AND SOCIETY
Hume's Prefiguration of Rorty
Andre C. Willis
41

3
ATHEISM AND POWER
Nietzsche, Nominalism, and the Reductive Spirit
Denys Turner
65

4
ATHEISM AND ETHICS
Recovering the Link between Truth and Transformation
Susannah Ticciati
85

5
ATHEISM AND METAPHYSICS
A Problem of Apophatic Theology
Henning Tegtmeyer
106

6
ATHEISM AND POLITICS
Abandonment, Absence, and the Empty Throne
Devin Singh
129

7
ATHEISM AND LITERATURE
Living without God in Dante's Comedy
Vittorio Montemaggi
155

8
ATHEISM AND THE AFFIRMATION OF LIFE
Dostoevsky's Response to Russian Nihilism
George Pattison
175

AFTERWORD
The Drama of Atheism
Constance M. Furey
199

Acknowledgments 203
Contributors 205
Index 209

INTRODUCTION

The Genealogy of Atheism

David Newheiser

Over the past fifty years religious identification has declined in many parts of the world. Although sociologists and scholars of religion have extensively studied secularization (seen as a social phenomenon), they have had less to say about atheism (understood as a personal identity).[1] Nevertheless, since forging a nonreligious life matters to many people, other commentators have written a great deal on the topic. Philosophers and public figures weigh the evidence for and against theistic belief, and this debate reverberates in community groups, conferences, and social media channels. Unfortunately, for all its vigor, this conversation tends to reflect a stereotyped understanding of religion, and as a result its vision of atheism is similarly two-dimensional. In response, this collection draws on the academic study of religion to demonstrate that atheism is more diverse (and therefore more interesting) than many acknowledge.

This introduction frames the essays that follow by developing a brief genealogy of atheism—from premodern Europe to the present. Atheism today is widely associated with the New Atheists, a group of commentators who claim that religion is irrational, unscientific, and morally corrosive. In order to justify the view that religion and atheism are squarely opposed, the New Atheists define them as competing hypotheses concerning the existence of a divine being. Although scholarly writing is generally less polemical, Anglophone philosophers tend to share the assumption that atheism and theism are incompatible beliefs. This reinforces the widespread impression that religious and nonreligious people are irredeemably at odds.

In response, I argue that defining atheism in terms of belief misrepresents its multiplicity. Just as scholars of religious studies have argued that it is misleading to equate religion with belief, the history of atheism makes clear that it is not simply a cognitive commitment—on the contrary, atheism incorporates ethical disciplines, cultural practices, and affective states. Against this background, these essays explore the complex relations of sympathy and resistance that connect particular atheisms with particular religious traditions. By developing a textured understanding of atheism's meaning and motivation, this collection opens new possibilities for conversation between those who are religious and those who are not.

ATHEISM AS HYPOTHESIS

Atheism has been subject to intense interest throughout the modern era, but it flashed into prominence fifteen years ago thanks to the New Atheists. Against the claim that religion and empirical science concern distinct dimensions of human life, these writers portrayed theism as a competitor to scientific explanation. As Richard Dawkins put it, "'The God Hypothesis' is a scientific hypothesis about the universe, which should be analysed as sceptically as any other."[2] At a time of growing anxiety about the danger posed by fundamentalist religious groups, this claim caught the popular imagination. In contrast to violent superstition, the New Atheists promised the dispassionate clarity of scientific knowledge.

The four books that inaugurated this movement each insists that fundamentalists are the true representatives of religion. Sam Harris opens *The End of Faith* by arguing that religious moderates abandon the clear teachings of their tradition to accommodate the norms of modern culture; according to Harris, the nature of religion is best expressed by extremists.[3] Christopher Hitchens begins *God Is Not Great* by dismissing the "nebulous humanism" of some theologians as ersatz religion.[4] In *Breaking the Spell* Daniel Dennett acknowledges that some religious adherents see practices like prayer as symbolic, but he claims that these people are not really religious: in his view, to be religious is to solicit the intervention of a superpowered agent.[5] As for Dawkins, the first chapter of *The God Delusion* explains that the transcendent wonder of some scientists is not religious, for religion is distinguished not by reverence but by an unscientific belief in supernatural events.[6]

The enthusiasm with which the New Atheists discount religious diversity suggests that they need fundamentalism as a foil. In fact, some religious communities embrace scientific inquiry and condemn violence done in the name of religion, but their existence complicates the distinction between atheistic rationality and religious dogma. Perhaps for this reason, the New Atheists focus on those with whom their differences are especially stark. Where the fundamentalist defenders of religion portray unbelief as the source of social ills, the New Atheists argue that the opposite is true, but both sides agree that religion and modernity are incompatible.

Because the New Atheists dismiss theological moderation, some commentators argue that they criticize a stereotype of religion.[7] What is more surprising is that, despite their status as the most prominent representatives of atheism today, their conception of atheism is similarly impoverished. In their view, religion is simply bad science, a set of beliefs that can be falsified through empirical observation. Although they worry about the behaviors that follow from religious beliefs, they see belief as the source of the problem, and so their solution is to replace irrational faith with scientific understanding. Depicting religion as a set of quasi-scientific assertions allows the New Atheists to claim that theism and atheism are incompatible hypotheses. However, just as religious practice is enormously diverse, there is reason to suspect that atheism is more varied than this dichotomy allows.

ATHEISM AS BELIEF

The scholarly literature on atheism is generally more measured than the public-facing debate, but it rests on similar assumptions.[8] In his classic essay "Why I Am Not a Christian" (1927), Bertrand Russell writes:

> Religion is based, I think, primarily and mainly upon fear. . . . Fear is the parent of cruelty, and therefore it is no wonder if cruelty and religion has gone hand-in-hand. It is because fear is at the basis of those two things. In this world we can now begin a little to understand things, and a little to master them by help of science, which has forced its way step by step against the Christian religion, against the Churches, and against the opposition of all the old precepts. Science can help us to get over this craven fear in which mankind has lived for so many generations.[9]

Russell's essay predates *The God Delusion* by eighty years, but its conceptual structure is remarkably similar. According to Russell, religion is fundamentally about belief, and the beliefs it requires are incompatible with scientific inquiry. In his view, religion suppressed progress throughout Western history, but science has come to dispel the ignorance on which dogma depends. Dawkins and Russell agree that religion obstructs moral progress, and they both claim that it only persists through the indoctrination of children.[10]

Like the New Atheists, Russell identifies religion with its most rigid adherents, and when he speaks of "religion" he seems to have Christianity mainly in mind. In his account, where modern Christians affirm claims that are suspiciously moderate, those in the past were clear in condemning unbelievers to damnation. "In those days," he says, "if a man said that he was a Christian it was known what he meant."[11] Although Russell thinks it is inhumane to say that some people are destined to everlasting punishment, he prefers to engage Christians who believe in a literal hell—after all, this is what allows him to argue that "the whole conception of God is a conception derived from the ancient Oriental despotisms."[12] Some Christians reject literalism for theological reasons, but Russell discounts such subtleties on the grounds that religion requires "definite belief."[13]

Following Russell, Anglophone philosophy has continued to define atheism in terms of belief. Anthony Flew's *God and Philosophy* (1966) focuses on the reasons given for belief in the Christian God, and it takes literalist Christianity as representative (without considering progressive Christianity, which Flew dismisses).[14] According to Flew, theological speech is intended as a statement of fact, but it fails to meet the standard of verification established by the physical sciences.[15] He writes: "In the sciences there is no doubt at all but that progress is possible. With a scientific hypothesis you can know where you stand. . . . The same does not appear to apply with the more sophisticated theistic statements."[16] Flew argues that talk about God is either empty or false, and so he concludes that there is no reason to accept what he calls "the religious hypothesis."[17]

Many defenders of religion agree that belief is the central question. In *The Existence of God* (1979) Richard Swinburne argues that belief in God's existence provides a causal explanation for a number of widely observable phenomena, including the existence of the universe and moral awareness.[18] Like Russell and Flew, Swinburne claims that religious beliefs should be seen as statements about the world, but unlike them he thinks theistic propositions are consistent with scientific explanation.[19] Where Swinburne gathers evidence, Alvin Plantinga's *Warranted Christian Belief* (2000) argues that Christian claims do not require argument to be rationally justified.[20] Yet although Plantinga's strategy differs from Swinburne's, both philosophers see religious beliefs as literal rather than symbolic, and they both suggest that the debate between atheism and Christianity hinges on the justification of propositional claims.[21]

In *The Oxford Handbook of Atheism* (2013) Stephan Bullivant provides a definition that is widely taken for granted: "'Atheism' is defined as an absence of belief in the existence of a God or gods."[22] Bullivant acknowledges that the term *atheism* is sometimes used in other ways, but he argues that it is necessary to stipulate a single meaning to avoid devolving into "contradictions and cross-purposes." This makes it possible to present theism and atheism as systems that are squarely opposed. However, such clarity comes at a cost. By defining atheism in terms of belief, the prevailing consensus is detached from the diversity of atheism as it actually exists.

ATHEISM AS ACCUSATION

The English word *atheist* derives from the Greek *atheos*, which applies a privative prefix (*a-*) to the word for "god" (*theos*). As this construction suggests, the meaning of *atheist* shifts depending upon the *theos* to which it is opposed. In Greek antiquity the term generally named those who were godless insofar as they lived as if there are no divine laws. The philosopher Socrates was famously accused of atheism in this sense. His opponents complained that "he does not believe in the gods of the state, and has other new divinities of his own."[23] Under Roman rule, second-century Christians such as Justin Martyr were also said to be *atheos*. Like Socrates, Christians believed in some form of divinity, but they were considered godless because they did not live according to polytheistic standards of piety.[24]

Modern commentators sometimes distinguish between theoretical and practical atheism, believing that there are no gods and acting as if there are no gods, but ancient authors saw the two as inseparable. In the second century CE, Theophilus of Antioch defended Christians against the charge of atheism by insisting that they are not cannibals.[25] With modern categories in mind, this seems strange. (Cannibalism has no connection with atheism as most understand it today.) However, because Theophilus and his opponents both presumed that godless beliefs and godless behavior go together, they agree that cannibalism would count as evidence of impiety. Rather than defining atheism in terms of belief, premodern Europeans understood it as a holistic phenomenon that includes ethics, aesthetics, and more.

The term *atheist* migrated from ancient Greek to modern languages in the sixteenth century. In this period Protestant and Catholic Christians frequently hurled the accusation at each other. Théophile Gautier comments, "Two savants and two theologians could not dispute without accusing each other reciprocally of sodomy and atheism."[26] In the seventeenth century the Catholic apologist François Garasse attributed atheism to a diverse group of people—including ancient philosophers such as Epicurus and Diogenes, biblical figures such as Nimrod and Cain, and Protestants like John Calvin and Martin Luther (who Garasse calls "a perfect atheist").[27] According to Garasse, it is impossible for a person to believe that there is no God, and in any case, many of the atheists he lists believed in the Christian God in particular. In this context *atheism* named a godlessness that is primarily moral.

This understanding of atheism continued into the early modern period. In eighteenth-century France a priest named Guillaume was arrested on the accusation that he was an atheist. Upon examination by a theological expert, he was judged to have made unsound claims concerning the nature of God's ideas about created beings—a question that is hardly central to Christian doctrine. Despite this indiscretion, Guillaume's examiner noted that "one could not accuse someone of impiety who has lost his way in matters so abstract, unless one found other proofs of his corrupted sentiments."[28] On this view, heterodox opinions were not enough to make one an atheist. In the end, the unfortunate Guillaume was convicted not for his beliefs but because of "the manifest debauchery and libertinism of his morals" (including, crucially, jokes on the topic of religion).[29]

From ancient Greece to early modern France, *atheist* was an accusation directed toward one's opponents rather than an identity to be claimed for oneself. At this point, however, the figure of the atheist finally took flesh. Philosophers such as Denis Diderot and Paul-Henri d'Holbach were among the first to call themselves atheists, and a century later the practice was suddenly widespread. Some historians argue that this development brought to light a current of unbelief that had been hidden until then.[30] As they observe, people have long held beliefs that diverged from the orthodoxy dominant in a particular place, and such dissent was sometimes suppressed. Nevertheless, to refer to these dissidents as atheists is misleading. It is only in the modern period that atheism and religion came to be equated with propositional belief; in premodern Europe a different network of concepts was in play.[31] For this reason, the emergence of atheism as an avowed identity transformed the term's significance.

ATHEISM AND RELIGION

Although some claim that rational unbelief and religious credulity have always been in conflict, the story of atheism is stranger than this suggests. In fact, people came to call themselves *atheist* through a series of cultural shifts motivated in part by dynamics at work within religious traditions. In the wake of the Protestant Reformation, some Christians began to seek a justification for their preferred form of Christianity in objective phenomena. Initially, this allowed each side to claim support from the newly emerging sciences, but the eventual result was that religious commitment became subordinated to empirical investigation. Whereas premodern Christians had argued that divine transcendence is invisible and inscrutable, some early modern theologians made God into an empirical hypothesis that was finally rendered superfluous.[32]

The vaunted conflict between religion and science originated in the course of this theological development. Medieval Christians understood *scientia* as an intellectual habit and *religio* as a moral habit.[33] On this understanding there could be no contradiction between *religio* and *scientia*, for they are not the same sort of thing. In the modern period, however, both science and religion came to be seen as bodies of objective knowledge that make propositional statements which are sometimes at odds. Where premodern *religion* referred to a piety that was independent of a single tradition, people began to speak of *religions* in the plural, each of which was seen as a system of doctrinal claims. Through the objectifying tendency of the time, religion and science were made to signify the opposite of what they once meant, and in the process a new attitude became possible—the rejection of religion on scientific grounds.[34]

These shifts in intellectual culture contributed to the development of atheism as an identity, but they are not enough to explain it. Alec Ryrie describes a seventeenth-century crisis of faith that was primarily affective.[35] Ryrie focuses on Protestant Europe, where some Christians expressed anger at the hypocrisy of the church while others felt a deep anxiety about the erosion of doctrinal certainties. In his analysis, this emotional ferment gave force to a moral critique of Christian commitment. The complaint was initially levied by one set of Christians against others, but it eventually blossomed into the explicit atheism of later centuries. Although some people in this period claimed that particular Christian beliefs were irrational, according to Ryrie the argument was motivated by morality and emotion rather than rationality alone.

Like the critics of Christianity that Ryrie describes, many nineteenth-century atheists drew on Christian thought in order to criticize Christianity. Ludwig Feuerbach, for instance, argued that God is a projection that functions to reinforce earthly power. By denying God any existence apart from human culture, Feuerbach dealt a serious blow to religious commitment, and he encouraged others to conclude that religion is a tool of political oppression. Feuerbach is therefore an important source for later atheism, and yet his critique of religion arose from a moral sensibility that was informed by Christianity.[36] Feuerbach was raised as a Lutheran, and he cited Luther hundreds of times—even referring to himself at one point as "Luther II."[37] Like Luther, Feuerbach's outrage at the complacency of many Christians was motivated by his concern for the values they espouse. It would be misleading to say that atheism is simply a form of heterodox Christianity (as some Christians imply), but Feuerbach exemplifies the way in which atheism often draws upon the traditions to which it responds.[38]

Because Feuerbach's atheism is driven by a passionate moral sensitivity, it cannot be reduced to the absence of belief in the existence of a God or gods. The same is true of other exemplars of nineteenth-century atheism: Friedrich Nietzsche, Karl Marx, Elizabeth Cady Stanton, Frederick Douglass, Percy Shelley, Hypatia Bonner, Mikhail Bakunin, and the Marquis de Sade.[39] These writers did reject religious beliefs, but that was not the sum—or even the focus—of their critique of religion. Some of them were concerned with the authority of science while others directed their attention toward ethics, politics, and aesthetics. Some attacked religion in declarative prose, and others sought to unsettle through poetry, fiction, memoir, and song. Modern atheism differs from its ancient precursors insofar as it became an identity people claimed for themselves rather than an accusation made by others. In both cases, however, atheism concerns motivations that run deeper than reason.[40]

ATHEISM IN PLURAL

This brief genealogy indicates that defining atheism in terms of belief obscures the cultural shifts through which modern atheism emerged, and it flattens the diversity of atheism in particular times and places. I have sought to show that atheism is instead a polyphonic assemblage that develops in conversation with religious traditions.[41] Despite its association with the cool light of reason, atheism is motivated by curiosity, defiance, delight, anxiety, anger, skepticism, and sympathy.[42] In each case it reflects the particularities of context, whether that context is European (as in the history I have sketched) or otherwise (as atheism grows increasingly global). To understand atheism it is therefore necessary to attend to the intersecting lines of affinity and resistance that connect particular atheisms with particular religious traditions.

My approach in this introduction reconsiders atheism using methods honed in the academic study of religion. Scholars such as Talal Asad argue that the modern concept of religion was invented in seventeenth-century Europe alongside a novel conception of the state as secular. Although these terms have become so familiar that we tend to take their meaning for granted, Asad and others have shown that they are far from neutral. Asad explains: "Defining what is religion is not merely an abstract intellectual exercise.... The act of defining (or redefining) religion is embedded in passionate disputes; it is connected with anxieties and satisfactions, it is affected by changing conceptions of knowledge and interest, and it is related to institutional disciplines."[43] By examining the genealogy of concepts such as religion, scholars of religion bring to light the hidden architecture of our self-understanding, thereby enabling us to think, feel, and work in new ways.[44]

To take a key example, religion today is often defined in terms of the cognitive commitments held voluntarily by individuals. As Asad and others have argued, both the definition of religion in terms of belief and the conception of belief in cognitive terms derives from one side in an old intra-Christian debate.[45] Insofar as it imposes a Protestant perspective, this vision of religion makes it harder to recognize other traditions on their own terms. Because it is enshrined in the legal systems of many Western societies, it has also disadvantaged groups (for instance, Muslims and Roman Catholics) that locate their identity in public, communal practice rather than the private realm of personal conviction.[46] Against this background, scholars of religion attend in detail to particular religious traditions while questioning the concepts that structure our imagination and our institutions.

This introduction has traced the genealogy of atheism in order to suggest that—just as religion encompasses ritual practice, moral formation, and more—atheism is not merely a matter of belief. The essays that follow develop this approach in detail. Since the history of atheism has generally centered on debates within and against Christianity, this collection focuses (though not exclusively) on the relationship between atheism and Christian traditions. The contributors look back, situating atheism in historical perspective, and they look forward, imagining a way past the dilemmas that dominate the existing literature. By untangling the stereotypes that characterize common accounts of European atheism, they open a space for a richer conversation to emerge—one that attends to the distinctiveness of atheisms emerging in other places.[47]

Each chapter addresses an issue with broad significance for the study of atheism, but each is animated by the glint of its author's particular curiosity. There are important differences among the group—regarding their normative attitude toward religious traditions, the relative priority of concepts and practices, and the need (or not) for metaphysical foundations. This diversity enables a shared set of interests to emerge—concerning contemplation, community, culture, humility, negativity, life, love, poetry, and protest. By bracketing the timeworn debate over the existence of God, this collection suggests that even passionate disputes can evolve beyond the grooves established by long-standing habit.

THE STRUCTURE OF THIS COLLECTION

The contents of this collection are organized into three broad groups. The first set of chapters develops an expanded understanding of atheism by revisiting three influential examples: Albert Einstein (in the twentieth century), Friedrich Nietzsche (in the nineteenth century), and David Hume (in the eighteenth century). In chapter 1, Mary-Jane Rubenstein reconsiders the relationship between atheism and science through the lens of Einstein's pantheism. Although Einstein was seen as an atheist by many of his contemporaries, Rubenstein suggests that his sense of the divinity of the cosmos complicates theism and atheism alike. In chapter 2, Andre Willis situates atheism as a social practice that has profound practical effects. Whereas statements of religious belief and unbelief are often evaluated as abstract theoretical claims, Willis's reading of Hume indicates that such utterances should be interpreted in terms of their pragmatic implications. And in chapter 3, Denys Turner draws upon Nietzsche to argue that a truly consistent atheism requires not simply a shift in belief but social transformation.

The second set of chapters asks how religious and nonreligious communities can better engage each other. In chapter 4, Susannah Ticciati argues that the debate over atheism has minimized the crucial role of ethics. Because she is herself a theologian, Ticciati is invested in theological claims, but she takes conversation with atheists as an opportunity to learn how to do Christian theology better. In chapter 5, Henning Tegtmeyer argues that Christian thought requires clarity on the question of metaphysics if it is to engage atheism productively. To avoid collapsing the distinction between atheism and theism, Tegtmeyer suggests that Christian theology ought to make claims that can be adjudicated by rational argument. Although Ticciati and Tegtmeyer offer contrasting visions, they both suggest that the conversation between atheism and Christianity would benefit from a new beginning.

The third set of chapters explores the unstable boundary between atheism and religious commitment. In chapter 6, Devin Singh takes atheism as an interpretive tool to highlight the ambivalence of Christian faith. Where protest atheism underscores the absence of a divine king who provides justice to all, Singh suggests that Christians can accept Jesus's absence as a sign that all sovereignty is suspect. In chapter 7, Vittorio Montemaggi asks what atheism might mean in the context of literature, which works through evocation and narrative rather than propositional assertion. In his reading, rather than condemning atheism, the medieval poet Dante Alighieri suggests that atheists and Christians might be able to recognize an unexpected affinity with each other. In chapter 8, George Pattison argues that the nineteenth-century novelist Fyodor Dostoevsky presents complex characters who struggle between atheism and faith. In this sense, Pattison suggests, Dostoevsky eludes the overly neat divisions that define the debate over atheism today.

In a concluding coda, Constance Furey traces atheism's affective resonance as it appears in each chapter—from the cool mood of Hume's communal inquiry to Nietzsche's revolutionary fire. As she describes, the drama of atheism depends on its capacity to unsettle and inspire. In keeping with this insight, these essays are driven not only by theoretical debates but by questions that resonate with the visceral energy of actual lives.

VARIETIES

In his classic book *The Varieties of Religious Experience*, William James distinguishes between institutional and individual religion: "Churches, when once established, live at secondhand upon tradition; but the founders of every church owed their power originally to the fact of their direct personal communion with the divine."[48] Without endorsing James's account of religious experience, this collection expands on his intuition that religious traditions cannot be reduced to the doctrinal statements made by ecclesiastical leaders.

Although James says relatively little about the varieties of nonreligious experience, he notes at one point that "the more fervent opponents of Christian doctrine have often enough shown a temper which, psychologically considered, is indistinguishable from religious zeal."[49] Read quickly, this sounds like a criticism, but in context it can be seen as a commendation. Whatever James himself thought about atheism, he implies that it is just as vibrant and diverse as religious commitment.

Those who define atheism in terms of belief often acknowledge that it has extracognitive implications. On this view, the theoretical conviction that a divine being does not exist might go on to influence the unbeliever's attitudes regarding ethics, politics, aesthetics, and so forth. The present collection explores a radical alternative: in keeping with James's understanding of religion, it suggests that atheistic affects and practices may be the cause (rather than the effect) of atheistic beliefs. Just as James sought to unsettle the tendency to identify religion with the pronouncements of its official representatives, these essays show that atheism is constituted by a complex network of which belief is only a part.

James offers a compelling account of the connection between thinking and the rest of life. He writes, "I do believe that feeling is the deeper source of religion, and that philosophic and theological formulas are secondary products, like translations of a text into another tongue."[50] Discursive claims are clearly important, but I think James is right that they express impulses that precede and exceed conscious thought. He continues a little later, "There is in the living act of perception always something that glimmers and twinkles and will not be caught, and for which reflection comes too late."[51] Rather than cutting atheism to a convenient size, each of these essays attends to an energy that evades easy encapsulation. This spark, I suggest, is what gives atheism its glimmering variety.

NOTES

1. For examples of the emerging literature on atheism by sociologists and scholars of religion, see Lois Lee, *Recognizing the Non-Religious: Reimagining the Secular* (Oxford: Oxford University Press, 2015); Jerome P. Baggett, *The Varieties of Nonreligious Experience: Atheism in American Culture* (New York: New York University Press, 2019); Hannah K. Scheidt, *Practicing Atheism: Culture, Media, and Ritual in the Contemporary Atheist Network* (New York: Oxford University Press, 2021).
2. Richard Dawkins, *The God Delusion* (London: Bantam Press, 2006), 2.
3. Sam Harris, *The End of Faith: Religion, Terror, and the Future of Reason* (New York: Free, 2004), 18–23.
4. Christopher Hitchens, *God Is Not Great: How Religion Poisons Everything* (New York: Twelve Books, 2007), 7.
5. Daniel Clement Dennett, *Breaking the Spell: Religion as a Natural Phenomenon* (London: Allen Lane, 2006), 10.
6. Dawkins, *The God Delusion*, 13–15.
7. See John Gray, *Seven Types of Atheism* (New York: Farrar, Straus, and Giroux), 2018.
8. In contrast to the Anglophone focus on scientific authority, European philosophers such as Jacques Derrida and Jean-Luc Nancy have considered atheism in connection with the ambiguities of history and personal experience. See Jacques Derrida, "Christianity and Secularization," trans. David Newheiser, *Critical Inquiry* 47, no. 1 (September 1, 2020): 138–48; Jean-Luc Nancy, *Dis-Enclosure: The Deconstruction of Christianity*, trans. Gabriel Malenfant, Michael B. Smith, and Bettina Bergo (New York: Fordham University Press, 2008). I have offered my own contribution to this conversation in David Newheiser, "Derrida and the Danger of Religion," *Journal of the American Academy of Religion* 86, no. 1 (2018): 42–61.
9. Bertrand Russell, *Why I Am Not a Christian: And Other Essays on Religion and Related Subjects* (London: Routledge, 2005), 18.
10. Russell., 17, 10.
11. Russell, 2.
12. Russell, 13, 18.
13. On Christian alternatives to biblical literalism, see (among many others) Origen of Alexandria, *Origen: On First Principles*, ed. John Behr (Oxford: Oxford University Press, 2018); David C. Steinmetz, "The Superiority of Pre-Critical Exegesis," *Theology Today* 37, no. 1 (April 1, 1980): 27–38.
14. Anthony Garrard Newton Flew, *God & Philosophy* (London: Routledge & K. Paul, 1966), 15–17.
15. Flew, 21–22; also see 171–72.
16. Flew, 21.

17. Flew, 170, 194.
18. Richard Swinburne, *The Existence of God* (Oxford, UK: Clarendon Press, 2004), 23, 49, 328.
19. Richard Swinburne, *The Coherence of Theism* (Oxford, UK: Clarendon Press, 1977), 88–96.
20. Alvin Plantinga, *Warranted Christian Belief* (New York: Oxford University Press, 2000).
21. It is worth making explicit that the most prominent partisans and opponents of atheism today are white men. This is another way in which (as I go on to argue) the discussion of atheism today is overly narrow. For more on the relation between atheism, gender, and race, see Anja Finger, "Four Horsemen (and a Horsewoman): What Gender Is New Atheism?," in *New Atheism: Critical Perspectives and Contemporary Debates*, ed. Christopher R. Cotter, Philip Andrew Quadrio, and Jonathan Tuckett (New York: Springer, 2017), 155–70; Tina Beattie, *The New Atheists: The Twilight of Reason and the War on Religion* (London: Darton, Longman and Todd, 2008); Anthony B. Pinn, *Humanism: Essays on Race, Religion, and Cultural Production* (New York: Bloomsbury, 2015); Nathan G. Alexander, *Race in a Godless World: Atheism, Race, and Civilization, 1850–1914* (New York: New York University Press, 2019).
22. Stephen Sebastian Bullivant, "Defining 'Atheism,'" in *The Oxford Handbook of Atheism*, ed. Stephen Sebastian Bullivant and Michael Ruse (Oxford: Oxford University Press, 2015).
23. Plato, *Euthyphro; Apology; Crito; Phaedo*, trans. Benjamin Jowett (Amherst, NY: Prometheus Books, 1988).
24. D. W. Palmer, "Atheism, Apologetic, and Negative Theology in the Greek Apologists of the Second Century," *Vigiliae Christianae* 37, no. 3 (1983): 234–59.
25. Theophilus of Antioch, "Theophilus to Autolycus," in *Ante-Nicene Fathers*, vol. 2, ed. Alexander Roberts, James Donaldson, and A. Cleveland Coxe (Buffalo, NY: Christian Literature Publishing, 1885). As a defensive maneuver, Theophilus argues that his pagan opponents are the real atheistic people eaters. See chapter 5, "Philosophers Inculcate Cannibalism," in the same volume.
26. Théophile Gautier, *Les grotesques* (Paris: M. Lévy, 1853), 71, qtd. in Alan Charles Kors, *Atheism in France, 1650–1729* (Princeton, NJ: Princeton University Press, 2016), 1:20.
27. François Garasse, *La doctrine curieuse des beaux esprits de ce temps, ou prétendus tels contenant plusieurs maximes pernicieuses à l'État, à la religion et aux bonnes moeurs* (Paris: Chappelet, 1623), 42, qtd. in Kors, *Atheism in France, 1650–1729*, 1:29–30.
28. François Ravaisson, *Archives de La Bastille: Documents inédits* (Paris, 1866), 14:197–201; Kors, *Atheism in France, 1650–1729*, 1:11–12.
29. Ravaisson, *Archives de La Bastille*, 14:221–22; Kors, *Atheism in France, 1650–1729*, 1:12.
30. E.g., David Wootton, "New Histories of Atheism," in *Atheism from the Reformation to the Enlightenment*, ed. David Wootton and Michael Hunter (Oxford: Oxford University Press, 1992), 13–53.
31. For a compelling defense of this view, see Dorothea Weltecke, "Beyond Religion: On the Lack of Belief during the Central and Late Middle Ages," in *Religion and Its Other: Secular and Sacral Concepts and Practices in Interaction*, ed. Heike Bock

and Jörg Feuchter (Frankfurt am Main: Campus Verlag, 2008), 101–14; Dorothea Weltecke, "L'athéisme et le doute au Moyen Âge: Un problème controversé," *Revue de l'Histoire des Religions*, no. 3 (September 1, 2015): 339–61.

32. For an influential exemplar of the premodern view, see Pseudo-Dionysius the Areopagite, *Pseudo-Dionysius: The Complete Works*, trans. Colm Luibhéid, Classics of Western Spirituality (New York: Paulist Press, 1987). I discuss this tradition in detail in David Newheiser, *Hope in a Secular Age: Deconstruction, Negative Theology, and the Future of Faith* (Cambridge University Press, 2019).

33. Peter Harrison discusses this development in two masterful books: *Religion and the Religions in the English Enlightenment* (Cambridge: Cambridge University Press, 2002); and *The Territories of Science and Religion* (Chicago: University of Chicago Press, 2015).

34. There is reason to think that neither religion nor science is as objective as each is sometimes taken to be. Lorraine Daston writes: "Because science in our culture has come to exemplify rationality and facticity, to suggest that science depends in essential ways upon highly specific constellations of emotions and values has the air of proposing a paradox.... I will nonetheless claim that not only does science have what I will call a moral economy (indeed, several); these moral economies are moreover constitutive of those features conventionally (and, to my mind, correctly) deemed most characteristic of science as a way of knowing." Lorraine Daston, "The Moral Economy of Science," *Osiris* 10 (1995): 3.

35. Alec Ryrie, *Unbelievers: An Emotional History of Doubt* (Cambridge, MA: Harvard University Press, 2019), 137.

36. For more on the moral motivations of atheists such as Feuerbach, see Dominic Erdozain, *The Soul of Doubt: The Religious Roots of Unbelief from Luther to Marx* (New York: Oxford University Press, 2015), chap. 6.

37. Wilhelm Bolin, *Ludwig Feuerbach: Sein Wirken und seine Zeitgenossen* (Stuttgart, 1891), 58, qtd. in Christy L. Flanagan, "The Paradox of Feuerbach: Luther and Religious Naturalism" (PhD diss., Florida State University, 2009).

38. Conversely, Feuerbach claims that "atheism... is the secret of religion itself"—on this view, religious fidelity may lead inexorably toward atheism. Ludwig Andreas Feuerbach, *The Essence of Christianity* (New York: Prometheus Books, 1989), xxvi.

39. Graham Oppy includes these figures in a list of 112 nineteenth-century atheists provided in his introduction to *A Companion to Atheism and Philosophy*, ed. Graham Robert Oppy (Oxford, UK: Wiley Blackwell, 2019), 7–8. However, quite a few of these figures (as well as Feuerbach himself) explicitly disavowed the label of atheism; by their own account, their critique only applied to certain forms of religion rather than to religion as such. This offers another example of the way in which the prevailing consensus flattens the complexity of historical experience by filtering everything through a manufactured dichotomy between theism and atheism (understood, according to Oppy, as a worldview).

40. Stephen LeDrew argues that the New Atheism is likewise motivated by political commitments rather than science alone. Stephen LeDrew, *The Evolution of Atheism: The Politics of a Modern Movement* (New York: Oxford University Press, 2016), 2. Susannah Ticciati develops a similar argument in her contribution to this collection.

41. For anthropologists such as Anna Tsing, the term *assemblage* names a formation that is constituted by shifting relationships (rather than a stable ontology).

Tsing writes: "In contrast to the unified harmonies and rhythms of rock, pop, or classical music, to appreciate polyphony one must listen both to the separate melody lines and their coming together in unexpected moments of harmony or dissonance. In just this way, to appreciate the assemblage, one must attend to its separate ways of being at the same time as watching how they come together in sporadic but consequential coordinations. Furthermore, in contrast to the predictability of a written piece of music that can be repeated over and over, the polyphony of the assemblage shifts as conditions change. This is the listening practice that this section of the book attempts to instill." Anna Lowenhaupt Tsing, *The Mushroom at the End of the World: On the Possibility of Life in Capitalist Ruins* (Princeton, NJ: Princeton University Press, 2015), 158.

42. See Lauren Berlant: "The seeming detachment of rationality, for example, is not a detachment at all, but an emotional style associated normatively with a rhetorical practice." Lauren Berlant, *Cruel Optimism* (Durham, NC: Duke University Press, 2011), 27.

43. Talal Asad, "Thinking about Religion, Belief, and Politics," in *The Cambridge Companion to Religious Studies*, ed. Robert A. Orsi, Cambridge Companions to Religion (Cambridge: Cambridge University Press, 2011), 37; see also Talal Asad, *Secular Translations: Nation-State, Modern Self, and Calculative Reason* (New York: Columbia University Press, 2018), 19, 25, 37, 50.

44. Michel Foucault explains: "It is a matter of making things more fragile through this historical analysis, or rather of showing both why and how things were able to establish themselves as such, and showing at the same time that they were established through a precise history. It is therefore necessary to place strategic logic inside the things from whence they were produced, to show that nonetheless, these are only strategies and therefore, by changing a certain number of things, by changing strategies, taking things differently, finally what appears obvious to us is not at all so obvious." Michel Foucault, "What Our Present Is," in *The Politics of Truth*, ed. Sylvère Lotringer (Los Angeles: Semiotext(e), 2007), 138–39.

45. See Asad, "Thinking about Religion," 46–48; Donald S. Lopez Jr., "Belief," in *Critical Terms for Religious Studies*, ed. Mark C. Taylor (Chicago: University of Chicago Press, 1998), 21–35; Robert A. Orsi, "Belief," in *Key Terms in Material Religion*, ed. S. Brent Plate (London: Bloomsbury Academic, 2015), 17–23; Saba Mahmood, *Religious Difference in a Secular Age: A Minority Report* (Princeton, NJ: Princeton University Press, 2016), 15.

46. Winnifred Fallers Sullivan, *The Impossibility of Religious Freedom* (Princeton: Princeton University Press, 2005), 7–9.

47. Since the nineteenth century, atheism has become (like everything else) increasingly globalized, and so it would be a mistake to assume that it is intrinsically Christian. In contexts like modern India, atheism has flourished, but it tends to address local forms of religiosity—for instance, Hindu practices of religious healing. For a fascinating window into Indian atheism, see Jacob Copeman and Johannes Quack, "Godless People and Dead Bodies: Materiality and the Morality of Atheist Materialism," in *Being Godless: Ethnographies of Atheism and Non-Religion*, ed. Roy Llera Blanes and Galina Oustinova-Stjepanovic (New York: Berghahn Books, 2017), 40–61.

48. William James, *Varieties of Religious Experience: A Study in Human Nature* (London: Routledge, 2002), 29.

49. James, 33.
50. James, 333–34.
51. James, 353.

REFERENCES

Alexander, Nathan G. *Race in a Godless World: Atheism, Race, and Civilization, 1850–1914.* New York: New York University Press, 2019.

Asad, Talal. *Secular Translations: Nation-State, Modern Self, and Calculative Reason.* New York: Columbia University Press, 2018.

———. "Thinking about Religion, Belief, and Politics." In *The Cambridge Companion to Religious Studies*, edited by Robert A. Orsi, 36–57. Cambridge Companions to Religion. Cambridge: Cambridge University Press, 2011.

Baggett, Jerome P. *The Varieties of Nonreligious Experience: Atheism in American Culture.* New York: New York University Press, 2019.

Beattie, Tina. *The New Atheists: The Twilight of Reason and the War on Religion.* London: Darton, Longman and Todd, 2008.

Berlant, Lauren. *Cruel Optimism.* Durham, NC: Duke University Press, 2011.

Bullivant, Stephen Sebastian. "Defining 'Atheism.'" In *The Oxford Handbook of Atheism*, edited by Stephen Sebastian Bullivant and Michael Ruse, 11–21. Oxford: Oxford University Press, 2015.

Copeman, Jacob, and Johannes Quack. "Godless People and Dead Bodies: Materiality and the Morality of Atheist Materialism." In *Being Godless: Ethnographies of Atheism and Non-Religion,* edited by Roy Llera Blanes and Galina Oustinova-Stjepanovic, 40–61. New York: Berghahn Books, 2017.

Daston, Lorraine. "The Moral Economy of Science." *Osiris* 10 (1995): 2–24.

Dawkins, Richard. *The God Delusion.* London: Bantam Press, 2006.

Dennett, Daniel Clement. *Breaking the Spell: Religion as a Natural Phenomenon.* London: Allen Lane, 2006.

Derrida, Jacques. "Christianity and Secularization." Translated by David Newheiser. *Critical Inquiry* 47, no. 1 (September 1, 2020): 138–48.

Erdozain, Dominic. *The Soul of Doubt: The Religious Roots of Unbelief from Luther to Marx.* New York: Oxford University Press, 2015.

Feuerbach, Ludwig Andreas. *The Essence of Christianity.* New York: Prometheus Books, 1989.

Finger, Anja. "Four Horsemen (and a Horsewoman): What Gender Is New Atheism?" In *New Atheism: Critical Perspectives and Contemporary Debates*, edited by Christopher R. Cotter, Philip Andrew Quadrio, and Jonathan Tuckett, 155–70. New York: Springer, 2017.

Flanagan, Christy L. "The Paradox of Feuerbach: Luther and Religious Naturalism." PhD diss., Florida State University, 2009.

Flew, Anthony Garrard Newton. *God & Philosophy.* London: Routledge & K. Paul, 1966.

Foucault, Michel. "What Our Present Is." In *The Politics of Truth*, edited by Sylvère Lotringer, 129–44. Los Angeles: Semiotext(e), 2007.

Garasse, François. *La doctrine curieuse des beaux esprits de ce temps, ou préten-*

dus tels contenant plusieurs maximes pernicieuses à l'État, à la religion et aux bonnes moeurs. Paris: Chappelet, 1623.

Gautier, Théophile. *Les grotesques*. Paris: M. Lévy, 1853.

Gray, John. *Seven Types of Atheism*. New York: Farrar, Straus and Giroux, 2018.

Harris, Sam. *The End of Faith: Religion, Terror, and the Future of Reason*. New York: Free Press, 2004.

Harrison, Peter. *Religion and the Religions in the English Enlightenment*. Cambridge: Cambridge University Press, 2002.

———. *The Territories of Science and Religion*. Chicago: University of Chicago Press, 2015.

Hitchens, Christopher. *God Is Not Great: How Religion Poisons Everything*. New York: Twelve Books, 2007.

James, William. *Varieties of Religious Experience: A Study in Human Nature*. London: Routledge, 2002.

Kors, Alan Charles. *Atheism in France, 1650–1729*. Vol. 1. Princeton, NJ: Princeton University Press, 2016.

LeDrew, Stephen. *The Evolution of Atheism: The Politics of a Modern Movement*. New York: Oxford University Press, 2016.

Lee, Lois. *Recognizing the Non-Religious: Reimagining the Secular*. Oxford: Oxford University Press, 2015.

Lopez, Donald S., Jr. "Belief." In *Critical Terms for Religious Studies*, edited by Mark C. Taylor, 21–35. Chicago: University of Chicago Press, 1998.

Mahmood, Saba. *Religious Difference in a Secular Age: A Minority Report*. Princeton, NJ: Princeton University Press, 2016.

Nancy, Jean-Luc. *Dis-Enclosure: The Deconstruction of Christianity*. Translated by Gabriel Malenfant, Michael B. Smith, and Bettina Bergo. New York: Fordham University Press, 2008.

Newheiser, David. "Derrida and the Danger of Religion." *Journal of the American Academy of Religion* 86, no. 1 (2018): 42–61.

———. *Hope in a Secular Age: Deconstruction, Negative Theology, and the Future of Faith*. Cambridge: Cambridge University Press, 2019.

Oppy, Graham Robert. Introduction to *A Companion to Atheism and Philosophy*, edited by Graham Robert Oppy, 1–12. Oxford, UK: Wiley Blackwell, 2019.

Origen of Alexandria. *Origen: On First Principles*. Edited by John Behr. Oxford: Oxford University Press, 2018.

Orsi, Robert A. "Belief." In *Key Terms in Material Religion*, edited by S. Brent Plate, 17–23. London: Bloomsbury Academic, 2015.

Palmer, D. W. "Atheism, Apologetic, and Negative Theology in the Greek Apologists of the Second Century." *Vigiliae Christianae* 37, no. 3 (1983): 234–59.

Pinn, Anthony B. *Humanism: Essays on Race, Religion, and Cultural Production*. New York: Bloomsbury, 2015.

Plantinga, Alvin. *Warranted Christian Belief*. New York: Oxford University Press, 2000.

Plato. *Euthyphro; Apology; Crito; Phaedo*. Translated by Benjamin Jowett. Amherst, NY: Prometheus Books, 1988.

Pseudo-Dionysius the Areopagite. *Pseudo-Dionysius: The Complete Works*. Translated by Colm Luibhéid. Classics of Western Spirituality. New York: Paulist Press, 1987.

Ravaisson, François. *Archives de La Bastille: Documents inédits.* Vol. 14. 19 vols. Paris, 1866.
Russell, Bertrand. *Why I Am Not a Christian: And Other Essays on Religion and Related Subjects.* London: Routledge, 2005.
Ryrie, Alec. *Unbelievers: An Emotional History of Doubt.* Cambridge, MA: Harvard University Press, 2019.
Scheidt, Hannah K. *Practicing Atheism: Culture, Media, and Ritual in the Contemporary Atheist Network.* New York: Oxford University Press, 2021.
Steinmetz, David C. "The Superiority of Pre-Critical Exegesis." *Theology Today* 37, no. 1 (April 1, 1980): 27–38.
Sullivan, Winnifred Fallers. *The Impossibility of Religious Freedom.* Princeton, NJ: Princeton University Press, 2005.
Swinburne, Richard. *The Coherence of Theism.* Oxford, UK: Clarendon Press, 1977.
———. *The Existence of God.* Oxford, UK: Clarendon Press, 2004.
Theophilus of Antioch. "Theophilus to Autolycus." In *Ante-Nicene Fathers*, vol. 2, edited by Alexander Roberts, James Donaldson, and A. Cleveland Coxe. Buffalo, NY: Christian Literature Publishing, 1885.
Tsing, Anna Lowenhaupt. *The Mushroom at the End of the World: On the Possibility of Life in Capitalist Ruins.* Princeton, NJ: Princeton University Press, 2015.
Weltecke, Dorothea. "Beyond Religion: On the Lack of Belief during the Central and Late Middle Ages." In *Religion and Its Other: Secular and Sacral Concepts and Practices in Interaction,* edited by Heike Bock and Jörg Feuchter, 101–14. Frankfurt: Campus Verlag, 2008.
———. "L'athéisme et le doute au Moyen Âge: Un problème controversé." *Revue de l'Histoire des Religions*, no. 3 (September 1, 2015): 339–61.
Wootton, David. "New Histories of Atheism." In *Atheism from the Reformation to the Enlightenment,* edited by David Wootton and Michael Hunter, 13–53. Oxford: Oxford University Press, 1992.

1

ATHEISM AND SCIENCE

On Einstein's "Cosmic Religious Sense"

Mary-Jane Rubenstein

PANTHEISM AS ATHEISM

From the moment the term was coined by an incensed eighteenth-century commentator, the position known as "pantheism" has been equated with atheism.[1] The year was 1709, and in an incensed response to the work of the Irish natural philosopher John Toland, the French author Jacques de la Faye wrote, "Toland believes in no God aside from nature, or the workings of the world. This is Atheism, or Pantheism (*hoc est Atheïsmum aut Pantheïsmum*)."[2] Thus we find the first recorded use of a word that centuries of philosophers would go on to use interchangeably with absurdity, irrationality, womanishness, primitivity, and—as we see from the moment of its invention—atheism. Even before the word existed, in fact, the heresy known as "pantheism" prompted the intellectual historian Pierre Bayle to denigrate its alleged forefather Baruch Spinoza as a "Jew by birth, and afterwards a deserter from Judaism, and lastly an *atheist*."[3]

For those with even a cursory knowledge of Spinoza, this accusation may seem perplexing. Against philosophical dualism on the one hand and popular theism on the other, Spinoza equated "God" with "Nature," explaining the entire world as a perfect expression of divinity itself. Such omni-theism prompted the German poet-mystic Novalis to call Spinoza a "God-intoxicated man."[4] Or in the words of that other poet-mystic Goethe, "Spinoza does not have to prove the existence of God; existence *is* God."[5] So if *everything* is God for Spinoza, then how does this all-God become in the eyes of critics a no-God? Why is pantheism so consistently equated with atheism, then and now, by theists and atheists alike?

There are two lines of thinking that produce this equation of pantheism with atheism. The first is theological, and it insists that a God who is the universe would be no God at all. A clear representative of this sort of logic is the Reverend Morgan Dix, rector of Manhattan's Trinity Episcopal Church in the mid-nineteenth century. Faced with an effervescent onslaught of transcendentalism—Emerson with his eyeball and Thoreau with his oversoul and Whitman with God in his lunchbox—Dix laments that in this bleak pantheist landscape "there is left no God. A substance, impersonal, there is; but we cannot imagine that unintelligible, unreasoning, unthinking, unloving state of impotence as our Father, our Creator, our Redeemer, our Sanctifier, our Friend. The God in whom we have believed is gone."[6] But what is "pantheism," and how does it obliterate the Father-Creator-Redeemer-Sanctifier-Friend in whom "we" have believed?

Etymologically, the term means "all-God," a patching together of the Greek words *pan* and *theos*. For pantheists, God does not just create the world; God *is* the world. But if God is the world, then God bears no greater resemblance to a father than to a forest, an elephant, or a tide pool. Hence Reverend Dix's horror in the face of the disappearance of his anthropomorphic God. The most pantheism can give us, he says, is a substance—and who on earth would pray to a substance? Or, for that matter, to an elephant or a forest? How could anyone relate meaningfully to an "impersonal," "unintelligible, unreasoning, unthinking, unloving state of impotence"?

To be sure, a hypothetical defender of pantheism might contest a number of these adjectives. For example, insofar as the pantheist God is the universe itself, and insofar as the universe does seem to produce things, it would certainly not be impotent. And insofar as it is possible to think of such a God-world, it would certainly not be unintelligible. Finally, although its attributes would differ radically from *human* reason, thought, and love, there is no reason the pantheist divinity could not be in some way personal—even omnipersonal. But Dix's primary concern with pantheism is not actually its impersonalism; his concern is its feminized *non*anthropomorphism. Traditional monotheism has understood God to be a singular, unchanging, disembodied (super)male. The pantheist God-world, by contrast, necessarily entails multiplicity, malleability, and materiality—traditionally feminine characteristics that interrupt nearly every traditionally theistic attribute. From Dix's perspective, then, the pantheist all-God is no God at all. To be a humanoid father-friend is what it means to be God in the first (and only) place.

The second line of thinking behind the perennial alignment of pantheism with atheism is more philosophical than theological. With Arthur Schopenhauer, it reasons that calling the world "divine" simply does not add anything to the concept of "world."[7] A universe-that-is-God is functionally and substantially equivalent to a universe-without-God, so as Schopenhauer has quipped, pantheism is nothing but "a euphemism for atheism."[8] From this perspective, it would be more honest just to call the world "world" than to dress it up with divinity; in the words of the pragmatist philosopher Nancy Frankenberry, "by assimilating *God* to *Nature* . . . [pantheists] raise the suspicion that one of the two of them is semantically superfluous."[9] The pantheist world creates and sustains itself, and as such, it is effectively atheistic.

As we endeavor in this volume to track the contours and subspecies of atheism—and to assess their fraught interconstitution with the positions they reject—my guiding question is whether pantheism amounts to the "atheism" with which it is so often and so polemically conflated. To assess this conflation, I will turn to a little-remembered scandal in the recent annals of intellectual history—namely, the panicked accusations of atheism hurled at the physicist-philosopher Albert Einstein, who professed an overwhelming awe at the mystery, order, and, indeed, divinity of the cosmos. By reading Einstein against himself, I will ultimately suggest that a pluralistic, perspectival pantheism would constitute even more of a threat than atheism to the anthropic father-friend of classical theism, whose toxic sovereignty Devin Singh exposes as the linchpin of imperial political theology, and whose monarchical attributes tend to be retained even in those positions—including Einstein's—that purport to kill him off.[10]

THE EINSTEIN CRISIS

The public outcry over "Einstein's God" or "Einstein's religion" flared up, and for the most part died down, in the second quarter of the twentieth century. Far from being a strictly ecclesiastical affair, this "Einstein crisis" was the hybrid product of a series of theological, political, scientific, economic, and epistemological convulsions, including the devastation of the First World War, the overturning of Newtonian physics by general and special relativity, the rupture between science and religion staged in the 1925 Scopes Trial, the rise of fascism in Europe, the crash of the US stock market, and Einstein's decade-long debate with Niels Bohr over quantum mechanics and the nature of reality. Arising from all these factors in complex relation, the Einstein crisis can be organized into three major waves.

The first wave hit in April 1929, one week before a lavish gala at the Metropolitan Opera House in honor of Einstein's fiftieth birthday, which would draw 3,500 people in support of the Jewish National Fund and the Zionist Organization of America.[11] As American Jews prepared to celebrate their most famous kinsman, Boston cardinal William Henry O'Connell delivered an address to the New England Province of Catholic Clubs of America, urging their members to pay no attention to the Jewish pseudo-prophet. Having previously denounced Hollywood and radio technology for proliferating a monstrous cadre of "masculine women" and "effeminate men," the cardinal charged Einstein's theory of relativity with endorsing the categorical indistinction of the topsy-turvy era.[12] The theory, he insisted, was nothing more than "befogged speculation producing universal doubt about God and his creation, cloaking the ghastly apparition of atheism."[13]

However camp it may sound to our ears, the word *ghastly* (from the German *geistlich*) still meant genuinely horrifying or terrifying in the early twentieth century. So Cardinal O'Connell warns us of a ghostly horror: of the apparition of an absence, namely, the absence denoted by atheism, which is less a substantive position than a refusal of substantiation. O'Connell's ghostly absence-presence is, moreover, "cloaked" in befogged speculation. A ghost in a fog that, furthermore, compels us even as it horrifies us—after all, O'Connell tells us our specter produces "*universal* doubt about God and his creation." According to this account, then, absolutely everyone is being drawn to the repellant account of the universe that general relativity provides.

If O'Connell's metaphors are hard to follow, his meaning is even foggier. He is clearly saying that relativity amounts to atheism, but he does not explain how, except to say that the theory is too confusing to be true and that it makes no mention of God.[14] But one can surmise from the ensuing controversies that the mere name of *relativity* connoted for O'Connell moral laxity—the sort that had in his eyes devoured law, economics, politics, and gender in the postwar era, and that he, along with nearly all his Catholic and mainline colleagues, believed could be held in check only by an unchanging, immovable, extracosmic lawgiver.[15] In short, relativity's denial of any absolute reference point for space and time seemed to O'Connell a denial of the Absolute altogether, and for that reason, it was both morally and empirically wrong.

Seeking to defend his assailed hero against the incensed cardinal, the Orthodox rabbi Herbert S. Goldstein of the Institutional Synagogue in New York sent a cable to Einstein in Berlin, asking, "Do you believe in God? Stop. Prepaid reply 50 words."[16] As it turned out, Einstein needed half as many words: "I believe in Spinoza's God who reveals himself in the orderly harmony of all things, not in a God who concerns himself with the fates and actions of human beings."[17] In an interview a few years later, Einstein would go on to clarify that his reply to Rabbi Goldstein "was not intended for publication. No one except an American could think of sending a man a telegram asking him: 'Do you believe in God?'"[18] Nevertheless, the earnest American rabbi took Einstein's cabled profession as proof that the physicist did, in fact, believe in God, and he went on to publish it in the *New York Times* as a rejoinder to Cardinal O'Connell. Einstein was by no means a ghastly atheist, Goldstein announced; after all, he had invoked Spinoza in a telegram. And "Spinoza, who is called 'the God-intoxicated man' and who saw God manifest in all of nature, certainly could not be called an atheist."[19] Of course, Goldstein's defense of Einstein was hardly beyond dispute; as we have already seen, Spinoza himself was called an atheist, as well as a pantheist, as well as an atheist disguised as a pantheist. And in an uncanny recapitulation of these seventeenth-century accusations, Pope Pius XI (the one who collaborated with the Nazis before realizing it was a mistake[20]) declared that Cardinal O'Connell was correct: Einstein's theory of relativity amounted to "authentic atheism even if camouflaged as cosmic pantheism."[21] So once again, pantheism amounts to atheism, but now our ghostly cloaking has become more militarily coded: atheism here is "camouflaged" in pantheism, lurking in its soft underbrush to launch a sneak attack on orthodoxy.

The second wave of controversy hit just seven months later, when Einstein published a piece in the *New York Times Magazine* entitled "Religion and Science."[22] Subtly informed not only by Spinoza but also by Kant, Nietzsche, Schleiermacher, Schopenhauer, and the colonial anthropology of the long nineteenth century, Einstein suggests in this short essay that "religion" develops in three historical stages. First comes the "religion of fear," in which so-called primitive peoples install anthropomorphic beings behind the terrifying forces of nature. As humans seek to please these beings, this first expression "develops" into a "moral religion," whose people are united under the eternally binding command of a single lawgiver. Although this moral stage dominates the so-called civilized religions, Einstein explains that it remains immature because it still worships an "anthropomorphic" God who concerns himself primarily with humanity. The highest stage of religion, he suggests, breaks free of this anthropomorphic deity and his anthropocentric carryings-on, and revolves instead around what Einstein calls a "cosmic religious sense," which is to say an appreciation of the astonishing, mysterious order of the cosmos. This awestruck, humbling feeling toward "the nobility and marvelous order . . . revealed in nature" exposes by comparison "the vanity of human desires and aims." And it is this "cosmic religious sense," Einstein concludes, that not only suffuses "the religious geniuses of all times" but animates scientific geniuses as well, inspiring the likes of Kepler and Newton to persist in their solitary labors to "understand even a small glimpse of the reason revealed in the world."[23]

Einstein's brief theory of religion and its relationship to science hit the New York newsstands early on a Sunday morning. Just hours later, it was decried in mainline Christian pulpits throughout the city, with Methodists, Presbyterians, Episcopalians, and Roman Catholics alike denouncing Einstein's "cosmic religious sense" as amoral, overly intellectual, impersonal, and anticlerical.[24] Einstein's lone defender—at least according to the next day's *Times*—was Rabbi Solomon B. Freehof, of Chicago, who maintained to the Free Synagogue congregation that Einstein was in no sense an atheist, because for Einstein, as for all pious men, "the universe is essentially mysterious. He confronts it with awe and reverence."[25] As we might remember, however, Einstein's previous rabbinic defender praised Einstein's belief, not in the mystery, but in the order of the universe. And this tension shows up throughout what one might call Einstein's philosophy of religion: for Einstein, the universe is at once totally rational and utterly mysterious, and this has something to do with God.

The final wave of "the Einstein crisis" crashed a full ten years after the publication of "Religion and Science," in response to an academic address Einstein made called "Science and Religion" (our hero's nearly unfathomable creativity seems to have bottomed out when it came to titles). Einstein offered the lecture as part of a symposium at Jewish Theological Seminary in New York that gathered scholars from a wide range of disciplines to confront the ongoing political "disintegration" of "Western civilization," a disintegration the conference organizers attributed to the disharmony of science and religion in the wake of Darwin's discovery of evolution. To reconcile these estranged partners, Einstein argued that religion and science occupy separate but supplementary "spheres." Science, he ventured, is concerned with "what *is*," whereas religion tells us "what *should be*"; science uncovers "facts," whereas religion prescribes "human thoughts and actions."[26] As such, neither is sufficient on its own; in Einstein's now-iconic words, "science without religion is lame, religion without science is blind" (46).

Whence, then, comes the perceived opposition between these mutually beneficial regimes? The largest impediment to the harmony between science and religion, Einstein ventures, is in the concept of a personal God (47). Channeling Spinoza, Einstein argues that science cannot affirm the existence of an anthropomorphic power who from time to time violates the order of nature in response to human petition. In addition to being scientifically inadmissible, he explains, such a God is ethically useless, relieving human beings of responsibility for their own actions. As an illustration, one might think of Representative Tim Walberg's explanation for Donald

Trump's 2017 withdrawal from the Paris accord: "As a Christian," he told his constituents, "I believe that . . . if there's a real problem . . . God will take care of it."[27] For ethical and scientific reasons alike, then, Einstein insists that *"teachers of religion must have the stature to give up the doctrine of a personal God"* (48, emphasis added). Once people are free from this divine overlord, Einstein promises they will also be free from egoistic concerns (like having the largest gross domestic product or the biggest sport utility vehicle), eventually attaining that comportment his earlier essay called the cosmic religious sense: a humble feeling of reverence for the mysterious yet rational whole. And in this way, the religious person becomes affectively identical to the scientist.

Again, Einstein had thought that this lecture might help his colleagues in the natural and theological sciences repair the rift between their disciplines. As far as most of his audience was concerned, however, Einstein's attempted reconciliation with religion amounted to a full-scale attack. As the *Chicago Daily Tribune*, the *New York Times*, the front page of the *Washington Post*, a flurry of local newspapers, and a feature article in *Time* magazine all declared, Einstein's call "to give up the doctrine of a personal God" amounted to a denial of God altogether.[28] In the words of an anonymous Roman Catholic priest, "There *is* no other God but a personal God. Einstein does not know what he is talking about."[29] In short, Einstein accomplished in this lecture precisely the opposite of what he had set out to do. By proclaiming the grandeur of a God his audience considered incoherent, he intensified the divisions among the spheres he thought he was unifying. Thus the *New York Times* reported that, as far as the conference organizers were concerned, this was a lecture in which "the famous unifier of time and space expounded his own atheism, which has been . . . never before so emphatically stated."[30]

As the physicist-philosopher Max Jammer has discovered in Einstein's personal letters, Einstein was baffled by this response and by the multidenominational excoriations that arrived by mail for months after the address was sensationally summarized in the press.[31] For the most part, the charges were predictable—many of them familiar from the sermonic drama ten years earlier, or indeed from the centuries-long critique of Spinoza. Einstein was an atheist; he was a pantheist; he was an atheist dressed as a pantheist; he had done away with God by denying God's personalism; he had done away with "man" by denying his resemblance to God; and his cosmic religion was "absurd," "the sheerest kind of stupidity and nonsense," and "full of jellybeans."[32] Although nearly all these critics were Christian, there were a few Orthodox and Conservative Jewish voices among them, including Rabbi Hyman Cohen, of Hudson County, who reported that "Einstein is unquestionably a great scientist, but his religious views are diametrically opposed to Judaism."[33]

One unprecedented set of claims, however—and one leveled exclusively by self-professed Christians—asserted that Einstein's atheistic pantheism was so ethically ruinous that it offered aid to the Nazi extermination of his own people. For example, Monsignor Fulton John Sheen, of Catholic University, objected that a cosmic divinity could hold no one responsible for his actions: "if God is only impersonal Space-Time," he reasoned, "there is no moral order; then Hitler is not responsible for driving Professor Einstein out of Germany. It was only a bad collocation of space-time configurations that made him act this way."[34] In fact, Einstein had made precisely the opposite claim in "Science and Religion," arguing that if God were personal, then God would be responsible for the violent convulsions of human behavior—including, presumably, Hitler's expulsion of the Jews. Yet Monsignor Sheen does not consider this position, taking it as given that an anthropomorphic lawgiver is necessary to securing moral conduct on earth (the obvious objection being, of course, that he doesn't seem to have done so).

Other incensed Christians pushed Einstein's alleged excusing of Hitler's behavior into a full-fledged justification of it. As one Roman Catholic attorney and self-described interfaith activist dared to assert, Einstein's denial of a personal God made a case for the "exp[ulsion of] the Jews from Germany" by making "Jewish theology" seem downright diabolical.[35] Masquerading as a defense of Judaism, this unsubtle anti-Jewishness is perhaps most clearly displayed in the missive by a Christian Zionist from Oklahoma, who writes:

> I have done everything in my power to be a blessing to Israel, and then you come along and with one statement from your blasphemous tongue do more to hurt the case of your people than all of the efforts of the Christians who love Israel can do to stamp out anti-Semitism in our Land. Professor Einstein, every Christian in America will immediately reply to you, "Take back your crazy, fallacious theory of evolution and go back to Germany where you came from, or stop trying to break down the faith of a people who gave you a welcome when you were forced to flee your native land."[36]

Perhaps needless to say, Einstein's major contributions to science had very little to do with any "theory of evolution." By associating Einstein with a teaching that twentieth-century "Fundamentalists" had determined to be anti-Christian, however, the author charges Einstein not only with aiding the destruction of Einstein's own people but also with refusing to assimilate himself into mainstream Christian culture—a refusal that amounted in the author's eyes to an act of aggression against it. Over the course of the letter, then, this critic's stated effort to "stamp out anti-Semitism" ends up reduplicating it.

FAITH IN REASON

Viscera and vitriol aside, what did Einstein mean when he professed adherence to "Spinoza's God"? On the most elementary level, he meant, as he insists in countless letters, that he was certainly not an atheist.[37] Depending on the day and context, he also meant either that he was a pantheist or that he was perhaps not a pantheist.[38] Regardless of whether he accepted this label, however, Einstein certainly used the word *God* interchangeably with *Nature*, an equation that has constituted the simplest formulation of pantheism since Spinoza equated the two. This identity of God and the natural world becomes clear in a conversation with a colleague who asked Einstein to explain what he had meant when he said, "Subtle is the Lord, but malicious He is not." Einstein replied that he meant, "Nature hides her secret because of her essential loftiness, but not by means of ruse."[39] If this second adage is indeed a translation of the first, then God and Nature are equivalent for Einstein, *and* this God-Nature is not deceiving us so long as we are thinking rationally. Indeed, what the heretical physicist means above all when he says "I believe in Spinoza's God" is that the world is so rationally structured that we can think of it as divine. Unlike Spinoza, however, Einstein admits that his unflagging faith in "the rationality or intelligibility of the world" is, precisely, a matter of faith.[40] As such, he falls far short of Nietzsche's madman, who as Ryan Coyne has demonstrated, loses faith not only in "God" but also in faith itself, which is theologically structured.[41] "The basis of all scientific work is the conviction that the world is an ordered and comprehensive entity," Einstein writes, "which is a religious sentiment."[42]

Insofar as the universe is fully rational, Einstein goes on to conclude that it must be fully determined. Again appealing to a supernatural source of this conviction, Einstein explains that "the scientist is possessed by the sense of universal causation. The future, to him, is every whit as determined as the past." And if the future and the past are both determined and rational, then neither humans nor God can be said to have free will. In response to a query from eleven-year-old Phyllis Wright, of the Riverside Church in New York, Einstein therefore asserts that scientists do not, in fact, pray, because nothing can be otherwise than it is. That having been said, he writes, "Our actual knowledge of these laws is only an incomplete piece of work, so that ultimately the belief in the existence of fundamental all-embracing laws also rests on a sort of faith."[43]

So faith grounds the reason that asserts the determinism of the nonetheless mysterious cosmos. Faith-reason, determinism-mystery—one might say that Einstein's cosmic religious sense amounts to reason at its limits: the more ardently it attempts to grasp the order of the universe, the more it understands how feebly it grasps it. And yet this constant falling short inspires the devout scientist only to intensify his effort to comprehend as much as he can. Einstein's universe is thus fully rational and persistently mysterious; as he famously encapsulates the matter: "The eternal mystery of the world is its comprehensibility. . . . The fact that it is comprehensible is itself a miracle."[44] Again, however, this commonly cited aphorism does not mean that the universe is fully comprehensible—at least not to the hopelessly insufficient human mind. Rather, it means that the universe is rationally structured and that the human mind participates to a limited extent in that universal reason. It is this dance between the comprehensible and the incomprehensible that constitutes for Einstein the essence of religion and science alike. Both practices aim to grasp in some way the rationally mysterious order of things called Nature or God, and both depend on what he calls faith in the ultimate rationality of existence—an admittedly indemonstrable faith in the perfect, unchanging, deterministic reason of the world.

At this point, we might want to assess the coherence of Einstein's cosmic religion. Regardless of whether or not it amounts to atheism, what does it mean for his unflagging reason to find its ultimate grounding in faith? To what extent can something as indeterminate as faith secure universal determinism? How can Einstein say that God is both impersonal and intelligent in the same breath? And above all, is Einstein really giving us a consistent pantheism? An alignment of God and world? If so, then how can his cosmic divinity be unchanging and absolute if the space-time it amounts to is dynamic and relative?

EINSTEIN VERSUS EINSTEIN

Relativity

In his universal theory of gravitation, Isaac Newton asserted the "absolute" nature of space and time.[45] To say that space and time are absolute is to say that they are independent of any particular perspective on them. Newtonian measurements therefore hold for all observers: regardless of the different vantage points of person A and person B, each will measure a mile as a mile and ten minutes as ten minutes. Moreover, to say that space and time are absolute is to say that they are independent of the objects within them, forming an inert grid across which beings move. Even if the universe were totally empty, space, according to Newton, would still be extended, and time would still pass from the past through the present to the future.

With his early twentieth-century papers on special and general relativity, however, Einstein demonstrated against Newton that space and time are not by any means independent of perspective, their inhabitants, or one another.[46] Rather, space is curved from one perspective and straight from another;[47] time passes differently depending on the velocity of the observer;[48] and space and time form a four-dimensional fabric that bends and warps according to the matter and energy "within" it. And this bending and warping of space-time is nothing other than "gravity" itself: the mass of the sun, for example, creates paths within which planets travel, while the mass of planets determines the path of the moons and comets that in turn exert their own gravitational force, all of them composing the dynamic shape of the solar system. Bound up as it is with space, time likewise does not progress uniformly throughout the cosmos; rather, it passes more slowly for bodies near massive, gravitationally powerful objects than it does for bodies far from them.

Therefore, as Niels Bohr summarizes it, Einstein's theory of relativity shatters the Newtonian clockwork, calling into question even the most elementary concepts of space and time, cause and effect. If it is the case that two bolts of lightning can hit a train sequentially from the perspective of the train, but simultaneously from the perspective of the embankment that runs alongside it, then there is an "element of subjectivity" built into everything we might try to say about the universe.[49] Einsteinian space-time therefore not only appears different; it *is* different from one constituent-observer to the next. Anything that takes place takes place differently, depending on your perspective.[50]

Now for Newton, the absolute nature of time and space reflected and reaffirmed the absolute nature of God. Space and time were effectively God's omnipresence and eternity, enacted as the material universe.[51] Insofar as Einstein revolutionizes our understanding of space and time, one might therefore imagine he would revolutionize our understanding of God, as well. Especially if Einstein's God is the order of the cosmos, one might imagine his divinity would be at least as manifold as trains and embankments and at least as relative as matter and space-time. And yet as we have already seen, Einstein does not come close to a theology of relativity. Rather, he asserts a theology of the absolute—of a single, unified, deterministic, cosmic divinity in which effect always follows cause, subject is separate from object, and God retains the sturdy invariance (and even the anthropomorphic rationality) "he" had enjoyed under the regime of classical and scholastic physics and theology alike.[52] What I am trying to suggest here is this: *Einstein's theology looks almost nothing like his cosmology.* And if he were setting forth a consistent pantheism, they would be effectively equivalent.

Quantum Disturbances

Granted, Einstein's absolutist theology is not the only instance of his recoiling from his own insights: he infamously couldn't stand the big-bang hypothesis his own equations produced, inventing a force out of thin air to assure himself that the universe wasn't expanding. But the conflict between Einstein's science and his metaphysics comes into clearest relief in his protracted debate with Niels Bohr over the nature of quantum mechanics.

Like relativity, quantum mechanics confronts us with irreducible perspectivalism; as both Bohr and Einstein realized, light can be fully described as a particle or as a wave, depending on the experimental arrangement one uses to observe it. So if a beam of light is sent through two slits, it will produce a wavelike pattern on the screen the light hits. But if one slit is closed, the same beam will produce a particle pattern. If photons are fired individually through two slits, they will collectively land in a wave. But if a "which-path" detector is added to determine how this is possible, the photons will behave as particles.[53] Niels Bohr's name for such mutually incompatible outcomes is *complementarity*: different experimental arrangements produce different realities. And just as special relativity proclaims it equally correct to say that the embankment is moving as that the train is moving, quantum mechanics proclaims it equally correct to say that light is a particle as it is to say that light is a wave.

As Bohr himself remarked, the "notion of complementarity" therefore "exhibits a certain resemblance [to] the principle of relativity."[54] In each case, the object of observation is inescapably bound up with the subject of observation, such that any accurate description of the phenomenon in question must specify the conditions that produce it in the first place. Given that Einstein himself had produced the insight that objectivity is perspectival, it is therefore surprising that he reacted as viscerally as he did against quantum mechanics. But as it turned out, he hated it.

Considering Einstein's faith in the rational, determinate nature of the universe, he couldn't stand the thought that tiny particles of matter might have no properties of their own—that these objects might gain properties only in relation to the subjects measuring them. Conversely, he couldn't quite bear the notion that such particles—such tiny little objects—might also behave as subjects: "it is quite intolerable," he wrote, "to think that an electron exposed to radiation should choose *of its own free will,* not only its moment to jump off, but also its direction."[55] Recall that Einstein's "Spinozism" had led him to deny free will to human beings and even God, so he found the notion that subatomic particles might have it intellectually inadmissible and, frankly, emotionally unbearable. "In that case," he confessed to Max and Hedwig Born, "I would rather be a cobbler or even an employee in a gaming-house, than a physicist."[56]

Far from serving as simple escape fantasy, however, Einstein's gaming house simultaneously encapsulates and ridicules the indeterminate universe of quantum mechanics. If physics can no more predict an effect from a cause than a gambler can foresee a roll of the dice, then what good is it? After all, if a physicist could calculate all the forces at work in a single roll (e.g., mass, velocity, torque, air resistance, distance to table, friction of surface), then she could, in fact, predict its outcome. There must, then, be some way to subject the quantum dice to a similar calculation—to do better than probability by getting at the determinate, determined reality of things. But as Einstein repeatedly admitted, this conviction stemmed from an instinct that was as theological as it was scientific. Thus, as he wrote in a constantly cited letter to Max Born: "Quantum mechanics is certainly imposing. But an inner voice tells me that it is not yet the real thing. The theory tells us a lot, but does not really bring us any closer to the secret of the 'old one.' I, at any rate, am convinced that *He* is not playing at dice."[57] *We* might be, but he's not. The quantum might look dicey to us here and now, but probability cannot possibly be the final answer to the mysteries of the universe.

Reality and Difference

Until the day he died, Einstein was convinced that there was something deeply wrong with what the quantum seemed to be saying about the nature of nature. And to return to the main thread of our inquiry, this conviction can be said to be the product of Einstein's theology, which asserted at once the mystery of the divine cosmos and its comprehensibility—a theology that, despite its "humility," nevertheless claimed to know the ways of the unknowable. This tension mirrors the tension between Einstein's relativistic physics and his absolutist metaphysics—a conflict that seems to have baffled Niels Bohr in particular. As Carl Sagan narrates one of their famous encounters, "Einstein said, 'God does not play dice with the cosmos.' And on another occasion he asserted, 'God is subtle but he is not malicious.' In fact Einstein was so fond of such aphorisms that the Danish physicist Niels Bohr turned to him on one occasion and with some exasperation said, 'Stop telling God what to do.'"[58] According to the historian of science and molecular biologist Gunther Stent, Bohr's irritation with Einstein's faith in a deterministic cosmos reveals that the "actual subject" of the famed "Great Debate" between Einstein and Bohr "not physical theory, but God."[59] What they were actually arguing about, Stent suggests, was whether or not there was a superrational power stabilizing the quantum-dicey universe, with Einstein holding onto "the traditional monotheistic viewpoint of modern science" and Bohr breaking through to a genuine, postmodern "atheism."[60] In this light, the Great Debate between Einstein and Bohr can be seen as enacting the final growing pains of an increasingly secular Western science, struggling to do away once and for all with its theological past.

It is striking, however, that Bohr's rebuke does not contest the existence of God so much as it contests Einstein's claim to know how God must behave—even to dictate how God should behave. Bohr was baffled not by Einstein's appeal to God, but by his presumption that God was a single, immutable order of things beyond the multitude of worldly phenomena.

PERSPECTIVAL PANTHEOLOGY

During his lifetime, Einstein was demonized as an atheist and a pantheist. Far from being atheistic, however, Einstein's cosmic religion held onto many of the characteristics of the God of classical theism; in particular, his singularity, omnipotence, eternity, impassivity, and his unchanging providential order. So one way to answer Einstein's critics is to simply say that his "pantheism" is really just theism in a more impersonal key. But in that case, it thereby ceases to be pantheism, preserving the abstract characteristics of the purportedly dead sovereign.[61] What, then, would a more consistent pantheism look like? From the foregoing discussion of the Einstein-Bohr debate, I would like to suggest that such a pantheism would need to align Einstein's perspectivally recoded "world" with the "God" that that world allegedly *is*. In that spirit, we might decide to read Bohr's critique of Einstein's theology not as a call to atheism, but as an invitation to a more pantheistic pantheism. A more Einsteinian pantheism, even—one whose God genuinely sheds the absolutism of determinism and the anthropocentrism of "reason" and assumes instead the complex perspectivalism of the universe itself.

Insofar as the quantum-relative universe is immanent, relational, mutable, and multiply perspectival, its divinity would share these attributes—to such an extent that pantheism thus construed collides with a certain kind of polytheism.[62] As D. H. Lawrence suggests, "All the gods that men ever discovered are still God, and they contradict one another and fly down one another's throats, marvelously. Yet they are *all* God: the incalculable Pan."[63] To affirm the divinity of such manifold, contradictory, and incalculable things would be to affirm endless, particular loci of divinity, or a kind of pancarnation: divinity's inability not to express itself in and as the endlessly untotalized run of all that is.

This is not, of course, to say that everything is divine to every perceiving agent. Far less is it to say that everything is the same. Rather, it is to acknowledge that what looks like an inert rock from one perspective is a sacred ancestor from another; that the catfish one person serves for dinner could be kin to her partner and a god to both of them; and that what looks in one light like the image of God is in another a blight on the planet, and in another still the billion-year product of bacterial collaboration. To borrow a distinction from the anthropologist Eduardo Viveiros de Castro, such a pancarnation would amount not to relativism (which is different from relativity), but to perspectivism. If relativism asserts that there are many ways to interpret the same world (or God), then perspectivism would assert that worlds-as-gods take shape differently, depending on the points of view and manifold agents who construct, destroy, and remake them.[64] This is what a consistent Einsteinian pantheism would look like—a theocosmology of relativity, dynamism, emergence, and perspective. And I suppose that, from some of those points of view, such pantheology would indeed amount to atheism. And from others, I think, it would not.

NOTES

Parts of this chapter are adaptations of material in Mary-Jane Rubenstein, *Pantheologies: Gods, Worlds, Monsters* (New York: Columbia University Press, 2018). Reprinted with permission of Columbia University Press.

1. The term *pantheist* first appears in a treatise by the Irish philosopher John Toland, who professes to be among their number without quite elucidating their doctrine: John Toland, *Socinianism Truly Stated; Being an Example of Fair Dealing in All Theological Controvrsys. To Which Is Prefixt, Indifference in Disputes: Recommended by a Pantheist to an Orthodox Friend* (London, 1705), 7. The noun *pantheism*, however, is initially attributable not to Toland, but to Jacques de la Faye.
2. Jacques de la Faye, *Defensio Religionis, Nec Non Mosis Et Gentis Judaicae, Contra Duas Dissertationes Joh. Tolandi, Quarum Una Inscribitur Adeisidaemon, Altera Vera Antiquitates Judaicae* (Ultrajecti: Apud Guilielmum Broedelet, 1709), 19, 23; with gratitude to Andrew Szegedy-Maszak for the translation. The work to which de la Faye is responding directly is John Toland, *Adeisidaemon, Sive Titus Livius. A Superstitione Vindicatus* (Hagae-Comitis: Apud Thomam Johnson, 1709).

3. Pierre Bayle, *Historical and Critical Dictionary: Selections* (Indianapolis, IN: Hackett, 1991), 288, emphasis added.
4. David W. Wood, *Novalis: Notes for a Romantic Encyclopedia/Das Allgemeine Brouillon* (Albany: State University of New York Press, 2007), xxv.
5. Goethe, letter to Jacobi (June 9, 1785) cited in Detley Pätzold, "Deus Sive Natura. J. G. Herder's Romanticized Reading of Spinoza's Physico-Theology," in *The Book of Nature in Early Modern and Modern History*, ed. Klaas van Berkel and Arjo Vanderjagt (Leuven, Belgium: Peeters, 2006), 161.
6. Reverend Morgan Dix, *Lectures on the Pantheistic Idea of an Impersonal Deity, as Contrasted with the Christian Faith Concerning Almighty God* (New York: Hurd and Houghton, 1864), 56.
7. "Against pantheism I have mainly the objection that it states nothing. To call the world God is not to explain it, but only to enrich the language with a superfluous synonym for the word world. It comes to the same thing whether we say 'the world is God' or 'the world is the world.'" Arthur Schopenhauer, *Parerga and Paralipomena*, trans. E. F. J. Payne, 2 vols. (Oxford, UK: Clarendon Press, 2000), 2:99.
8. Schopenhauer, 1:114.
9. See Nancy Frankenberry, "Classical Theism, Panentheism, and Pantheism: On the Relation between God Construction and Gender Construction," *Zygon* 28, no. 1 (March, 1993): 44.
10. Devin Singh, "Fragile Belief and the Empty Throne: Theology and Politics after Ascension," in this volume.
11. "Thousands Attend Einstein Jubilee Celebration in New York City," *Jewish Daily Bulletin*, April 18, 1929.
12. "Death of a Cardinal," *Time*, May 1, 1944.
13. "Einstein Believes in 'Spinoza's God,'" *New York Times*, April 25, 1929.
14. J. D. B. Mail, "Cardinal O'Connell's Full Statement against Professor Einstein's Theories," *Jewish Daily Bulletin*, April 18, 1929.
15. "Is there any standard that has not been challenged in our post-war world? Is there any absolute system of ethics, of economics or of law, whose stability and permanence is not assailed somewhere?" George Sylvester Viereck, *Glimpses of the Great* (New York: Macauley, 1930), 356. On the connection between this creeping moral relativism, the theory of relativity, and a generalized waning belief in God as the moral lawgiver, see "Dr. Ward Attacks Einstein Theories," *New York Times*, November 10, 1930.
16. Cited in Max Jammer, *Einstein and Religion: Physics and Theology* (Princeton, NJ: Princeton University Press, 1999), 49.
17. "Ich glaube an Spinozas Gott der sich in gesetzlicher Harmonie des Seienden offenbart, nicht an Gott der Sich mit Schicksalen und Handlungen der Menschen abgibt," qtd. in "Einstein Believes in 'Spinoza's God,'" translation altered slightly.
18. Viereck, *Glimpses of the Great*, 372, 375.
19. "Einstein Believes in 'Spinoza's God.'"
20. See David Kertzer, *The Pope and Mussolini: The Secret History of Pius XI and the Rise of Fascism in Europe* (New York: Random House, 2014).
21. "Vatican Finds Professor Einstein Is an Atheist," *Jewish Daily Bulletin*, May 26, 1929.

22. Albert Einstein, "Religion and Science," *New York Times Magazine*, November 9, 1930.
23. Einstein, "Religion and Science."
24. See "Dr. Ward Attacks Einstein Theories"; "Dr. Coffin Praises Child's Simplicity," *New York Times*, November 10, 1930; "'Intellectual' View of God Is Assailed," *New York Times*, November 10, 1930; "Urges Faith in Leaders: Dean Gates Deplores Followers Who Are Critical," *New York Times*, November 10, 1930.
25. By contrast, "the anti-religious view of the universe looks upon the world as a clearly understood machine in which every 'riddle' is either solved or on the way to solution." "Einstein's Faith Defended," *New York Times*, November 10, 1930.
26. Albert Einstein, "Science and Religion" (1940), in *Ideas and Opinions*, ed. Cal Seelig and Sonja Bargmann (New York: Three Rivers Press, 1982), 45. Subsequent page references will be cited internally.
27. Walberg cited in Jacob J. Erickson, "'I Worship Jesus, Not Mother Earth': Exceptionalism and the Paris Withdrawal," *Religion Dispatches*, June 2, 2017.
28. "Give Up Idea of Personal God, Einstein Urges," *Chicago Daily Tribune*, September 11, 1940; "Religion of Good Urged by Einstein," *New York Times*, September 11, 1940; "Einstein Urges Abandonment of Personal God Doctrine," *Washington Post*, September 11, 1940; Einstein, "Science and Religion." For a summary of the local news pieces, see Jammer, *Einstein and Religion*, 98–103.
29. Cited in Jammer, *Einstein and Religion*, 98.
30. "Religion of Good Urged by Einstein," 27.
31. See Jammer, *Einstein and Religion*, 103–7.
32. See Jammer, 98–101.
33. Jammer, 99.
34. Cited in Jammer, 102.
35. Jammer, 104–5.
36. Jammer, 106.
37. "There are yet people who say there is no God. But what really makes me angry is that they quote me for support of such views." Einstein cited in Jammer, *Einstein and Religion*, 97.
38. In his nearest avowal of pantheism, Einstein explains, "this firm belief . . . in a superior mind that reveals itself in the world of experience, represents my conception of God. In common parlance, this may be described as 'pantheistic' (Spinoza)." Albert Einstein, "On Scientific Truth" (1929), in *Ideas and Opinions*, ed. Cal Seelig and Sonja Bargmann (New York: Three Rivers Press, 1984), 262. In his nearest disavowal of pantheism, Einstein writes: "I am not an Atheist. I do not know if I can describe myself as a Pantheist." Viereck, *Glimpses of the Great*, 372–3. Either way, he did not seem particularly attached to or repelled by the label; it simply was not his focus. As he explained to Viereck, "I am fascinated by Spinoza's Pantheism. I admire even more his . . . deal[ing] with the soul and body as one, and not two separate things" (373). Insofar as Spinoza's unification of mind and body are predicated upon his unification of God and Nature, however, an acceptance of the former would logically require an acceptance of the latter. If it is the case that Spinoza can be called a pantheist (and if he cannot, it is not clear who can), then it is also the case that Einstein can be called a pantheist.
39. Einstein cited in Abraham Pais, *Subtle Is the Lord: The Science and the Life of Albert Einstein* (1982; Oxford: Oxford University Press, 2005), vi.

40. Einstein, "On Scientific Truth," 262.
41. Ryan Coyne, "The Death of God and the New Contemplative Life," in this volume.
42. Albert Einstein, "On Science," in *Cosmic Religion with Other Opinions and Aphorisms, with an Appreciation by George Bernard Shaw* (New York: Covici-Friede, 1931), 98.
43. Einstein cited in Jammer, *Einstein and Religion*, 92.
44. Einstein cited in Yehuda Elkana, "Einstein and God," in *Einstein for the 21st Century: His Legacy in Science, Art, and Modern Culture*, ed. Peter L. Galison, Gerald Holton, and Silvan Schweber (Princeton, NJ: Princeton University Press, 2008), 36.
45. Isaac Newton, *The Principia* (1687), trans. Andrew Motte, Great Minds Series (Amherst, NY: Prometheus Books, 1995), 13.
46. Albert Einstein, "On the Electrodynamics of Moving Bodies (1905)," in *The Collected Papers of Albert Einstein, Volume 2: The Swiss Years: Writings, 1900–1909* (Princeton, NJ: Princeton University Press, 1989); Albert Einstein, "The Field Equations of Gravitation (1915)," in *The Collected Papers of Albert Einstein, Volume 6: The Berlin Years: Writings, 1914–1917* (Princeton, NJ: Princeton University Press, 1997).
47. "I stand at the window of a railway carriage which is travelling uniformly, and drop a stone on the embankment, without throwing it. . . . I see the stone descend in a straight line. A pedestrian who observes the misdeed from the footpath notices that the stone falls to earth in a parabolic curve. . . . The stone traverses a straight line relative to a system of co-ordinates rigidly attached to the carriage, but relative to a system of co-ordinates rigidly attached to the ground (embankment) it describes a parabola." Albert Einstein, *Relativity: The Special and the General Theory*, trans. Robert W. Lawson (New York: Three Rivers Press, 1961), 10–11.
48. Einstein's most famous example in this regard concerns a train struck by lightning in two places, A (toward the back of the train) and B (toward the front). From the perspective of the embankment, the two bolts strike simultaneously, whereas from the perspective of the train, bolt B hits before bolt A. Neither of these is more correct than the other; rather, the measure of correctness depends upon the specification of the vantage point. In short, "events which are simultaneous with reference to the embankment are not simultaneous with respect to the train and *vice versa*. . . . Every reference body . . . has its own particular time." Einstein, 30–31.
49. Niels Bohr, "Physical Science and the Study of Religion," in *Studia Orientalia Ioanni Pedersen Septuagenario A. D. VII Id. Nov. Anno MCMLIII a Collegis Discipulis Amicis Dicata* (Copenhagen: Munksgaard, 1953), 387.
50. We should note that such full-fledged perspectivism did not emerge until Einstein developed the theory of general relativity, and even at that point, Einstein himself was notoriously allergic to declarations like "everything in life is relative and we have the right to turn the whole world mischievously topsy-turvy." Einstein cited in Viereck, *Glimpses of the Great*, 356–57. In fact, he had initially wanted to call his special theory of relativity "invariance theory" by virtue of the inalterable— indeed, absolute—nature, neither of space nor of time, but of their totality. For although "constantly moving observers will disagree about the difference in time (Δt) or the difference in space (Δx) separately," they must agree about the differ-

ence in space-time itself. Technically speaking, then, "the 'space-time distance squared' $[(\Delta x)^2 - (\Delta y)^2]$ does *not* depend on the inertial reference frame." Lorraine Daston and Peter L. Galison, *Objectivity* (New York: Zone Books, 2007), 303. As Einstein came to realize, however, this referential independence holds only for bodies in "uniform rectilinear and non-rotary motion"; in other words, it leaves out gravity. Einstein, *Relativity*, 69. Once the consideration of gravity pushes Einstein from special to general relativity, spacetime loses its invariance because "space and time become players in the evolving cosmos. They come alive. Matter here causes space to warp there, which causes matter over there to move, which causes space way over there to warp even more, and so on. General relativity provides the choreography for an entwined cosmic dance of space, time, matter, and energy." Brian Greene, *The Fabric of the Cosmos: Space, Time, and the Texture of Reality* (New York: Vintage, 2005), 73.

51. Stephen Snobelen, "'The True Frame of Nature': Isaac Newton, Heresy, and the Reformation of Natural Philosophy," in *Heterodoxy in Early Modern Science and Religion*, ed. John Hedley Brooke and Ian Maclean (Oxford: Oxford University Press, 2005), 254.
52. The Protestant theologian Dean Fowler makes a similar argument, asserting that "Einstein's cosmic religion develops in a direction opposite [to] that of the implications of his thought." Fowler, "Einstein's Cosmic Religion," 277. In the context of the rest of Fowler's work, however, it seems that he sets forth this argument to lay the groundwork for a specifically Christian process theology rather than to push Einstein's theory of relativity into the pantheism his espousal of Spinoza seems to promise. See Dean R. Fowler, "A Process Theology of Interdependence," *Theological Studies* 40, no. 1 (March 1, 1979): 44–58.
53. For a diagrammed explanation of these experiments, see Karen Barad, *Meeting the Universe Halfway: Quantum Physics and the Entanglement of Matter and Meaning* (Durham, NC: Duke University Press, 2007), 97–106.
54. Bohr, "Physical Science," 388.
55. Albert Einstein to Max and Hedwig Born, April 29, 1924, in Albert Einstein, Max Born, and Hedwig Born, *The Born-Einstein Letters: Correspondence between Albert Einstein and Max and Hedwig Born from 1916 to 1955*, trans. Irene Born (New York: Walker & Co., 1971), 82.
56. Einstein to Max and Hedwig Born.
57. Albert Einstein to Max Born, December 4, 1926, in Einstein, Born, and Born, *Born-Einstein Letters*, 91.
58. Carl Sagan, "The Other World That Beckons: A Profile of Albert Einstein," *New Republic*, September 16, 1978, https://newrepublic.com/article/117028/world-beckons.
59. Gunther Stent, "Does God Play Dice?," *The Sciences* (March 1979), 21–22.
60. Stent, 22.
61. On the long history of such denials, see Devin Singh's chapter "Fragile Belief," in this volume.
62. See Ryan Coyne's Nietzschean retrieval of a "pagan faith in temporal becoming" in his chapter "Death of God," in this volume
63. D. H. Lawrence, "The Novel" (1925), in *Selected Critical Writings*, ed. Michael Herbert, *Oxford World Classics* (Oxford: Oxford University Press, 1998).
64. Viveiros de Castro, "Exchanging Perspectives," 471.

REFERENCES

Barad, Karen. *Meeting the Universe Halfway: Quantum Physics and the Entanglement of Matter and Meaning.* Durham, NC: Duke University Press, 2007.

Bohr, Niels. "Physical Science and the Study of Religion." In *Studia Orientalia Ioanni Pedersen Septuagenario A. D. VII Id. Nov. Anno MCMLIII a Collegis Discipulis Amicis Dicata,* 385–90. Copenhagen: Munksgaard, 1953.

Daston, Lorraine, and Peter L. Galison. *Objectivity.* New York: Zone Books, 2007.

"Death of a Cardinal." *Time,* May 1, 1944, 54.

Einstein, Albert. "The Field Equations of Gravitation (1915)." Translated by Alfred Engel. In *The Collected Papers of Albert Einstein, Volume 6: The Berlin Years: Writings, 1914–1917,* 117–20. Princeton, NJ: Princeton University Press, 1997.

———. "On Science." In *Cosmic Religion with Other Opinions and Aphorisms, with an Appreciation by George Bernard Shaw,* 97–103. New York: Covici-Friede, 1931.

———. "On Scientific Truth." 1929. In *Ideas and Opinions,* edited by Cal Seelig and Sonja Bargmann, 261–62. New York: Three Rivers Press, 1984.

———. "On the Electrodynamics of Moving Bodies (1905)." Translated by Anna Beck. In *The Collected Papers of Albert Einstein, vol. 2, The Swiss Years: Writings, 1900–1909,* 140–71. Princeton, NJ: Princeton University Press, 1989.

———. *Relativity: The Special and the General Theory.* Translated by Robert W. Lawson. New York: Three Rivers Press, 1961.

———. "Religion and Science." *New York Times Magazine,* November 9, 1930, 1.

———. "Science and Religion." 1940. In *Ideas and Opinions,* edited by Cal Seelig and Sonja Bargmann, 41–49. New York: Three Rivers Press, 1982.

Einstein, Albert, Max Born, and Hedwig Born. *The Born-Einstein Letters: Correspondence between Albert Einstein and Max and Hedwig Born from 1916 to 1955.* Translated by Irene Born. New York: Walker & Co., 1971.

Elkana, Yehuda. "Einstein and God." In *Einstein for the 21st Century: His Legacy in Science, Art, and Modern Culture,* edited by Peter L. Galison, Gerald Holton, and Silvan Schweber, 35–47. Princeton, NJ: Princeton University Press, 2008.

Faye, Jacques de la. *Defensio Religionis, Nec Non Mosis Et Gentis Judaicae, Contra Duas Dissertationes Joh. Tolandi, Quarum Una Inscribitur Adeisidaemon, Altera Vera Antiquitates Judaicae.* Ultrajecti: Apud Guilielmum Broedelet, 1709.

Fowler, Dean R. "Einstein's Cosmic Religion." *Zygon* 14, no. 3 (September 1979): 267–78.

———. "A Process Theology of Interdependence." *Theological Studies* 40, no. 1 (March 1, 1979): 44–58.

Frankenberry, Nancy. "Classical Theism, Panentheism, and Pantheism: On the Relation between God Construction and Gender Construction." *Zygon* 28, no. 1 (March 1993): 29–46.

Greene, Brian. *The Fabric of the Cosmos: Space, Time, and the Texture of Reality.* New York: Vintage, 2005.

Jammer, Max. *Einstein and Religion: Physics and Theology*. Princeton, NJ: Princeton University Press, 1999.
Lawrence, D. H. "The Novel." 1925. In *Selected Critical Writings*, edited by Michael Herbert, 179–90. Oxford World Classics. Oxford: Oxford University Press, 1998.
Newton, Isaac. *The Principia*. 1687. Translated by Andrew Motte. Great Minds Series. Amherst, NY: Prometheus Books, 1995.
Pais, Abraham. *Subtle Is the Lord: The Science and the Life of Albert Einstein*. 1982; Oxford: Oxford University Press, 2005.
Pätzold, Detlev. "Deus Sive Natura: J. G. Herder's Romanticized Reading of Spinoza's Physico-Theology." In *The Book of Nature in Early Modern and Modern History*, edited by Klaas van Berkel and Arjo Vanderjagt, 155–66. Leuven, Belgium: Peeters, 2006.
Sagan, Carl. "The Other World That Beckons: A Profile of Albert Einstein." *New Republic*, September 16, 1978. https://newrepublic.com/article/117028/world-beckons.
Schopenhauer, Arthur. *Parerga and Paralipomena*. Translated by E. F. J. Payne. 2 vols. Vol. 1. Oxford, UK: Clarendon Press, 2000.
———. *Parerga and Paralipomena*. Translated by E. F. J. Payne. 2 vols. Vol. 2. Oxford, UK: Clarendon Press, 2000.
"Science and Religion." *Time*, September 23, 1940, 52–53.
Snobelen, Stephen. "'The True Frame of Nature': Isaac Newton, Heresy, and the Reformation of Natural Philosophy." In *Heterodoxy in Early Modern Science and Religion*, edited by John Hedley Brooke and Ian Maclean, 223–62. Oxford: Oxford University Press, 2005.
Stent, Gunther S. "Does God Play Dice?" *The Sciences* (March 1979): 18–23.
Toland, John. *Adeisidaemon, Sive Titus Livius: A Superstitione Vindicatus*. Hagae-Comitis: Apud Thomam Johnson, 1709.
———. *Socinianism Truly Stated; Being an Example of Fair Dealing in All Theological Controvrsys. To Which Is Prefixt, Indifference in Disputes: Recommended by a Pantheist to an Orthodox Friend*. London, 1705.
Viereck, George Sylvester. *Glimpses of the Great*. New York: Macauley, 1930.
Viveiros de Castro, Eduardo. "Exchanging Perspectives: The Transformation of Objects into Subjects in Amerindian Ontologies." *Common Knowledge* 10, no. 3 (2004): 463–84.

2

ATHEISM AND SOCIETY

Hume's Prefiguration of Rorty

Andre C. Willis

> Poetry cannot be a substitute for a monotheistic religion, but it can serve the purposes of a secular vision of polytheism.
>
> RICHARD RORTY, *Pragmatism as Romantic Polytheism*

> That the corruption of the best things produces the worst, *is grown into a maxim, and is commonly proved, among other instances, by the pernicious effects of* superstition *and* enthusiasm, *the corruptions of true religion.*
>
> HUME, *Essays Moral, Political and Literary* X.1

Public disputes between those who hold the idea that God exists and those who reject this idea are often fanned on one side by hostility for the Abrahamic traditions and fueled on the other side by animus for skepticism. This is why these polemical and often performative debates between so-called theists and so-called atheists often strike me as disingenuous; they masquerade as serious intellectual argument as a way to conceal low-grade animus. Their either-or quality reflects and reinscribes a dangerous binary thinking that reinforces the illusion that grand, existential questions are reducible to a simple choice between two mutually exclusive positions. We see deleterious effects when this divisive mode of thinking seeps into the political realm. To prevent its proliferation at the register of "God-talk" we must generate thoughtful considerations of the variety of interwoven issues that link atheism and theism (like the current volume). This work reveals the fluidity of each term and demonstrates their mutual dependence. When we consider atheism and theism as overlapping ideas rather than solely oppositional ones, a number of interesting questions arise.

Questions around theism can bear on more than reductive issues about religious belief. They may say something about the dynamism of human community and the breadth of the human imagination, as well as our propensity to create symbols and engage in particular kinds of grammars over time. For example, when we press beyond the simple theist-atheist binary we position ourselves to understand the function of things like "atheist churches" and the appeal of "secular theists." We also get a clearer view on how nontheistic concepts of deity (especially pantheistic worldviews like panentheisms and pandeisms) may also usefully inform the human quest for meaning. Finally, to escape the uncomplicated binary theism-atheism is to open oneself to consider, in nuanced ways, how different kinds of beliefs—theistic, nontheistic and atheistic ones—might differently shape our moral actions and ethical connections.

The Western philosophical tradition is full of thinkers that have attended to questions of theism in productive ways. In this chapter, I consider two well-known critics of religion who have figured prominently in Western thought, David Hume and Richard Rorty. My premise is that when approached via complicated reflections on questions of theism-atheism, their writing reveals certain resemblances. I find similarly provocative Hume's eighteenth-century claim that the dispute between atheists and theists was "merely verbal" and Rorty's twentieth-century statement that both theism and atheism were irrational.

It is worth noting that on Rorty's own account, his engagement with questions around theism was not primarily informed by Anglo-Enlightenment figures like Hume, Locke, and Berkeley but by Hegel, Nietzsche, Heidegger, and Dewey. Along with the three continental philosophers, it makes sense that Dewey's thoughts about religion would have an impact on Rorty, as both men are considered foundational to American philosophy. These "American Pragmatists" generally turn away from "otherworldly," supernatural and metaphysical concerns to more "this worldly," natural, and empirical ones. Thus, they redirect the "conventional" theological questions about the ontological status of the deity (e.g., Does God exist?, How do we gain knowledge of the Divine?, What are the characteristics of God?) toward concerns about the impact that beliefs in "God" have on human experience, particularly at the social or public level.[1] For pragmatists, claims like "I believe in God" (theism) or "I do not believe in God" (atheism), when taken on their own, are largely uninteresting. They become interesting when we consider their implications, how they tie into other commitments, and how they shape our habits.

One might wonder what really is at stake in arguing that some of the central ideas in the work of the eighteenth-century thinker David Hume can be viewed as anticipating the crucial insights of American pragmatism, particularly concepts articulated by Richard Rorty in his 1989 text *Contingency, Irony, and Solidarity*.[2] The simple answer is that elucidating traces of Hume's thought in Rorty's work invites us to better understand the overlaps between theism and atheism. For the connections I make between Hume and Rorty are neither random nor isolated; they bear on debates between theists and atheists in at least two important ways. The first is that in distinct yet overlapping fashions, each thinker confirmed that atheism and theism were both species of belief that presupposed a notion of God. Hume and Rorty started from an awareness that both crude atheisms and unsophisticated theisms were grounded in the core idea of the existence of a deity.[3] Their work revealed the extent to which the hubris of a confident theism that knows "all too well what [it] is affirming when [it] says 'God exists'" is the "mirror image" of a bold atheism that "know(s) all too well what it [is] denying when [it] says 'God does not exist.'"[4] Maybe this is what Hume was suggesting when he wrote that the dispute between theists and atheists was "merely verbal" and "incurably ambiguous" (*Dialogues Concerning Natural Religion* 12.6) and what Rorty was signifying when he observed that "Christian theism . . . [was] no more irrational than atheism."[5]

Second, Hume and Rorty both challenged the conventional pillars of the Western philosophical enterprise—rational certainty, formal argumentation, and ethical persuasion—which, to them, had proved insufficient tools to combat idolatry. They recognized that literature (especially Rorty's notion of philosophy as poetics), captivating narratives (especially Rorty's idea of redescription as a literary practice), multivocality (Hume's numerous dialogues), and close attention to literary form (especially Hume's essays, philosophical treatises, political arguments, historical writings, and letters) were just as important as, if not more important than, the formal philosophical grammars of metaphysics and epistemology, particularly when it came to contending with belief in deities and embracing tenets of a religious tradition. It follows that Hume and Rorty both relied on literature and literary devices, history, and cultural politics as idioms to express their dynamic sociocritical and philosophical views on theisms or atheisms.

More specifically, my hope in this chapter is to show that Hume's historical redescriptions, his moderate skepticism, and his use of the psychological quality "sympathy" can be usefully thought of as prefiguring Rorty's approach to the categories of contingency, irony, and solidarity. This is not to merely set up Hume in the Rortyean lineage and to draw attention to this largely underrecognized feature of Rorty's thought; it is, in addition, to consider connections between theism and atheism and to reveal affinities between Hume and Rorty. Hume and Rorty were soundly anticlerical and extremely critical of religious practices that led to social instability, and they both held disdain for religious beliefs that generated political division. Interestingly, however, they seemed to realize that the character of religion in a society is important for the flourishing of that particular society and that claims about God could be thought of as linguistic truths—that is, cultural and social—rather than as metaphysical truths.

RORTY'S "CONTINGENCY" AND HUMEAN APPROACH TO HISTORY AND COMMON LIFE

Rorty's central argument in chapter 1 of *Contingency, Irony, and Solidarity* is that human language is historically contingent. He writes: "Our language and our culture are as much a contingency, as much a result of thousands of small mutations finding niches (and millions of others finding no niches), as are the orchids and the anthropoids" (16). One consequence of conceiving of language as fully contingent is that it means that our speech about God is dynamic and ever changing, and that this speech is not handed down to us from above. Rather, it arises naturally from the human imagination and is thus soaked in history and community. The prevailing truths of religion, theism (and even atheism) are, then, thoroughly grounded in fleeting systems of language, culture, and community.

As is typical to his overall philosophic style, Rorty tends to make strong claims that he immediately wants to situate, and in some ways to justify, within a wider philosophical heritage. To that end, he crafts a broad philo-historical narrative that hooks his emphasis on historical contingency to an antecedent intellectual tradition. Rorty's creative reinterpretation of the thinkers he highlights—Nietzsche, Freud, Wittgenstein—positions their work such that it bolsters his socionormative and political aim: secular liberal society. For him, society must "try to get to the point where we no longer worship anything, where we treat nothing as a quasi-divinity, where we treat everything—our language, our conscience, our community—as a product of time and chance" (22). This secularizing sociopolitical goal fuels Rorty's way of thinking of language as fully contingent and opens us to the idea that we can understand the three-lettered symbol *G-O-D* as a product of the human imagination that points beyond that which can be known.

To be preoccupied with contingency in language, culture, and community is, for Rorty, to summon a form of creative, albeit private, heroism. For if language, culture, and community are fully provisional and ever shifting, then human agents constantly create and re-create grammars, describe and redescribe culture, and make and remake community. The heroes of the projects of re-creation and redescription are not philosophers; they are poets. Poetry is thus elevated above conventional philosophy, because "only poets, Nietzsche suspected, can truly appreciate contingency. The rest of us are doomed to remain philosophers, to insist that there is really only one true lading-list, one true description of the human situation, one universal context of our lives. We are doomed to spend our conscious lives trying to escape from contingency rather than, like the strong poet, acknowledging and appropriating contingency" (28).

The "strong maker, the person who uses words as they have never before been used, is best able to appreciate her own contingency" (28), and this private appreciation forms a kind of aesthetic heroism. In some ways, this poetic response to contingency coupled with a public vision could support the development of new historical narratives that might effectively diagnose communal experience in ways that serve communal interests. For without any neutral moral ground on which to stand or "any plain moral facts out there in the world" (173), liberals, "the people who think that cruelty is the worst thing we do," creatively redescribe historical events to support their sociopolitical vision. Yet Rorty's public-private split renders the strong poet impotent for bringing about the effective liberal society. In short, to state it crudely, Rorty's heroic poet is no political activist.

Perhaps the diverse reading choices of sixteen-year-old David Hume, "sometimes a philosopher, sometimes a poet," in the summer of 1734 reflected his unique attempt to avoid reducing philosophy to the realms of the distant and contemplative, and displayed his enthusiastic tendency to embrace poetry as the art of the provisional and present. Hume's veneration of poetry can be taken as a challenge to conventional approaches to theism. One the one hand, it flags a certain openness to new possibilities for language—particularly metaphors and analogies—to express things beyond this world. In doing so, it removes transcendence from the realm of the philosophical discourse and places it in the realm of the theo-poetic. On the other hand, Hume's writings suggest that if it is to remain provisional, any reference to a transhistorical being (a God) is one that is always incomplete because its description is *within* history, community, and language.

Hume's letter to his boyhood pal Michael Ramsay articulated his foundational self-understanding as both a poet and a philosopher. Citing Virgil, Hume remarked that the "one solace in his suffering" was his daily reading of both poetry and philosophy.[6] For, he claimed, the "wiseman" and the "husbandman" agreed in "peace of mind, in a liberty and independency on fortune, and contempt of riches, power, and glory. Everything is placid and quiet in both persons, nothing perturbed or disordered."[7] It's fair to say that Hume believed that creative philosophical work and complex poetry fostered a sense of harmony, which he described as follows: "They enjoy an untroubled calm. A life that knows no falsehood."[8]

My point here is that Hume articulated links between poetry and philosophy in ways that Rorty could well have been thinking of when he argued for the strong poet. Hume, of course, was not the first philosopher to think of the connections between poetry and philosophy. He was, however, unique as an early modern "man of letters" whose writing poignantly demonstrated that style and content were mutually constitutive, not independent, variables. Hume's body of work reflected his acute awareness that philosophy was always articulated in and constituted by literary form: his essays, dialogues, historical writings, philosophical texts, and religious tracts probed the limits of form and plumbed the depths of different genres. It is not far-fetched to imagine Hume as antecedent to that line of thinkers Rorty elevated: Nietzsche, Freud, Wittgenstein, and others.

To think of Hume as a Rortyan strong poet of the English-speaking Enlightenment is to consider thoroughly Hume's "boldness of temper" and his being "led to seek out some new medium" in terms that approximate a kind of poetic heroism. In his famous "Letter to a Physician" (most likely Dr. George Cheyne) in 1734, Hume described the inclinations of his literary energies: "You must know then that from my earliest Infancy, I found alwise a strong Inclination to Books & Letters. As our College Education in Scotland, extending little further than the Languages, ends commonly when we are about 14 or 15 Years of Age, I was after that left to my own Choice in my Reading, & found it encline me almost equally to Books of Reasoning & Philosophy, & to Poetry & the polite Authors" (letter 3). Hume's sense of the links between poetry and philosophy and his creative predilections for redescription inform his idea of the "true philosopher" and shape his work as a "true historian." Allow me to say a brief word about Hume's "true historian."

Hume's longest (more than a million words) and, arguably, his most time-consuming work (nearly fifteen years), was his six-volume *History of England* (published between 1754 and 1762). The historian Nicholas Phillipson described this text as "designed to encourage modern readers to think about the stories they had been told about the history of civilization in their country."[9] We can think about this major historical writing and Hume's *Natural History of Religion* (which describes the historical development of vulgar theism from polytheism) as revising, redescribing, and reappropriating earlier narratives and antecedent histories. Among other things, the *Natural History of Religion*'s discussion of the evolution of polytheism highlights the close connections between theism and atheism, and the *History of England* depicts how religious vocabularies shift over time.

An often overlooked feature of Hume's *History of England* is the extent to which Hume writes as a quasi poet of redescription (per Rorty's language) that recasts historical events and characters in ways that emphasize the moral, social, and political qualities that both generate and are consequences of "greatness of mind" and the "sentimental sublime."[10] Siebert contends that in the *History*, "Hume has refashioned the familiar sentimental character into a new type, one we might term the 'hero of feeling.'" Eerily presaging Rorty's "strong maker," Siebert contends, "The creation of this hero is part of the redefinition of virtue that Hume undertakes."[11] Siebert describes Hume historical writing as a kind of quasi-poetic enterprise where Hume is the artist of redescription pressing against the boundaries of historical writing such that he conjures the "sentiment for the sublime." This conjuring requires Hume to harness the "talent itself of the poets" (*Enquiry Concerning the Principles of Morals*, 259), which, on Siebert's argument, allows him to re-create the "hero of feeling" and re-describe the sentimental sublime in the *History of England*.

In spite of Siebert's unique interpretation of Hume, it is important to remember that not all historical work is reducible to (Rortyan) redescription. It is Hume's preoccupation with the dynamism of history, his emphasis on its persistent motion, what he calls its "flux and reflux," that permits his creative rearticulations and the new descriptions he gives throughout his historical narrative. This historical dynamism is also displayed in the *Natural History of Religion*, where Hume recasts the historical arc (against that of his contemporaries) to suggest that polytheism preceded monotheism. The cyclical movement of history will, it seems, render atheism, then polytheism, as future historical phases. The point is that Hume's philosophy of history as flux and reflux bears on the debate between theism and atheism. Hume writes, "It is remarkable, that the principles of religion have kind of flux and reflux in the human mind, and that men have a natural tendency to rise from idolatry to theism, and to sink again from theism into idolatry" (*Natural History of Religion* 8.1).

It is safe to say that Hume's history affirmed historical contingency. Yet his way to "acknowledge" and "appropriate" contingency was not explicitly to call for strong poets, obsess on invention, and fixate on redescription (à la Rorty); it was, rather, to exemplify a "true philosopher," one who understood the contingencies of history and embraced them while locating the background ideas, habits, and practices that sustained in the face of contingent languages, cultures, and communities. That is, Hume balanced, in ways Rorty chose not to, the contingent with the consistent. Like Rorty, Hume resisted simple notions of transcendence and easy universals. Unlike Rorty, Hume welcomed the background ideas, categories, concepts, and stories. One of the ways he did this was by affirming "common life," a discursive category that serves as an important but often overlooked part of Hume's intellectual legacy.

For Hume, "common life" was the mode of thought and action that confirmed the importance of our dynamic customs, ever-shifting prejudices, and natural propensities against skeptical reason and the contingencies of history. Hume's "common life," as argued by Donald W. Livingston in *Philosophical Melancholy and Delirium,* worked dialectically with his notion of false philosophy. The resolution and overcoming of this division was the rare, "true philosophy."

Hume's argument for true philosophy over false philosophy and vulgar forms of thinking is grounded in his notion of common life.[12] Hume described the tension between these two modes as follows: "In considering this subject we may observe a gradation of three opinions that rise above each other, according as the persons, who form them, acquire new degrees of reason and knowledge. These opinions are that of the *vulgar,* that of a *false philosophy* and that of the *true*; where we shall find upon enquiry, that the true philosophy approaches nearer to the sentiments of the vulgar, than to those of a mistaken knowledge" (Treatise I.IV.III.9, italics mine). Hume's true philosopher, the philosopher of common life, approached the contingency of language, culture, and community in ways that strike me as supportive of Rorty's argument for the historical contingency of language and the strong maker. Rorty's rejection of the wisdom of Hume's "common life"—that is, Hume's embrace of both the contingent and the consistent—reflects Rorty's philosophical temperament as well as his historical moment.

THE RORTYAN LIBERAL IRONIST AND THE HUMEAN MODERATE SKEPTIC

For the Rortyan "liberal ironist," the debate between theists and atheists has nothing to do with discovering or rejecting an ontological truth, embracing or discarding metaphysical reality, or satisfying or ignoring a spiritual need; rather, it is simply a matter of temporarily orienting oneself within a vocabulary.[13] The liberal ironist creatively redescribes history and poetically narrates social life; in so doing, she becomes a master of her grammar and an author of her identity. In this way, the liberal ironist challenges the authority of both her conscience and her community. She becomes a hero in a liberal society that recognizes, as Rorty writes, that "it is what it is, has the morality it has, speaks the language it does, not because it approximates the will of God or the nature of man but because certain poets and revolutionaries of the past spoke as they did" (*Contingency, Irony, Solidarity* 60–61). To recognize the contingency of language, and hence, authority, is to reject a flat-footed theism that places all power in the hands of deity and to shun the fixed and unalterable claims of an uncomplicated atheism.

The fecund character of the liberal ironist has provoked criticism and generated support from across the wide swath of the philosophical spectrum. Progressive political philosophers tend to be dismayed by what appears as a lack of a public program for the liberal ironist,[14] and analytic philosophers, by definition, scrap the argument that philosophy should aspire to a form of poetry. At the same time, philosophers of law laud the "jurisprudential ambition" of a "narrative reconstitution of political morality" driven by the liberal ironist,[15] and philosophically inclined liberal pluralists cite Rorty's philosophical pluralism as provocative.[16] But what exactly is significant about Rorty's "liberal ironist"? How, if it all, might we connect it to the thought of David Hume? Finally, what is the use-value, if any, of these matters on the question of atheism?

Rorty creates the character of the liberal ironist while describing philosophy as a form of poetry in the fourth chapter of *Contingency, Irony, and Solidarity* (*CIS*, 1989). In this chapter, "Private Irony and Liberal Hope," he builds a case for the "ironist" from his description of our ultimate set of commitments, which he dubs our "final vocabulary":

> All human beings carry about a set of words which they employ to justify their actions, their beliefs, and their lives. These are the words in which we formulate praise of our friends and contempt for our enemies, our long-term projects, our deepest self-doubts and our highest hopes. They are the words in which we tell, sometimes prospectively and sometimes retrospectively, the story of our lives. I shall call these words a person's "final vocabulary."
>
> It is "final" in the sense that if doubt is cast on the worth of these words, their user has no noncircular argumentative recourse. Those words are as far as he can go with language; beyond them there is only helpless passivity or a resort to force. (*CIS*, 73)

I want to make two initial observations related to this citation. First, an example: a Buddhist monk would be described as using a "Buddhist final vocabulary." Second, an explanation: Rorty's point in drawing our attention to our final vocabulary is to suggest that there is no ultimate court of appeal to determine which beliefs we hold as true, and no final arbiter to rationally confirm our ideals as justifiable. For Rorty, the decisive grammar we use to support our actions and ideas is not grounded in anything beyond itself.

To turn back to my example and extend it: how is this Buddhist monk, or anyone, to relate to the fact that her "final vocabulary" is not justifiable on terms outside of itself? Rorty describes an attitude one might take: that of the "ironist":

> I shall define an "ironist" as someone who fulfills three conditions: (1) She has radical and continuing doubts about the final vocabulary she currently uses . . . ; (2) she realizes that arguments phrased in her present vocabulary can neither underwrite nor dissolve these doubts; (3) insofar as she philosophizes about her situation, she does not think that her vocabulary is closer to reality than others, that it is in touch with a power not herself. Ironists who are inclined to philosophize see the choice between vocabularies as made neither within a neutral and universal metavocabulary nor by an attempt to fight one's way past appearances to the real, but simply by playing the new off against the old. (*CIS*, 73)

The distinctive mood of the ironist is informed by a healthy dose of skepticism. That is, our Buddhist "ironist" recognizes the fundamental instability of her views on, for example, impermanence, and realizes that these positions are rationally indefensible outside of themselves. If our Buddhist ironist is a philosophical and reflective type—that is, an intellectual—it is likely that she would embrace the idea that the belief she holds that "all existence is temporary" is no more than a strategic way of thinking that she learned in community with others who had been taught some similar version of it. They likely came to understand this view as helping them process parts of their life experience in ways they found to be effective.

Since the "opposite of irony is common sense" (*CIS*, 74), the commonsense realist stands against the ironist. "Common sense," Rorty explains, is "the watchword of those who unselfconsciously describe everything important in terms of the final vocabulary to which they and those around them are habituated" (*CIS*, 74). At its most basic level, common sense functions within the parameters of our habits and confirms our prejudices: a common sense (i.e., non-ironist) Buddhist—that is, a Buddhist "practitioner"—lives according to his Buddhist final vocabulary without any tension or doubt. He accepts impermanence and other Buddhist principles and beliefs as they were taught to him—as universal truths—and he uncritically and nonreflectively lives with them.

More reflective than the commonsense practitioner Buddhist is the commonsense metaphysician Buddhist. This non-ironist Buddhist thinks he can give a full intellectual account of his Buddhist final vocabulary. Rorty explains:

> The metaphysician is someone who takes the question, "what is the intrinsic nature of (e.g. justice, science, knowledge, Being, faith, morality, philosophy)?" at face value. He assumes that the presence of a term in his own final vocabulary ensures that it refers to something which *has* a real essence. The metaphysician is still attached to common sense, in that he does not question the platitudes which encapsulate the use of a given final vocabulary, and in particular the platitude which says there is a single permanent reality to be found behind the many temporary appearances. *He does not redescribe but, rather, analyzes old descriptions with the help of other old descriptions.* (74, italics mine)

Our Buddhist metaphysician considers his final vocabulary as a reflection of reality. He believes that there is such a thing as the "real" and that his Buddhist final vocabulary depicts reality.[17] This is distinct from our Buddhist ironist, who rejects realism entirely. For "the ironist . . . is a nominalist and a historicist. She thinks nothing has an intrinsic nature, a real essence." Against the two strands of commonsense approaches (the practitioner and the metaphysician), the ironist "spends her time worrying about the possibility that she has been initiated into the wrong tribe, taught to play the wrong language game. She worries that the process of socialization which turned her into a human being by giving her a language may have given her the wrong language, and so turned her into the wrong kind of human being. But she cannot give a criterion of wrongness" (75).

I highlight Rorty's fecund category "final vocabulary," and focus on his liberal ironist as well as two of its opposing characters, the metaphysician and the practitioner, to demonstrate the "presence" of Hume's thought in these figures, particularly the Humean approach to irony and, relatedly, Hume's engagement with metaphysical questions. In some ways it is surprising that Rorty makes no mention of Hume's contributions here. Rather, he elevates Proust's grasp of contingency and focuses on Proustian literary redescription as fundamental for the development of liberal autonomy.[18] Hume never gets mentioned.

Yet John Vladimir Price's *The Ironic Hume* (1965) contended that Hume's ironic mode was quite visible and that it operated bidirectionally: Price argued that Hume both recognized the space between human hopes and human accomplishments as ironic and also used irony as a literary style to mask his skepticism. Rorty's liberal ironist does not mask her skepticism—her worries are on the surface. But Hume's choice to use irony as a literary style, according to Price, is not simply to hide and conceal a profound skepticism; it is, rather to display a more moderate skepticism. Hume's moderate skeptic shares the attitude of Rorty's liberal ironist: both thought similarly about metaphysics. The philosopher Michael Williams, a well-known student of Rorty's, supports this idea when he describes this convergence of Rorty's categories with Hume's as a "Humean turn."[19] Williams situates Rorty's metaphysician as a type of "metaphysical realist" and locates his liberal ironist in line with the "moderate skeptic" (both Enlightenment terms). In doing so, he places Rorty's argument in alignment with Hume's framework.[20]

Williams's point reminds the reader that skepticism plays a significant role in Hume's thought project. Of course, scholars grapple about the depth and intensity of Hume's skepticism, whether it is a form of Pyrrhonism, and how (and whether) he resolves it.[21] Hume's writings, particularly his early *Treatise* and the first *Enquiry,* display an openness to Pyrrhonism—an extreme form of skepticism that fully suspends judgment on every issue—but ultimately his positions rely on tacit forms of "belief as fundamental for our ordering of experience."[22] I think of Hume's conciliation between skepticism and belief as a form of intellectual humility. Like Rorty's liberal ironist, who has continuing doubts about her final vocabulary, Hume's moderate skeptic is "diffident of his philosophical doubts, as well as of his philosophical convictions" (Treatise I.IV.VII.14). The similarities here are glaring.

Hume's moderate skeptic also recognizes that Pyrrhonian skepticism leads to a logical dead end, that it undermines the capacity for action, and that it paralyzes our ability to make judgments regarding sources of our beliefs. Hume writes in the *Enquiry Concerning Human Understanding* (1749) that he prefers an "easy philosophy" that considers man chiefly as born for *action,* a philosophical approach whose "species of philosophers paint her [virtue] in the most amiable colours"; "borrowing all helps from poetry and eloquence, and treating their subject in an easy and obvious manner, and such as is best fitted to please the imagination, and engage the affections. . . . They make us *feel* the difference between vice and virtue; they excite and regulate our sentiments; and so they can but bend our hearts to the love of probity and true honour, they think, that they have fully attained the end of all their labours" (1.1, original italics). There are at least three resonances between Hume's "easy philosophy" and the approach of Rorty's liberal ironist that are worth noting. First, Hume says that it "borrows all helps from poetry." Recall from my discussion of Rorty's contingency and Hume's history and common life earlier that Rorty's argument for the liberal ironist occurs within his larger interest in philosophy as a form of poetry. Second, similar to the affective strengths of the Rortyan ironist, Hume's "easy philosophy" appeals to our feelings and sentiments, not reason alone. And third, Hume's easy philosophy understands humans as "born for action" in ways that the ironist is driven to the action of redescription.

In terms of metaphysics, the approaches of Hume and Rorty overlap. Rorty's basic bifurcation between the ironist and the metaphysician share resonances with Hume's division between the moderate skeptic and abstract philosopher. The moral component of Rorty's project, solidarity, and Hume's psychological mechanism of "sympathy" provide a third and final area for consideration.

RORTY'S SOLIDARITY AND HUME'S SYMPATHY

In "Solidarity," the closing chapter of *Contingency, Irony, and Solidarity*, Rorty offers a moral strategy grounded in his personal final vocabulary. He calls for "our recognition of one another's common humanity" (189). Rorty admits that the call for solidarity can easily be read as the kind of transhistorical claim that stands in opposition to the historical contingency he has trumpeted, and he acknowledges that the notion of recognition that he invokes summons epistemological foundations counter to those of the liberal ironist he has championed. Still, he "urges" us—via a refrain that rings of atheism—to "try *not* to want something which stands beyond history and institutions" (189), yet he promotes belief in North American liberal society and its concomitant "moral obligation to feel a sense of solidarity with all other human beings" (190).

In spite of the belief in liberal secular democracy, Rorty shows no interest in securing theological support for his moral approach, and he distinguishes his version of solidarity from the "traditional philosophical way" of thinking about it. He writes, "The traditional philosophical way of spelling out what we mean by 'human solidarity' is to say that there is something within each of us—our essential humanity—which resonates to the presence of this same thing in other human beings" (189). Solidarity is neither part of our human "essence," nor given to us by God. It is, for Rorty, a practice thoroughly grounded in human personality, situated in a moment of human history, and connected to the dynamic needs of a human community. It must be enacted.

From one angle, Rorty's solidarity is exceedingly practical: it is driven by a specific aim (social hope for a secularized community), comes at a particular moment (the present), and requires a human community (liberal North Americans). From another angle, these practical considerations invite broad, general speculation. For example, what does a fully secular community actually look like? Who, precisely, are groups of "liberal North Americans" that Rorty references, and why would they show solidarity? Rorty's answer to the latter invites more questions than it resolves. He writes, "Our sense of solidarity is strongest when those with whom solidarity is expressed are thought of as 'one of us,' where 'us' means something smaller and more local than the human race" (191). A lot of options remain.

Rorty's "urging" for a human solidarity that cannot be justified via any "philosophical presuppositions" aims, ultimately, to function as a way to link suffering human agents. To recognize our "similarities with respect to pain and humiliation" (192) is, for Rorty, to create togetherness across various divisions and to generate connections where it feels unnatural to do so. To my ear, this way of thinking about generating connections carries a religious residue, has a teleological dimension, and relies on, in some ways, something like a quasi-theological—or at least not-fully-comprehensible—power. That is, I think of the obligation toward Rorty's practice of solidarity as something greater than that solidarity itself. It drives toward an end. And it works somewhat mysteriously, this "practice."[23]

It makes sense to think about Rorty's version of solidarity as shaping a particular sort of ethical formation that begins from the suggestions of sentiment and works toward the practices of solidarity. This kind of moral binding—a form of labor—retains the "contingent historical character" that Rorty's project demands. That is, it is derived from human community not antecedent to it. Rorty's public philosophical project for a more democratic politics stems from the sentiment of solidarity, which—he emphasizes—is grounded in the moral deliberations of a particular community at a distinct moment, for a unique end. His concluding paragraph hits this home: "To sum up, I want to distinguish human solidarity as the identification with 'humanity as such' and as the self-doubt which has gradually, over the last few centuries, been inculcated into inhabitants of the democratic states—doubt about their own sensitivity to the pain and humiliation of others, doubt that present institutional arrangements are adequate to deal with this pain and humiliation, curiosity about possible alternatives" (198).

Hume observed (in his *Treatise* and *First Enquiry*) that there was no epistemologically sound argument for a deity with moral attributes, and he wrote in the *Natural History of Religion* that history confirmed popular religion to be ineffective at transmitting effective moral judgment. Hume thus started his considerations of ethical formation from the perspective of human agents fully situated in history and community. He thought that their moral judgments were both fueled by the sentiments and dependent on social approval. Hume grounded his moral project in shared feeling, that is, a sentiment, generated by a mechanism he named "sympathy." Like Hobbes—a major influence on Hume's moral thought—Hume was not a moral realist; he did not support the idea that our moral judgments reflected some preexistent and transcendent truth. He thought our moral imaginations, filtered through history and social life, projected a schema of values onto the world. This ever-present schema served as a kind of moral background for our ethical choices.

For Hume, if the sentiments were to gain approval from conventions of community (Hume calls this "approbation") and combine with a "natural motive to action,"[24] they might progress to a moral obligation, the active manifestation of our affective bond with others. For Hume, the psychological mechanism of sympathy is crucial to this binding. Sympathy was foundational for our deeper connection to and stronger cooperation with our fellow human beings.

It is easy to mistake Hume's notion of sympathy for the virtue of empathy, but to crudely equate the two is to misrepresent Hume's moral project. Sympathy, on the account Hume gives in *Treatise* II.I.XI,[25] might be thought of as a naturally occurring psychological feature of the mind that sparks moral judgments. It differs from empathy, the idea that one can put oneself in someone else's shoes, in that sympathy emphasizes experiencing the same or similar feelings as someone else while remaining in one's own shoes. Hume wanted to track how the motives of the moral actor could be transferred, how they could gain public approval, and he used this mechanism of sympathy to enable him to do so.

There is much more to say about Hume's category "sympathy." The problems and challenges of this category, as well as its usefulness for Hume's moral thinking, are well documented in the secondary literature. I want to make just two points to support my position that Hume's "sympathy" could have served as a kind of antecedent moral category to Rorty's idea "solidarity." The overlaps between the moral projects of both Hume and Rorty are obvious: both emphasized that there was no transcendent, transhistorical, and independent truth-value for our morals. Moral judgment was a product of social and historical factors (among other things). First, Rorty's solidarity shared the idea with Hume's sympathy that our capacity to risk feeling more connected to others was a product of our social world and a consequence of public life. Second, Rorty's hope that our feelings of solidarity will expand was grounded in Hume's notion that the sentiments progress. Rorty writes:

> Hume is a better advisor than Kant about how we intellectuals can hasten the coming of the Enlightenment utopia for which both men yearned. Among contemporary philosophers, the best advisor seems to me to be Annette Baier. Baier describes Hume as "the woman's moral philosopher" because Hume held that "corrected (sometimes rule-corrected) sympathy, not law-discerning reason, is the fundamental moral capacity." . . . Baier would like us to get rid of both the Platonic idea that we have a true self, and the Kantian idea that it is rational to be moral. . . . This substitution would mean thinking of the spread of the human rights culture not as a matter of our becoming more aware of the requirements of the moral law, but rather as what Baier calls "a progress of sentiments." . . . This progress consists in an increasing ability to see the similarities between ourselves and people very unlike us as outweighing the differences. It is the result of what I have been calling "sentimental education." (Rorty, *Truth and Progress*, 181)

CONCLUSION

Hume's view of philosophy as a synthetic mode of thinking that challenges abstruse philosophy, embraces historicism and perspectivalism, and invests in the usefulness of ideas over their logical certainty anticipates Rorty's. And there is significant overlap and a surprising similarity in some of their terms and categories, which bear on debates about atheism and theism. To consider God as G-O-D—a historically contingent symbol of common life crafted by heroic poets and true religionists who elevate solidarity via the mechanism sympathy—is to leave room for both theism and atheism. It is to note a merely "verbal dispute" between the two sides.

The distinctions between Rorty's work and Hume's can also be useful for thinking about theism and religion. As I noted earlier, Rorty's desire to abandon conventional philosophical language and emphasize both the historical contingency of language and poetic redescription as a heroic response has symmetry with Hume's approach to ideas and also overlaps with his notion of the true philosopher. The difference between Rorty's strong poet and Hume's true philosopher rests on the degree to which the true philosopher (of common life) engages with the public and the strong poet does not. Hume's rare, true philosopher reconciles the popular opinions of common life with the vulgar conclusions of false philosophy. Unlike the false philosopher, Hume's true philosopher is not alienated from the traditions of common life that produced her. She explains, describes, and organizes the conclusions of common life as she quietly challenges them. "The true philosopher," Livingston writes, "having worked through the errors of false philosophy, recognizes the authority of the popular [vulgar] system in his own thought."[26]

Rorty's strong poet, unlike the Humean true philosopher, does not affirm the traditions of common life. She seems to be a thoroughly private figure. For, as Williams states, "In our active, public lives, we cannot be ironists, nor would it be desirable for us to try to be. But in our private, reflective moments we can contemplate the fragility and contingency of even the language in which we express our most heartfelt commitments."[27]

Let me turn back to the Buddhist practitioner, the Buddhist metaphysician, and the Buddhist ironist. The relation of each of these figures to their final vocabulary is meaningfully different for Rorty. The Buddhist ironist is so insecure, unstable, and distant from common sense that she can only react. On Rorty's own argument, "Irony seems inherently a private matter" (87). He continues: "On my definition, an ironist cannot get along without the contrast between the final vocabulary she inherited and the one she is trying to create for herself. Irony is, if not intrinsically resentful, at least reactive. Ironists have to have something to have doubts about, something from which to be alienated." Rorty's points lead him to conclude that the ironist has "an inability to empower" (91).

Hume's Buddhist true philosopher, however, would feel a strong kinship with fellow Buddhists. She is less invested in firm theological content and philosophical language of her tradition—which she recognizes are final vocabularies in the Rortyan sense and thus unstable, but she revels in the practices and ceremonies. The Buddhist true philosopher affirms common life and rejects its contamination by abstract thought. She empowers because her skepticism is not a private affair. It makes us *feel* the difference between vice and virtue, excite and regulate our sentiments, and "bend our hearts to the love of probity and true honour" (E, 1.1).

The Buddhist false philosopher—to continue in the Humean frame—takes a "vulgar" way of conceiving what we do: his approach verifies the infestation of metaphysics into false philosophy—that is, how modern religion strives for philosophical legitimation above all. True religion counters this impulse: it neither aims for legitimacy in the terms of abstract thought nor opts for easy answers. It tries to provide stability in the face of the life's vicissitudes. One might ask, how is this "religion"? Rorty's ironist answers: because this redescription expands "our chances of being kind, of avoiding the humiliation of others" (*CIS*, 91).

On Livingston's reading, Hume contends that we can be in the business of either certifying or invalidating long-standing artifacts of our culture (e.g., reason, religion). On Rortyan terms, this would be taking a commonsense approach to a final vocabulary. More rarely, a true philosopher might bring attention to these practices, trace their origins, and formulate "critical rules, principles or ideals which seem to reflect the practice[s]."[28] Hume's framing designates "true philosophy" to indicate the rare harmony of common life and philosophical self-reflection. It distinguishes between the surface of experience and that which precedes it. In this way, the true philosopher can assume a natural order if she needs to but not necessarily take it to be real (although she may).[29]

He does not make it explicit, but Rorty's interventions here, his categories "ironist" and "final vocabulary," are obsessed with the epistemic status of certain ideas and beliefs. Rorty clarifies that we are not able to confirm ideas as real and justify beliefs as true. Hume's philosophy of common life does not share this obsession; it aims to explain the process of formation of our ideas and beliefs to shed light on the surface of experience and, inadvertently, what lies below it. To do so, "true philosophy" must take into account the categories and prereflective convictions of common life, whose sources remain inscrutable. The epistemological humility of the Humean true philosopher positions her to embrace the most useful and naturally occurring beliefs with a quiet confidence.

For Rorty, our final vocabularies, when approached from common sense, divide and compete. A Protestant Evangelical final vocabulary bumps up against a Roman Catholic final vocabulary. For Hume, the tacit wisdom of common life as well as the natural functioning of our minds generates our human impulse to embrace a basic theism, the belief that the world is a result of purposive activity, in spite of the fact that this belief flies in the face of the standards of evidence required by abstract thought. In this way, Hume's true philosophy and true religion connect human communities via this "natural" sense of theism.

But the Humean true philosopher is historically astute. She is aware that basic theism, although it helps us function by allowing us to order and organize experience, will get deformed by the human passions and ultimately manifest in some form of "religious" activity, divisive final vocabularies, or factionalism. This is also Rorty's worry. But Hume has an answer: the rare true religion can "methodize and correct" the distortions. Rorty only allows us redescription.

On the parameters of Livingston's argument, true theism—that we tend to think of the world as ordered by "springs and principles"—is a foundation for true philosophy. It affirms that the sources of our "belief in basic theism" lie beyond both actual experience and our final vocabulary. This leaves us open to genuine theism and true religion, a rare form of religion that contributes "to the amendment of men's lives, and their improvement in morality and social virtue" (*Enquiry Concerning the Principles of Morals*, 9.2.1). Rorty might balk at the idea of a genuine theism and true religion, but he would be similarly unhappy with a genuine atheism, and he would find little value in false religion. For him the debate about theism is of little use—the move toward secular liberal society, a kind of de-theologizing writ large, moves Rorty's interests away from narrow claims for either theism or atheism.

NOTES

1. I think of pragmatists as intervening in disputes about atheism in slightly different ways at distinct moments across three historical periods of American pragmatism, yet this loose and imprecise periodization (proto-pragmatist, classical pragmatist, and neo-pragmatist) is used as a heuristic. Instead of emphasizing traditional theological inquiries into God's existence, the proto-pragmatist Ralph Waldo Emerson highlighted how our rhetoric and reflection about God affected our moral choices. For more on Emerson, see Jeffrey Stout, "The Transformation of Genius into Practical Power: A Reading of Emerson's Experience," *American Journal of Theology and Philosophy* 35, no. 1 (January 2014): 3–22. See also Emily Dumler-Winckler, "Romanticism as Modern Re-enchantment: Burke, Kant, and Emerson on Religious Taste," *Zeitschrift für Neuere Theologiegeschichte* 22, no. 1 (2015): 1–22. Rather than centering conventional theistic concerns about the nature of divinity, the "Classical" pragmatists C. S. Peirce, William James, and John Dewey drew attention to the multiplicity of belief experiences and the consequences of those experiences on our moral conduct. See Cornel West, *The American Evasion of Philosophy: A Genealogy of Pragmatism* (Madison: University of Wisconsin Press, 1989); Jeffrey Stout, "Commitments and Traditions in the Study of Religious Ethics," *Journal of Religious Ethics* 25, no. 3 (1997): 23–56. And in lieu of the focus on the biblical concept of God, the neo-pragmatists Jeffrey Stout, Cornel West, and Richard Rorty stressed the importance of history, politics, and language in framing our always-revisable theological views, which—importantly—both shape and are shaped by our overlapping public and private lives.
2. In this essay I limit my comments to Richard Rorty, *Contingency, Irony, and Solidarity* (Cambridge: Cambridge University Press, 1989). This is the seminal text from the second half of Rorty's career. I am not the first thinker to consider Hume and Rorty together, although I am one of a very few who seem to recognize some of the important links between the two thinkers. Insightful work on both thinkers has come from Colin Koopman, "Challenging Philosophy: Rorty's Positive Conception of Philosophy as Cultural Criticism," in *Richard Rorty: From Pragmatist*

Philosophy to Cultural Politics, ed. Colin Koopman Alexander Groeschner and Mike Sandbothe (New York: Bloomsbury 2013), and Michael Williams, "Rorty on Truth and Knowledge," in *Richard Rorty: Contemporary Philosophy in Focus*, ed. David R. Hiley and Charles Guignon (Cambridge: Cambridge University Press, 2003).

3. See David Newheiser's comment in the introduction to this collection: "Although scholarly writing is generally less polemical, Anglophone philosophers tend to share the assumption that atheism and theism are incompatible beliefs" (1).

4. Denys Turner, *How to be an Atheist: An Inaugural Lecture Given in the University of Cambridge* (Cambridge: Cambridge University Press, 2002), 13.

5. Hume wrote that the dispute between theists and atheists was "merely verbal" and "incurably ambiguous" in the *Dialogues Concerning Natural Religion* (12.6). It is both their relatedness—described by Lord Shaftesbury as the "mix" of theism and atheism (*Characteristicks of Men*, 1732, 14)—that is, the extent to which we might understand these forms of belief as on a fairly narrow continuum, and Hume's stark provocations around the topic that link him with the neo-pragmatist Richard Rorty. For Rorty's claim regarding the irrationality of atheism and theism, see Stephen Louthan, "On Religion: A Discussion with Richard Rorty, Alvin Plantinga and Nicholas Wolterstorff," *Christian Scholar's Review* 26, no. 2 (1996): 179–80.

6. "Ea sola voluptas solamenque mali," from the *Aeneid*, qtd. in David Hume and J. Y. T. Greig, "Letter I," in *The Letters of David Hume*, 2 vols. (Oxford, UK: Clarendon Press, 1932), 1:8.

7. "Letter to Michael Ramsey," July 4, 1727, in Hume and Greig, *Letters of David Hume*.

8. In his letters, Hume misquotes Virgil's *Georgics*: *At secura quies, et nescia fallere vita*. See Hume and Greig, *Letters of David Hume*, 10.

9. N. T. Phillipson, *David Hume: The Philosopher as Historian*, rev. ed. (New Haven, CT: Yale University Press, 2012).

10. Donald Siebert, "The Sentimental Sublime in Hume's History of England," *Review of English Studies* 40, no. 159 (August 1989): 325–72.

11. Siebert, 352.

12. Hume interpreter Donald Livingston writes, "In the end Hume argues that true philosophy and true religion are the same." Donald W. Livingston, *Philosophical Melancholy and Delirium: Hume's Pathology of Philosophy* (Chicago: University of Chicago Press, 1998), 57.

13. Dennis Sansom writes that Rorty's "'liberal ironist' represents the truly modern person, one who is emancipated from traditional problems of truth, God and the natural law, and who continually remakes her or himself by adopting new metaphors for living." Dennis Sansom, "Where Are We Going? Dante's Inferno or Richard Rorty's Liberal Ironist," *Religions* 10 (2019): article 49, https://doi.org/10.3390/rel10010049.

14. For example, see William Connolly's remarks in T. Ball, W. Connolly, P. Dews, and A. Malachowski, "Review Symposium on Richard Rorty," *History of the Human Sciences* 3, no. 1 (1990): 101–22. Also Chantal Mouffe, "Deconstruction, Pragmatism and the Politics of Democracy," in *Deconstruction and Pragmatism*, ed. Chantal Mouffe and Simon Critcheley (London: Routledge, 1996): 1–12.

15. Ian Ward, *Shakespeare and the Legal Imagination*, Law in Context (London: Butterworths, 1999), 10.
16. See Cheryl Misak, "Pragmatism and Pluralism," *Transactions of the Charles S. Peirce Society* 41, no. 1 (2005): 129–35. Misak prefers the Peircean view of pluralism to the Rortyan one because Peirce allows for the existence of truth. From my view, Rorty also allows for a "truth of the matter."
17. Here Rorty's bias is revealed. The idea that there is "a single permanent reality" is a Western notion that would not be a part of a Buddhist's final vocabulary.
18. Rorty thus positions Proust, the "ironist novelist" par excellence, against the "ironist theorists" Heidegger, Nietzsche, and Hegel. He makes the case that Proust is the proper kind of ironist because his work was uninterested in bringing together our public and private final vocabularies.
19. Williams, "Rorty on Truth and Knowledge."
20. Williams, 74.
21. There is a significant amount of quality scholarship on Hume's skepticism. For example, Nicholas Capaldi, "The Dogmatic Slumber of Hume Scholarship," *Hume Studies* 18, no. 2 (1999): 117–35; David Fate Norton, *David Hume, Common-Sense Moralist, Sceptical Metaphysician* (Princeton, NJ: Princeton University Press, 1982); Peter Jones, *Hume's Sentiments: Their Ciceronian and French Context* (Edinburgh: Edinburgh University Press, 1982); J. P. Wright, "Hume's Academic Scepticism: A Reappraisal of His Philosophy of Human Understanding," *Canadian Journal of Philosophy* 16 (1986): 407–35; and Nicholas Capaldi, *David Hume: The Newtonian Philosopher*, Twayne's World Leaders Series (Boston: Twayne, 1975); D. C. Ainslie, "Hume's Scepticism and Ancient Scepticism," in *Hellenistic and Early Modern Philosophy*, ed. Jon Miller and Brad Inwood (Cambridge: Cambridge University Press, 2003); and Robert J. Fogelin, *Hume's Skepticism in the Treatise of Human Nature*, International Library of Philosophy (London: Routledge & Kegan Paul, 1985). Both Ainslie and Fogelin read the *Enquiry* as concluding with a calm, mitigated skepticism and the *Treatise* as more Pyrrhonian. My position borrows more from Miriam McCormick, "A Change in Manner: Hume's Skepticism in the *Treatise* and *First Enquiry*," *Canadian Journal of Philosophy* 29 (1999): 413–31.
22. Willis, *Towards a Humean True Religion*.
23. It is fair to say that at this point in his career, Rorty is less "religiously musical" than he will become. Yet here he understands himself as thoroughly secular; his moral emphasis on solidarity is not dependent on or driven by any recognizable forms of theism. Instead, it is a democratic obligation.
24. Annette Baier, *Death and Character: Further Reflections on Hume* (Cambridge, MA: Harvard University Press, 2008), 69.
25. "No quality of human nature is more remarkable, both in itself and in its consequences, than that propensity we have to sympathize with others, and to receive by communication their inclinations and sentiments, however different from, or even contrary to our own." *Treatise* 2.1.11.1. David Hume, *A Treatise of Human Nature*, 1739.
26. Donald W. Livingston, *Hume's Philosophy of Common Life* (Chicago: University of Chicago Press, 1984), 22.

27. Williams, "Rorty on Truth and Knowledge," 74.
28. Livingston, *Hume's Philosophy of Common Life*, 56.
29. It is important to remember that Hume's "true philosophy" does not intend to establish the true as the "real" or the "certain" as in some forms of rationalism and empiricism. As a malleable, background vocabulary (not a "final" one) it was primed to make a rhetorical difference, that is, to inspire character development and social stability.

REFERENCES

Ainslie, D. C. "Hume's Scepticism and Ancient Scepticism." In *Hellenistic and Early Modern Philosophy*, edited by Jon Miller and Brad Inwood, 251–73. Cambridge: Cambridge University Press, 2003.

Baier, Annette. *Death and Character: Further Reflections on Hume*. Cambridge, MA: Harvard University Press, 2008.

Capaldi, Nicholas. *David Hume: The Newtonian Philosopher*. Twayne's World Leaders Series. Boston: Twayne, 1975.

———. "The Dogmatic Slumber of Hume Scholarship." *Hume Studies* 18, no. 2 (1992): 117–35.

Connolly, W., T. Ball, P. Dews, and A. Malachowski. "Review Symposium on Richard Rorty." *History of the Human Sciences* 3, no. 1 (1990): 101–22.

Dumler-Winckler, Emily. "Romanticism as Modern Re-enchantment: Burke, Kant, and Emerson on Religious Taste." *Zeitschrift für Neuere Theologiegeschichte* 22, no. 1 (2015): 1–22.

Fogelin, Robert J. *Hume's Skepticism in the Treatise of Human Nature*. International Library of Philosophy. London: Routledge & Kegan Paul, 1985.

Hume, David, and J. Y. T. Greig. *The Letters of David Hume*. 2 vols. Oxford, UK: Clarendon Press, 1932.

Jones, Peter. *Hume's Sentiments: Their Ciceronian and French Context*. Edinburgh: Edinburgh University Press, 1982.

Koopman, Colin. "Challenging Philosophy: Rorty's Positive Conception of Philosophy as Cultural Criticism." In *Richard Rorty: From Pragmatist Philosophy to Cultural Politics*, edited by Colin Koopman, Alexander Groeschner, and Mike Sandbothe, 75–106. New York: Bloomsbury, 2013.

Livingston, Donald W. *Hume's Philosophy of Common Life*. Chicago: University of Chicago Press, 1984.

———. *Philosophical Melancholy and Delirium: Hume's Pathology of Philosophy*. Chicago: University of Chicago Press, 1998.

McCormick, Miriam. "A Change in Manner: Hume's Skepticism in the *Treatise* and First *Enquiry*." *Canadian Journal of Philosophy* 29 (1999): 413–31.

Misak, Cheryl. "Pragmatism and Pluralism." *Transactions of the Charles S. Peirce Society* 41, no. 1 (2005): 129–35.

Mouffe, Chantal. "Deconstruction, Pragmatism and the Politics of Democracy." In *Deconstruction and Pragmatism*, edited by Chantal Mouffe and Simon Critcheley, 1–12. London: Routledge, 1996.

Norton, David Fate. *David Hume, Common-Sense Moralist, Sceptical Metaphysician*. Princeton, NJ: Princeton University Press, 1982.

Phillipson, N. T. *David Hume: The Philosopher as Historian*. Rev. ed. New Haven, CT: Yale University Press, 2012.

Rorty, Richard. *Contingency, Irony, and Solidarity*. Cambridge: Cambridge University Press, 1989.

Sansom, Dennis. "Where Are We Going? Dante's Inferno or Richard Rorty's Liberal Ironist." *Religions* 10 (2019): article 49. https://doi.org/10.3390/rel10010049.

Siebert, Donald. "The Sentimental Sublime in Hume's History of England." *Review of English Studies* 40, no. 159 (August 1989): 352–72.

Stout, Jeffrey. "Commitments and Traditions in the Study of Religious Ethics." *Journal of Religious Ethics* 25, no. 3 (1997): 23–56.

———. "The Transformation of Genius into Practical Power: A Reading of Emerson's Experience." *American Journal of Theology and Philosophy* 35, no. 1 (January 2014): 3–24.

Ward, Ian. *Shakespeare and the Legal Imagination*. Law in Context. London: Butterworths, 1999.

West, Cornel. *The American Evasion of Philosophy: A Genealogy of Pragmatism*. Madison: University of Wisconsin Press, 1989.

Williams, Michael. "Rorty on Truth and Knowledge." In *Richard Rorty: Contemporary Philosophy in Focus,* edited by David R. Hiley and Charles Guignon, 69–75. Cambridge: Cambridge University Press, 2003.

3

ATHEISM AND POWER

Nietzsche, Nominalism, and the Reductive Spirit

Denys Turner

"When I use a word," Humpty-Dumpty said in rather a scornful tone, "it means just what I choose it to mean—neither more nor less."
"The question is," said Alice, "whether you can make words mean so many different things."
"The question is," said Humpty-Dumpty, "which is to be master—that's all."

NOMINALISM

Is Nietzsche a nominalist? You might wonder why I ask; and you might be irritated by the fact that I don't answer the question itself, nor explain why I ask it, until the end of this chapter. Please be patient, for the journey itself is quite interesting and not just where it gets us. My purpose is to situate Nietzsche's atheism within a small part, a fragment, of the history of a broad set of positions in logic and epistemology the narrative of which seems to illuminate a distinctive feature of that atheism: Nietzsche comes from somewhere, and why not place him philosophically *en scène*? So, is he a nominalist?

It's hard to say, but here's how a three-year-old child becomes nominalist for the nonce. She plays games with a new word and, fascinated by its sound, repeats the word over and over again until the sound and the sense fall apart, what had once seemed to be a natural connection having come to seem arbitrary. Thereupon it seems to her as if there is no longer any mechanism or rule to hand that might pull off the trick of getting sound and sense back together, causing her to wonder how they were ever connected up with such natural ease in the first place. Perhaps, she thinks, it is just that she had become accustomed to it by no more than habit, but now her experiment has troublingly disabused her of that impression of semantic naturalness. Perhaps it is as it can seem, upon the breakdown of a personal relationship, of a marriage or a friendship, that there never had been a real one there in the first place—which might of course be true, although the breakdown is not by itself evidence that it is. The experience is familiar in such cases. But they are special, being induced in the one case artificially by a child's repetitive play, by an adult's personal misfortune in the other.

Nonetheless, for all the prima facie implausibility of such an inference, there are philosophers who set out in earnest from where children end up in play and propose a general account of meanings as somehow only contingently taking a ride in their linguistic vehicles: it's as if because it is true that for any given word in a language its meaning might be otherwise, then for all language meaning is in general fortuitous, contingent, so as in turn to inform a correspondingly rule-free epistemology, a general theory of knowledge.

In either case, whether of meaning or of knowing, it is a proposition underlying much modern philosophy on all sides, whether rationalist or empiricist. It is a sort of presumption in favor of reductive radicalism, a conceptual tidying up, a clearing away of unnecessary assumptions, as in the parsimony of an Ockham—don't overburden explanation with unneeded hypotheses, still less entities—or as when the skeptical Hume speculates that causal stories that seem to embody necessary connections in fact narrate nothing more than contingently acquired habits of mind: the thing just happens, he says, and you get used to it. On the rationalist side Descartes seems in a similar reductively skeptical spirit to be in one way more radical still: unlike Hume he regards all questions to be open, even in such formal disciplines as arithmetic, so that it makes sense for him to ask—at least for the sake of setting out the limits of what can be doubted—whether 2 + 2 might not equal 5, and on what account we can be certain it equals 4. Whence he calls on theology, the will of God, to explain the fact that 4 is the answer—its being but a "fact," and not, as he thinks, a necessary truth, being the inevitable consequence, like it or not, of the supposition that it might have been 5.[1] In another way, though, it is Hume who wears the radical laurels, as we will see: for Descartes the suspension of belief is merely methodological and provisional, and the point of the exercise is to show that any generalized skepticism is self-defeating, thus to establish some bedrock of certainty. Hume, by contrast, means it unconditionally, and he wants to persuade you to accept the skeptical result and to be of an untroubled mind about it.

And although Hume's sort of case that any statement of fact is contingent and could be false seems plausible—for a statement's being possibly false is no more than a consequence of its being a statement of fact—all the same it isn't true that all states of affairs in the natural world could be other than how our experience tells us they are. Just because any empirical claim requires evidence for its truth, and could be false for the want of it, it doesn't follow that all experience is contingent and might be false. For "any statement of fact might be false" is of course true; but even so "every statement of fact might be false" doesn't follow, and certainly isn't true, such a line of argument being no more sound than the inference that because every husband is married to some wife there is, alas for her, some wife every husband is married to. Doubt what you may one thing at a time, you can't doubt everything all at once. For knowledge, as Otto Neurath said, is like the rotting ship of Theseus. You may be able to replace one timber at a time while at sea; what you cannot do while tossing about thereupon is all at once replace the lot.[2]

There are philosophers, and nominalists are among them, who think thoughts about causal connections in a way similar to Hume's but generalize them for language and meaning as a whole, so as to represent the relationship between all language and the world as in the same way contingent. What is distinctive about nominalist ways of getting to that general conclusion is their model of linguistic meaning as such, which takes as its paradigm of meaningful utterance the act of naming, specifically the act of imposing a proper name upon an individual, as when calling a person "Peter" or "Beatrice," or a dog "Fido"—their "given" names as we say. For of course, such acts of naming are indeed at the choice of the person naming, we do indeed "give" them, as when parents decide on what to call their child: and here it is their act that gets the name to hook on to her, it's simply up to them and for everyone else to take their word for it. So in general you don't need to know anything about a thing to name it; it's up to you how you do so, that is, as Humpty-Dumpty says, if you are in a position to impose your will.

But if the act of naming is taken to be the bedrock linguistic act, all other such acts being in some way or other reducible to it, then you are likely to get an account of how we build names into their concatenations in judgments, akin to what Peter Geach calls the "two name" theory of predication, according to which "in an affirmative predication the subject is a name and so is the predicate, and the predication is true if and only if the subject-name and the predicate-name stand for the same thing or things."[3] Of course nominalists do not maintain that every linguistic act is an act of imposing a proper name, for clearly that is not so: "Socrates is a man," they will say, predicates a grammatically general term, "man," of the individual

Socrates. But as Geach says, a nominalist has to parse the phrase out in some such way as will eliminate all general terms, so as to treat "man" as the name of what "Socrates" names, the two names "standing for the same thing or things." Generalizing from such cases, nominalists maintain that you can always analyze universal terms and the propositions formed out of them into names of, and statements about, individuals.

One such nominalist is Thomas Hobbes, whose political theories come into the nominalist picture in ways that I explain further down the line, but for now let us attend to his theory of predication that underlies them. He says of names that "some are *Proper*, and singular to one onely thing; as Peter, John, This man, this Tree: and some are *Common* to many things; as *Man, Horse, Tree*," but for all that such is a distinction in grammar there is a point in logic going along with it, and he adds, "There is nothing in the world Universall but Names; for the things, are every one of them Individual and Singular." And if you ask on what account a universal term is predicated of some number of individuals, Hobbes replies that it will be on account of some accidental features that they happen to share, some "similitude in some quality, or other accident: And wheras a Proper name bringeth to mind one thing onely; Universalls recall any one of those many."[4]

Generally speaking, then, the logical picture of language as nominalists conceive of it is of names as semantic atoms, building up to sentences as semantic molecules, that is, names in combination, and of reason as constructing the combination of such molecular sentences into the chemical mixtures of argument. Or you can say that for nominalists language is like a watch that a watchmaker can disassemble into its bits and pieces and put back together again in good working order, unlike a cat or a human being that is not amenable to such treatment. And then we can add that for many nominalists the world and logic correspond—as the basic semantic unit is the name, so the basic ontological unit is the individual, for only individuals actually exist, and there are no universal entities. And then naturally, if not inevitably, there will go together with the ontology an antirealist epistemology. For antirealist nominalists maintain that there are no universals in the mind either, but only freely constructed classes of individuals connected at will by way of highlighted features that are, as Hobbes puts it, "accidentally" (i.e., inessentially) common only to them: as "man is a featherless biped," though but contingently true, will do for a universal, since every human being has but two legs and no feathers, and nothing else does. So then, logic, metaphysics, and epistemology converge: individual names are the basic units of speech, individuals alone exist, and the proper object of all knowledge is the individual. In short, nominalists of this species are strong individualists: they are logical individualists as to meaning and reference, they are ontological individualists—only individuals actually exist—and, as we will see, they are commonly individualists as to ethics and in consequence as to politics. But also nominalists are as commonly voluntarists, Hobbes again being one such, the voluntarism following from the nominalism.

For given that names have no natural connections with their objects, something has to account for the way they hook up in the relatively stable connections that they do. And since nothing else does the work, the will rushes into the semantic vacuum to pull off the job. If names are the semantic atoms, will is what sets them in motion so as to form those semantic concatenations, the congealing molecules formed by the power of speech out of the atoms of meaning. Naturally, then, there is a question as to whose intentional act is to deliver which combinations in which connections, or, as Humpty-Dumpty says, the question is, "Who is to be master?" and that's all there is, or can be, to it—if you are a nominalist.

OCKHAM AND CONCEPTUALISM

Hobbes's nominalism is particularly radical and is rare in the history of semantic theory, most versions of nominalism being closer in one way or another to some form of conceptualism. More moderately, conceptualists maintain that although there are no existent universals outside the mind, there are universal concepts in the mind, conventional groupings or classifications of individuals under common names. Concepts function in relation to individual instances like a library's classifications of books under topics, and therein by alphabetical sequences of authors, the mind working in some such way as a librarian; or as a copy editor works, indexing a book; or perhaps the mind is envisioned as a taxonomist with a language to hand to do the work of classification.

Such forms of conceptualism represent the turn away from pure and Hobbesian forms of nominalist individualism and toward something like a factually more complex, and certainly a logically more plausible, account of the child's repetition experiment. For in the real world the child quickly learns to turn from her nominalist experiment and to repeat the word no longer in isolation but in its occurrence in as many true and false sentences as she can think of, and, upon finding that her semantic alienation occurs no more, her nominalist problem simply evaporates. For the experience of semantic emptiness was the consequence of the experiment's having removed the utterance of words from any communicative context, and the child had artificially to induce the problem before it was in need of any solution. Once the repetition experiment is abandoned, and semantic life gets back to normal, it will once again seem obvious that the meanings of words are learned through a community's shared habits of affirming and negating appropriate sentences, so that names, like all other grammatical parts of speech, get their meanings from the shape and form of the great variety of sentences they occur in, from whole vocabularies and practices of utterance. For a word needs a role within a literature to own a meaning; it cannot do it on its own, every word being "part of the main," and none but an island. Thereupon nominalism as a theory of meaning begins to look like a solution in search of the problem it solves. Whereas, then, a pure nominalist like Hobbes thinks that a sentence gets its meaning from the concatenation of the names it assembles, conceptualists are commonly conventionalists and hold that names get their meanings from the sweep and scope of the sentences in a natural language that assemble them. If the nominalist intuition about meaning is an artifice of thought supported only by such as the child's repetition games, the conceptualist intuition is supported by routine practices of adult linguistic competence. Nominalists believe that the meanings of words, being attached to them by way of no given conventions, are in the end what someone—I, or someone else, or a group, or community—has the power to *decide* them to be; conceptualists believe that the meanings of words are *given* in commonly received practices of communication.

In the fourteenth century, William of Ockham, usually deemed a nominalist,[5] seems sometimes rather to be of this conceptualist cast of mind. He begins, like the nominalist, by rejecting a form of what today we would probably call essentialism. "There is no universal outside the mind," he says, "really existing in individual substances or in the essences of things . . . the reason is that everything that is not many things is necessarily one thing in number and consequently a singular thing."[6]

And this is where nominalists and conceptualists are of one mind, negatively in the rejection of a common enemy: essentialism. For both nominalists and conceptualists there are no actually existent natural kinds, no existent essences, there are only individuals and collections of them; and if the mind sorts individuals under universal kinds by way of concepts, it is *only* the mind that does this, and in its doing so, it is unconstrained by the real world that it conceptualizes. In short, Ockham is ontologically nominalist—there are only individuals—and epistemologically a conceptualist: we can construct universals of collections of individuals that are more than the nominalist's empty names. But if we are to understand the full force of the joint rejection of essentialism—Hobbes's and Ockham's—it is necessary to distinguish two forms of it, a Platonist ultrarealism, and a moderate form of realism such as is represented by, say, the ontology of Thomas Aquinas. What is common to both as the objects of criticism is the proposition that there are universal essences that exist in reality.

Agreed that universal essences actually exist, Plato and Aquinas differ as to how they exist outside the mind and in the world. In its Platonist form, the claim of the essentialist is not only that universals actually exist outside the mind; it is that universals outside the mind are what properly exist.[7] For on Plato's account individual instantiations of a universal, Peter, or this cat of mine named Tonks, exist only "more or less," more in the degree to which they participate in the universals, humanity or felininity, they instantiate, less in the degree to which they don't. But Aquinas rejects this idealism and, while agreeing with Plato that universals exist outside the mind, denies they exist in reality otherwise than as individuated: there can be no subsistent universal essences, Aquinas says.[8] But Ockham's rejection of essentialism targets both Plato's and Aquinas's form of it: in rejecting the Platonist form of it, he is at one with Aquinas; but he denies also Aquinas's moderate form of realist essentialism.

Aquinas's position makes no sense, Ockham says; for were there existent individualized essences, it would follow that not even God could annihilate any individual substance without thereby annihilating every substance of the same kind: on Aquinas's account, the destruction of the individualized universal, Peter, says Ockham, would entail the destruction of the universal individualized, humanity. But that consequence is absurd: of course an individual of any kind can cease to exist without the kind ceasing to exist with it. For even when the last dodo dies, what a dodo is, Ockham says, doesn't die with it; otherwise, we wouldn't be able to say intelligibly, "Now there are no dodos." And we can say there are no dodos because the concept "dodo" is a mental construct that survives the destruction of all its instantiations, so that the sense of "there are no dodos" is that the mentally constructed class of dodos is emptied of instances. And if the consequent (the death of any dodo is the end of every dodo) is false, as obviously it is, then too the antecedent that entails it (dodos are individuated essences) must be false too, and Aquinas's version of logical realism thereby fails along with the Platonist form of it.[9] The result: for Ockham as for Hobbes there are no essences existing outside the mind. And if there are no essences, then there are no necessary connections, causal or otherwise, outside the mind either. Everything is contingent, except what we may, for this or that purpose, or in this or that context, construe otherwise.

NIETZSCHE AND HUME

Let us, then, rephrase the question: Is Nietzsche a nominalist, like Hobbes, or a conceptualist like Ockham? Or is he neither? For sure he says some nominalist-sounding things, and whether or not he would identify himself explicitly as a nominalist he draws some of the conclusions that are consistent with a nominalist logic and epistemology. At the very least he is anti-essentialist, insofar as essentialism is, among other assertions, the claim in either Plato's or in Aquinas's form that there are necessary connections in the world because there are real essences—though of course there is nothing distinctively Nietzschean in his rejection of that, he is simply following in a long nominalist tradition. So when he said of the classical doctrine of cause and effect—that "there is probably never such a duality"—he is saying no more than Hume had said over a century before him. Indeed, an innocent first reader of the texts of both might be forgiven for thinking (contrary to fact) that Nietzsche was quoting Hume when he asserts that where classical rationalism, or even, as he thinks, the philosophical underpinnings to natural science, requires necessary connections between antecedent causes and their effects as being determined by their natures or essences, "in truth a continuum faces us, from which we isolate a few pieces, just as we always perceive a movement only as isolated points, i.e. we do not really see, but infer."[10] Therefore, "we should not erroneously *objectify* 'cause' and 'effect' like the natural scientists do (and whoever else thinks naturalistically these days—) in accordance with the dominant mechanistic stupidity which would have the cause push and shove until it 'effects' something; we should use 'cause' and 'effect' only as pure *concepts*, which is to say as conventional fictions for the purposes of description and communication, *not* explanation."[11] One hundred years before Nietzsche, Hume had said the same:

> When I see ... a Billiard-ball moving in a straight line towards another ... may I not conceive, that a hundred different events might as well follow from that cause? ... May not the first ball return in a straight line, or leap off from the second in any line or direction? All these suppositions are consistent and conceivable. Why then should we give the preference to one, which is no more consistent or conceivable than the rest? All our reasonings *a priori* will never be able to show us any foundation for this preference.[12]

Unsurprisingly the logic of their deconstructions of causality leads to the same result for doctrines of substance. For, Nietzsche says, "In order for the concept of substance to originate," "which is indispensable to logic though nothing really corresponds to it in the strictest sense, it was necessary that for a long time changes in things not be seen, not be perceived; the beings who did not see things exactly had a head start over those who saw everything 'in a flux,'"[13] which is no more than Hume had said about the impression we have on the billiard table upon observation of the impact of one ball on another: therein is contained, "it is commonly supposed," some secret of indiscernible necessary connection. Not so, he says, for "in considering of motion communicated from one ball to another we [can] find nothing but contiguity, priority in the cause, and constant conjunction," there being nothing in the regularity with which the conjunction is observed to justify the claim that "there is a necessary connexion betwixt the cause and the effect, and that the cause possesses something, which we call a *power*, or *force*, or *energy*." Therefore, "when we take the assistance of experience, it only shows us objects contiguous, successive, and constantly conjoined."[14]

Relentlessly does the deconstructive work press on. For if our commonsense notions of identity in general fall foul of it, it is inevitable that Hume takes the criticism forward on to notions of the identity of persons. That identity cannot be located in "the soul," he says, for

> the soul ... is nothing but a system or train of different perceptions, those of heat and cold, love and anger, thoughts and sensations; all united together, but without any perfect simplicity or identity. *Des Cartes* maintained that thought was the essence of the mind, not this thought or that thought, but thought in general. This seems to be absolutely unintelligible, since every thing, that exists, is particular.... The mind is not a substance, in which the perceptions inhere.... We have no idea of substance of any kind, either material or spiritual.[15]

And it is in the same deconstructive mood that Nietzsche asks, concerning what he calls the "soul superstition that still causes trouble as the superstition of the subject or I,"[16]

> What gives me the right to speak about an I, and, for that matter, about an I as cause, and, finally, about an I as the cause of thoughts? ... [For w]hen I dissect the proposition "I think," I get a whole set of bold claims that are difficult, perhaps impossible, to establish,—for instance that *I* am the one who is thinking, that there must be something that is thinking in the first place, that thinking is an activity and the effect of a being who is considered the cause, that there is an "I," and finally that it has already been determined what is meant by thinking,—that I *know* what thinking is.[17]

Still, true—and also remarkable—as is the common ground thus far between Hume and Nietzsche in the criticism of the metaphysical concepts of cause, substance, and personal identity; such coincidences of thought assembled in isolation from wider contexts are wholly misleading if it is thought they are evidence of some shared critical program. For Hume's deconstruction is principally skeptical and ironic in purpose, and his philosophy is empiricist only in further consequence of that primary skeptical intent. Hume doesn't really want to prove anything much; his criticism is motivated more by an unambitious concern to stay within the bounds of what you can't deny, howsoever skeptical you may be in denying what you can, and in that wholly general sense he does not differ from Descartes. Where he differs significantly from Descartes is in the matter of what are the indisputable grounds on the basis of which doubt is possible.

Perhaps above all Hume's target is Descartes' conviction that doubt stops short in the certainty of the "I," in the "I exist" that for him is given even in the act of doubting itself. For doubt whatsoever you please, there is within that doubt an I who doubts. But Hume, and together with him Nietzsche, knows that you can very well challenge Descartes' *cogito*. For, Hume says, even if it is conceded that for any given thought there is an I thinking it, nothing establishes that for any sequence of thoughts there is a single "I" who thinks that sequence: for even if for thought 1 there is an I thinking it and for thought 2 a second I thinking that, what is there to show that I-1 and I-2 are the same I? An appeal to memory as supplying the link between the continuity of the thinking acts with the continuing identity of a thinking subject will serve Descartes no good, since a memory-act is of course but another thought, thought 3. "The stream of thoughts is mine," you say, "how could I *not* know that?" But, Hume and Nietzsche reply, that is no better than to say: "There is but the stream of thoughts, there is no 'mine' in it anywhere; and what is more there isn't a reason for describing the succession of thoughts even as constituting a single sequence." Which seems right. For not even the thought of the sequence as a whole adds anything to Descartes' solution; it only extends his problem with thought following thought, and, the solution being endlessly postponed, it fails ad infinitum. Thus does the Cartesian ego undermine itself, and Hume correctly identifies the conclusion that must follow from it: if a self must be, as Descartes supposes, a direct object of thought, an "I" given in every conscious act, then the condition cannot be met.[18] There is no such object of thought, and, as Hume says, self-reference can yield only a theater in which there are players but no stage, no substantive self, nothing but a "hank of self-suspending onions hung from a string that doesn't exist."[19] And thus far Hume and Nietzsche are agreed.[20]

For Nietzsche, of course, this critique of the Cartesian self is but a step taken with a far more radically deconstructive purpose that cannot be allowed to stop there. But Hume balks at anything further. It is as if he sees where this line of thought is going and recoils from the danger his skepticism is running into. And in case that "as if" is too speculative, what is certain is that Hume shows no inclination to push the argument to any point at which it would place under threat the three conditions that limit the extent of his skepticism: the possibility of Newtonian science, of conventional morality, and of a Whiggish conception of society and political community. For though on his account none of these is any longer grounded in metaphysical foundations, by no means does he intend to leave thought without foundations of any kind. Hume will keep his science, morality, and politics intact, so long as he can have them grounded in sense experience and without metaphysics; indeed, he thinks not only can he have them, but also they are all the more stably justified for their not being in thrall to shaky and uncertain foundations in a supposed metaphysical bedrock. Ockham's parsimonious principle lives on in Hume's skepticism in that the less you have to assume by way of foundations, the more secure are the structures that rest on those you have. Skepticism is Hume's method, the empiricism, rationalist vulnerabilities once skeptically stripped out, yield the desired result. For no longer resting on necessary causes, Newtonian mechanics are rendered secure on the ground of sense experience; the identity of persons can the more confidently be reasserted precisely for not requiring grounds in a Cartesian self; and morality is in place because it no longer relies on moral obligation's being derived by unfounded inference from natural fact. All these are left standing, and they are all the safer for their epistemological grounds having been cut back to a secure minimum. Hume's skepticism is but halfway radical. In the end it is wholly conservative, which is why even his atheism is so easygoing. He doesn't need strenuously to deny God. God simply disappears from a picture in which there is no greater need of that hypothesis generally than there was for Laplace in natural science. And that is also why he can philosophize happily in the daytime and repair easy of mind to the billiard table for the evening.

Not so Nietzsche. Far from welcoming Hume's species of empiricist skepticism for having got at least some way down toward a wholesale subversion of epistemic foundations, he seems to think of empiricism as the last resort of a complacent foundationalist frame of mind intent on not letting skepticism take him anywhere further. And that, for Nietzsche, is all the more dishonest intellectually for its having the appearance of critical deconstruction. It could not have surprised Nietzsche that Hume's critique of metaphysics is so lacking in radicalness, since it carries with it its own principle of containment, of set purpose falling short. Here an objectivist account of science, left intact by Hume, is Nietzsche's target, specifically its empiricist and materialist reductivism. Of course, Nietzsche says (with heavy irony), "materialistic atomism" is "one of the most well-refuted things in existence," but while we may have learned from Copernicus that the Earth does not stand still, and then from Boscovich that nothing at all stands still, not even matter itself, that "residual piece of earth and clump of an atom,"[21] nonetheless all that falls far short of a consistent deconstruction.

For even if science itself has formally abandoned the styles of eighteenth-century materialistic atomism, that last resort of materialist foundationalism, the scientific mentality is still haunted by the ghost of ultimate foundations, which continues to haunt in the form of anxiety at the loss of them, in nostalgia for that materialistic "standing still" that is "left still standing" in the need for an explanatory bedrock somewhere. It is not enough for Nietzsche that the demand for ultimate foundations has been in theory abandoned if natural science, even understood as empiricists do, in practice itself stands in for them. This inconsistent and incoherent appeal to the authority of natural science is, for Nietzsche, every bit as pernicious as, and retains every bit as tenacious a hold on, explanatory mentalities as does either any "metaphysical need," or any moral need. Therefore, Hume's empiricist reliance on the authority of sense experience exhibits the same failure of deconstructive nerve as do the halfhearted atheisms of Nietzsche's own times, the atheisms of those who deny the existence of God in the name of science but refuse to follow through to the consequences of that denial. Such a "kind of consequential reasoning," Nietzsche notes, is peculiarly "*English*"; it is the reasoning of those who "are rid of the Christian God and are now all the more convinced that they have to hold on to a Christian morality." But "English fatheads notwithstanding," you can't have the one without the other, whether what is in question is a moral fundamentalism or a scientific, whether in the one case in his times it is George Eliot, "that moralizing little woman,"[22] or in the other case in ours it is a Richard Dawkins or a Daniel Dennett, those dogmatic, and intellectually spineless, half-atheist "little" men. The God denied is still there in the intellectual bad faith of the materialists who think they have seen God off in the name of science and of the metaphysical Christian "soul believers," who would see science off in the name of God. Either way it is the same failure of intellectual and moral nerve, half-baked atheists and evangelical theists cuddled up in cozy complicity.

HOBBES

Besides, even as such partially reductivist forms of empiricism go, Hume's is hardly the most radical. Hume may strip science of metaphysical necessity, but in Hume's own time Roger Boscovich, and a century before him Hobbes, had stripped away even the static atomism that sustained classical eighteenth-century materialisms well into the late nineteenth century, and so into Nietzsche's own times. In fact, Hobbes's materialism is closer in some ways to that of Einstein and special relativity, expounded in 1905 a mere five years after Nietzsche's death, than to the atomic theories of the earlier Enlightenment. For Hobbes the explanatory fundamental is not the static particle of the antique atomists, impossibly at once possessing mass, and so dimensions, and at the same time indivisible. The base unit of explanation to which all else can be reduced, from gross inert matter to the most complex of social structures, is, Hobbes said, energy, motion, force. Explanation is needed not of those forces in motion, for they are fundamental, but of the existence of the observable phenomena of continuing relatively stable identities. We need to know what those processes are by which those constructions of the flux are formed into temporary parallelograms of forces, the interactions of whose motions cancel one another out in inevitably precarious equilibria. Across the explanatory board, from physics, through psychology, to social theory, force is primitive and absolute, stability provisional and conditional. And in the world of human social interaction it is power and the desire for it that is the motion driving everything. Given, then, that on their own the tendency of the elementary forces in interaction is centripetal and fundamentally unstable, the goal of explanation for Hobbes is to find a way in which those interactions can be so constructed as to create and, so far as such things can achieve stability, stabilize a Leviathan, a commonwealth.

The problem generated in what he calls the "state of nature" is acute. For on Hobbes's voluntarist model, the motion of a person, that by which every human is driven, is the desire for power; and every person must seek some power, life being but the drive endlessly to seek some "future apparent good" for oneself. And as one desires any good whatsoever, Hobbes says, so one necessarily desires such power as "is a present means to obtain" it.[23] Herein is the key to the central inference that Hobbes makes, as he puts it, "from the passions": power, is to be understood in relative, not in absolute, terms, not as a settled condition of equilibrium, but as unstable excess.[24] For my power consists only in its "eminence" over that of others, so that if, insofar as I desire anything I desire the power required to attain it, I must in consequence desire the excess of my power over all others who either actually do, or for all that I know might, also desire to obtain it.[25] And if that is true for me, it is true for anyone else. For it is a general truth that if you do not know whether I do or do not desire that power which, being "eminent," would extinguish yours, then you must always anticipate that I might be doing so. And because of that veil of ignorance as to what I seek come what may, you in turn must seek power over me, so that both of us must ceaselessly seek such power as is eminent over that of the other. The desire for any power thus being always the desire for more power, the competitive struggle must spiral endlessly up, in a "general inclination of all mankind, a perpetuall and restlesse desire of Power after power, that ceaseth onely in death. And the cause of this, is not alwayes that a man hopes for a more intensive delight, than he has already attained to; or that he cannot be content with a moderate power; but because he cannot assure the power and means to live well, which he hath present, without the acquisition of more."[26] And from that general and intrinsically restless inclination follows the famous description of the state of nature, inherently unstable, essentially conflictual, as a "state of Warre," this being the condition human affairs would be in were there no reason for each person to remove themselves from it. It is a condition in which there can be no morality, because if there can be nothing just, there can be nothing unjust either. For if there is no common power, there can be no law; and if no law, then no justice, and if none of these, then "Force, and Fraud, are in Warre the two cardinal vertues"; and then, in such a state of affairs, there could be nothing but "continuall feare, and danger of violent death; And the life of man, solitary, poore, nasty, brutish, and short."[27] Such, then, is the condition that all mankind would be in—now without any science at all, not even of Hume's epistemologically attenuated sort, hence no engineering, no art, no letters, no building, no means of transport, for now there is no Humean constraint of any kind. Here at last, you might say, is a fully deconstructed world wherein there is no foundation of any sort, for where once there has been some equilibrium, some stability, there is only will in an endless spiral of excess, the nominalism finally entailing consistently a wholly unconstrained desire, pure will operating in a moral vacuum: the desire for power has become an entirely abstract excess.

NIETZSCHE AND HOBBES

Why does Hobbes's program of reduction seem so uncannily close to Nietzsche's? Both, after all, strip explanation back as far as it can possibly go but only so as to reach a point at which there is no firm ground, only shifting instabilities. Is it because both pushed through to the full consequences of their nominalism with a consistency that is unrivaled within the history of philosophy in the modern period, although Hobbes stands close to the beginning of that period and Nietzsche at its end? It might seem so. More particularly, is it that Nietzsche shares with Hobbes a combination of that nominalist logic with a voluntarist psychology of which in the modern era Hobbes is one of the most radical proponents? It would seem so too. But then is it also true that Nietzsche shares with Hobbes a reductivist conception of the ethical as but the rationalization of a fundamentally egoist psychology, altruism derived from a consistent egoism, a psychology that purports to demonstrate why a rational agent who is motivated by nothing but self-referring interests has a reason, precisely out of that pure egoism, to hand over the governance of those interests to a common sovereign whose power overwhelms all equally? Undoubtedly that he does not share. Why, then, do Hobbes and Nietzsche, sharing that common nominalist logic, and with it the voluntarist psychology entailed by it, differ as radically as they do as to the consequences of that conjunction? Both are engaged in a program of ultimately radical deconstruction, driving explanation back to a starting point that constantly moves and to a finishing line that you can never reach, like the running track of the "Caucus race" in *Alice's Adventures in Wonderland*. Yet they differ just as radically as to what the outcome of their deconstructions leaves you with. In what way?

Nietzsche's explicit target is Christianity as a cultural and moral practice, and perhaps above all it is of Christianity as a mentality, as a deceiving and self-deceived civilization, a complex of beliefs and practices that survives even the gradual and progressive decline of explicit Christian faith. In fact it survives even into forms of positive disbelief and explicit atheism. For Nietzsche, the genius of Christianity is shown in the overwhelming success of the bad faith by which historically it overthrew the proud, ecstatic, joyfully aesthetic, Dionysian, civilization of the ancient world in the name of the "pale Galilean,"[28] the bloodless way of the joyless philistine who converts everything into its opposite, displaces the aesthetic by means of the ascetic, overpowers the world by means of a parade of powerlessness, and by way of its false humility subverts the truly proud. And one of the devices of this campaign of bogus humility is its protean ability to transform itself into the appearance even of its opposite in pursuit of retaining its grip on power—even atheism nowadays, he says, is doing God's dirty work, and with reason does he say it. For, as Terry Eagleton says, in pure Nietzschean spirit, "modern secular societies . . . have effectively disposed of God, but find it morally and politically convenient—even imperative—to behave as though they have not."[29] "I come too early . . . my time is not yet," says the madman wielding a lantern in the midday sun,[30] for his message of God's death is too demanding for the casual English atheists of the marketplace. God is not yet dead; he has been kept alive. And in a final irony his corpse has been propped up by Dawkins and Dennett, and perhaps most deceivingly by them, who but scoff at the madman, happy to flaunt their denial of God at so low a price in the consequences of doing so, keeping thereby "a-hold of nurse for fear of finding something worse."

And so it is with Hobbes—so near to Nietzsche in appearance, so far from him in truth—ready to entertain his state of nature stripped bare logically, morally, and theologically, on condition that the antifoundationalist logic that got him there in the state of nature will magically fetch him straight out of it, the egoistic nature entailing an altruistic resolution, the radical nominalism generating the conservative politics of Leviathan, the radical freedom in the state of nature self-alienated in submission to the will of an absolute sovereign. And in the end we do get it: Nietzsche is not after all to be represented as a sort of Hobbes minus the social compact, as if we could get to his "overman" by way merely of pulling out from the contract into civil society, the Leviathan, and turning back to the unlimited egoism of the state of nature.

It is true that Nietzsche was calling for a return to such radically egoistic foundations as a pure voluntarism can reach, but, he says, there are two egoisms, one "worth a great deal" and the other "worthless and contemptible," the one representing the "ascendant," and the other the "descendent line of life"; the "individual" of this latter is "an error" as the "philosophers have understood him thus far," representing an individualism that is "nothing," an empty and valueless abstraction.[31] Thus described is the individual of Hobbes's political theory. This individual *is,* after all, an abstraction, although it parades as the concrete—and Marx is here at one with Nietzsche—it is the empty fiction of the individualist at the center of a distinctly modern, bourgeois interest; there is in fact no such thing as this individual, and the passions Hobbes's inferences are made from are correspondingly abstract. For Hobbes's passions have no natural objects, they are desires in pursuit of anything whatever, it matters not what, except that it has always to be that vacuous, abstract, "more," its character consisting in nothing but its "eminence." Hobbes is not in the least Nietzschean, any more than his egoism is of the sort that is "worth a great deal." Hobbes's egoism is of the "worthless and contemptible sort," just as his presocial and self-denying state of nature is the opposite of Nietzsche's society-transcending aestheticism, which says "yes to life." And in his last words before he collapsed into insanity and finally fell silent, Nietzsche explains, "even in its strangest and hardest problems, the will to life rejoicing in the *sacrifice* of its highest types to its own inexhaustibility—*this* is what I called Dionysian, *this* is what I sensed as the bridge to the psychology of the *tragic* poet. *Not* freeing oneself from terror and pity, not purging oneself of a dangerous emotion through its vehement discharge . . . but, over and above terror and pity, *being oneself* the eternal joy of becoming."[32]

So, then, is Nietzsche a nominalist? He is. Perhaps he is the first truly consistent nominalist, grasping fully, and joyously, nominalism's atheist implications in an unconstrained affirmation of will. Nominalist that he is, though, it is not nominalism that is his point. He takes that battle in semantic theory to be over, and he is right historically, for between them Hobbes and Hume have effectively cleared the ground of any trace of an opposed essentialism, or so they say; and pretty much everyone else since appears to agree. But that won't do for Nietzsche: here at the end, we get to where Nietzsche begins, since for him what is yet to be completed is the task, sociologically and above all psychologically, of convincing a civilization, a mentality, and a culture to conform to the atheistic truth of its nominalist self. For only then will God be truly dead, and Nietzsche fully alive.

NOTES

1. René Descartes, *Meditations on First Philosophy*, in *Discourse on Method and Meditations on First Philosophy*, trans. Donald A. Cross (Indianapolis, IN: Hackett, 1998), 61.
2. Otto Neurath, *Anti-Spengler*, vol. 1 of *Empiricism and Sociology*, Vienna Circle Collection (Munich: Callweg Verlag, 1921).
3. P. T. Geach, "Nominalism," in *Logic Matters* (Los Angeles: University of California Press, 1980), 289. Although in this essay, Geach attributed the two-name theory to Ockham, in my view it is found less ambiguously in Hobbes.
4. Geach, 289. Note that Hobbes says that a universal term "calls to mind any *one*" of the individuals that it distributively includes, not "*every* one" collectively of them.
5. Although Jenny Pelletier offers a reading of Ockham as less hostile to a "metaphysics of being" than is the more common opinion, see her *William Ockham on Metaphysics, the Science of Being and God* (Leiden, Netherlands: Brill, 2012). I doubt her reading, though, for the concept of being that Ockham is left with, on her account, is so thinned out as to be vacuous and doing no work. We might as well say that there is no concept there at all.
6. William of Ockham, *Expositionis in Libros Artis Logicae Prooemium et Expositio in Librum Porphyrii de Praedicabilibus*, vol. 2 of *Opera Philosophica* (St. Bonaventure, NY: Franciscan Institute, 1978), 11–12.
7. Plato, *Republic* VII.
8. At any rate this is so in our sublunary world. For, of course, he thinks that there are subsistent universal forms: they are angels. But angels are not mundane.
9. What is more, on Ockham's argument against realism, the Platonist form of it is the less vulnerable of the two. For on the Platonist account, the existence of universal essences survives any number of failed instantiations; as the Platonist would have it, it is the essence itself that truly exists, not those individual instantiations.
10. Friedrich Nietzsche, *The Gay Science*, bk. III, ed. B. A. O. Williams, trans. Josefine Nauckhoff, Cambridge Texts in the History of Philosophy (Cambridge: Cambridge University Press, 2001), 113.

11. Friedrich Nietzsche, *Beyond Good and Evil*, ed. and trans. Rolf-Peter Horstmann and Judith Norman, Cambridge Texts in the History of Philosophy (Cambridge: Cambridge University Press, 2002), 21.
12. David Hume, *An Enquiry Concerning Human Understanding*, ed. and with introduction by Eric Steinberg (Indianapolis, IN: Hackett, 1995), bk. 4, 18–19.
13. Nietzsche, *Gay Science*, 112.
14. David Hume, *An Abstract of a Treatise of Human Nature*, ed. and with introduction by Eric Steinberg (Indianapolis, IN: Hackett, 1995), 134.
15. Hume, *Abstract*, 135. See Geach on the significance of Sir John Cutler's silk stockings, which, having been continuously darned with wool so that no silk remains, are nonetheless one and the same stockings as they were at the outset. The identity is in the continuity of the material process.
16. Nietzsche, *Beyond Good and Evil*, preface, 3.
17. Nietzsche, 16, 16–17.
18. On this matter Hume and Thomas Aquinas agree. For Aquinas, the knowledge of the self is either simply the concomitant awareness of a conscious act's being mine, the self-awareness that goes along within an act of knowing or perceiving its proper object, or else it is simply the theoretical knowledge I may have of what the self is, the knowledge of which is the product of a *diligens et subtilis inquisitio*—in other words, of the philosophy of mind. See *Summa Theologiae* Ia q87 a1 corp.
19. I no longer recall the exact form of words here, or the source of them. I used to think that William James said something like this of Hume's account of the self, but I can find it nowhere in his published work. I doubt that I made it up myself, much as I would like to think that I had the wit to do so.
20. Although Aquinas disagrees here. From the fact that we can legitimately talk about "self-knowledge," it does not follow, he says, that what is known is some self, other than that known *in* what I do and know and feel. Nor does he believe it follows that there is no *persona* that does and knows and feels. There seems to be a residually Cartesian assumption in the view of Hume and Nietzsche that just when Descartes' doctrine of the self as the direct object of knowledge is rejected, it follows that there is no substantive self at all.
21. Nietzsche, *Beyond Good and Evil*, 12, 14. Roger Joseph Boscovich was a Croatian physicist, astronomer, mathematician, philosopher, diplomat, poet, theologian, and Jesuit priest who worked at the Pontifical Gregorian University in Rome in the mid- to late eighteenth century.
22. The first quote is from Friedrich Nietzsche, *Twilight of the Idols; or, How to Philosophize with a Hammer*, trans. and with introduction and notes by Duncan Large (Oxford: Oxford University Press, 1998), ix, 5, 45. The second from p. 45.
23. Thomas Hobbes, *Leviathan*, ed. Richard Tuck, Cambridge Texts in the History of Political Thought (Cambridge: Cambridge University Press, 1994), bk. I, 10, 62.
24. *Leviathan*, I, 13, 89.
25. *Leviathan*, I, 10, 62.
26. *Leviathan*, I, 11, 70.
27. *Leviathan*, I, 13, 90; *Leviathan*, I, 13, 89.
28. *Vicisti, Galileaee*. "Thou hast conquered, O pale Galilean: the world has grown grey from thy breath." Algernon Charles Swinburne, "Hymn to Proserpine," in *Poems and Ballads* (London, 1866).

29. T. F. Eagleton, *Culture and the Death of God* (New Haven, CT: Yale University Press, 2014), 157.
30. Nietzsche, *Gay Science,* 120.
31. Nietzsche, *Twilight,* ix, 33, 59.
32. *Twilight,* x, 5, 81.

REFERENCES

Aquinas, Thomas. *Summa Theologiae.*
Descartes, René. *Discourse on Method and Meditations on First Philosophy.* Translated by Donald A. Cross. Indianapolis, IN: Hackett, 1998.
Eagleton, T. F. *Culture and the Death of God.* New Haven, CT: Yale University Press, 2014.
Geach, P. T. "Nominalism." In *Logic Matters.* Los Angeles: University of California Press, 1980.
Hobbes, Thomas. *Leviathan.* Edited by Richard Tuck. Cambridge Texts in the History of Political Thought. Cambridge: Cambridge University Press, 1994.
Hume, David. *An Abstract of a Treatise of Human Nature.* Edited and with an introduction by Eric Steinberg. Indianapolis, IN: Hackett, 1995.
———. *An Enquiry Concerning Human Understanding.* Edited and with an introduction by Eric Steinberg. Indianapolis, IN: Hackett, 1995.
Neurath, Otto. *Anti-Spengler, Vienna Circle Collection.* Vol. 1 of *Empiricism and Sociology.* Munich: Callweg Verlag, 1921.
Nietzsche, Friedrich. *Beyond Good and Evil.* Edited and translated by Rolf-Peter Horstmann and Judith Norman. Cambridge Texts in the History of Philosophy. Cambridge: Cambridge University Press, 2002.
———. *The Gay Science.* Edited by B. A. O. Williams. Translated by Josefine Nauckhoff. Cambridge Texts in the History of Philosophy. Cambridge: Cambridge University Press, 2001.
———. *Twilight of the Idols, or How to Philosophize with a Hammer.* Translated and with an introduction and notes by Duncan Large. Oxford: Oxford University Press, 1998.
Ockham, William. *Expositionis in Libros Artis Logicae Prooemium et Expositio in Librum Porphyrii de Praedicabilibus.* Vol. 2 of *Opera Philosophica.* St. Bonaventure, NY: Franciscan Institute, 1978.
Pelletier, Jenny. *William Ockham on Metaphysics.* Vol. 109 of *The Science of Being and God.* Leiden: Brill, 2012.
Swinburne, Algernon Charles. *Poems and Ballads.* London, 1866.

4

ATHEISM AND ETHICS

Recovering the Link between Truth and Transformation

Susannah Ticciati

THE NEW ATHEISTS AND THEIR THEOLOGICAL INTERLOCUTORS

One of the aims of this volume is to show that atheism (like theism) is not a univocal phenomenon, and thus to de-polemicize debate between atheists and theists. If there is variety among atheists and theists alike, then a binary opposition between them—in which atheists of all types are ranged against theists of all types—is brought into question. Instead, one is invited to seek local divergences and convergences between particular atheists and theists, with the possibility of discovering, for example, that certain theists may find themselves closer in important respects to certain atheists than to other theists. If that indeed turns out to be the case, then the labels lose much of their potency, and attention can be given instead to the particulars of a position, no longer obscured by the homogenizing and polemical label.[1]

The present chapter attends to a controversy that has excelled in vicious and verbose polemic: the debate with the "new atheists." There have been a good number of theological responses, some of which mimic the combative, point-scoring character of much of the new atheist writing, and some of which press beyond polemic to more measured engagement. These responses cover a wide range of theological ground. The thin narrative of progress underpinning some of the new atheist writings is exposed by Terry Eagleton (from a Marxist perspective) for its failure to recognize the radical nature of sin, and its political impotence in the face of the horrors of capitalism.[2] David Bentley Hart offers a counterhistory in which the evils allegedly brought about by "religion" are placed in the context of an account of the Christian tradition as that which has (uniquely) fostered an ethic of love and compassion.[3] Less sweepingly polemical, but sharing the dismissive tone of Eagleton and Hart, is Denys Turner's apophatically rooted critique that such atheists deny a God that no self-reflective Christian would affirm, and that their denials are outstripped by the much more thoroughgoing denials of the apophatic tradition.[4] Voicing a perspective from beyond the male-dominated battleground of the debate, Tina Beattie exposes from a feminist perspective the ideological situatedness of the new atheism's scientism.[5] Her nonpolemical approach arguably enables her to offer all the more deeply devasting a critique. David Fergusson, most measured of all, deliberately seeking a respectful engagement, points (among other things) to the complexity of the theological tradition as something that already houses the challenges thrown at it as if for the first time by the new atheists.[6] Several of the theological contributors, finally, highlight the complementary rather than competitive relationship between science and theology.[7]

While some of these responses are more compelling than others, surely from the theologian's perspective (from which I also write) enough has been said: the new atheists have no ground left on which to stand. Why, then, revisit the debate? The beef I take up in this essay, however, is not with the new atheists but with the theologians. I argue—as a theologian—that they have missed an important opportunity in their response to the new atheists. If some of them succeed in moving beyond mimicry of new atheist polemic, then they largely share a tendency to mirror a structural feature of the writings of the new atheists that prevents them from hearing and responding to what is arguably the deepest concern being voiced by the new atheists—an ethical concern. My aim is to expose and repair this structural feature, and thereby respond to the atheists' ethical concern. The resultant rapprochement may in turn make way for more constructive disagreement.

The structural feature in question has to do with the relationship between truth and transformation. There is a tendency among the atheists and the theologians alike (albeit with notable exceptions) to divorce truth from transformation, if not in theory, then nevertheless in practice. Let me take time to spell out what I mean.

First, it is clear even from a superficial acquaintance with the new atheists that they are concerned not only about the truth or falsity or religious truth claims, but—and perhaps more fundamentally—about their practical effect. This tends to be framed in the general terms of whether religion is harmful. For example, Daniel Dennett's *Breaking the Spell*, after offering a scientific hypothesis to account for religion as a natural phenomenon in evolutionary terms, turns to the driving question of whether religion does more good than harm,[8] exploring this question in terms of the relationship between religion and morality, and in the final chapter asking in the light of his findings what we should do, particularly in response to the problems of religious fanaticism. The unapologetically practical agenda is striking (and the recommendation he makes, to "educate the people of the world,"[9] interestingly noncontroversial even to the theologian). Sam Harris's whole agenda is to expose the connection between religion and violence, taking Islamic extremism as his paradigm but finding the same logic in moderate forms of religion and other religions: that is, a logic of belief "beyond the scope of rational discourse" and "in the absence of evidence."[10] Assuming the falsity of religious beliefs on the basis of their manifest absurdity, Harris takes his task to be that of showing how beliefs lead to action, and that religious beliefs "are leading us, inexorably, to kill one another."[11] Richard Dawkins's *The God Delusion*, despite having a title that appears to emphasize the truth question, reveals its underlying agenda in the highly emotive penultimate chapter in which Dawkins argues that bringing children up religious should be regarded as a form of child abuse (arguably a form that is even worse than sexual abuse).[12] His concern is arguably less with the mere falsity of the God hypothesis than with its perniciousness.[13]

Dawkins, like Harris and Dennett, is ultimately worried about the effect that religion has on people. Dennett, on top of this, explicitly separates the question of effect (good or bad?) from the question of truth. Commenting on the connection between religion and health, he remarks on "how independent these questions are from whether or not any religious beliefs are *true.*"[14] Although Dawkins does not make such a theoretical separation, his argument exhibits a structural separation between them insofar as he spends most of his book treating the truth question in abstraction from the question of effects. By contrast with Dennett and Dawkins, Harris's whole argument seeks to display a connection between the irrationality of faith and its violent effects. While assuming the falsity of religious belief, he nevertheless succeeds in opening up the question of the relation between belief and action, and thus (in my terms) between truth and transformation.[15] While Harris is something of an exception, I argue that the onus is nevertheless on the theologians to respond to the new atheists in a way that speaks precisely to this relationship between truth and transformation.

A different strain of contemporary atheism is found in Alain de Botton, who begins his *Religion for Atheists* with the claim that "the most boring and unproductive question one can ask of any religion is whether or not it is *true.*"[16] While agreeing heartily with those who believe that of course the answer is "no, it is not true," he goes on to consider, and argue for, the benefits of (a variety of forms of) religious practice. Once again, truth is separated from effect, although this time the effects are considered in sociological terms, and the judgment is largely positive. Julian Baggini is similarly appreciative of some forms of religion, arguing for an "immanent atheist religiosity," a form of atheism that denies "the supernatural" but that has in common with religion (at its best) an orientation to the immanent that recognizes its richness and meaningfulness.[17] In his *Atheism: A Very Short Introduction* he distinguishes the charge that religion is false from the charge that it is harmful (both leveled at religion by "militant atheists").[18] While he holds (albeit nondogmatically) that religion is false, he is far from thinking that it is harmful (as becomes even clearer in his plenary paper delivered at the 2018 annual conference of the Society for the Study of Theology).

Baggini and de Botton have in common with Dennett and Dawkins a separation of the question of effect from the question of truth (although in Dawkins's case the separation is felt in practice rather than in theory). Sam Harris is the exception. All, however, share a powerful concern about the effect of religion on people, or what we might call more descriptively its enhancement or diminishment of human flourishing. Their driving concern, in short, is an ethical one.

The theologians are also interested in both truth and effect (or what I will come to call *transformation*). Where most of them depart from the dominant tendency among the atheists, however, is in their explicit recognition, at least in theory, of their inseparability. Take the following claims. Beattie suggests that "it only makes sense to say that God 'exists' insofar as we embody that existence within the fabric of our own lives."[19] Eagleton proposes that "religious faith is not in the first place a matter of subscribing to the proposition that a Supreme Being exists. . . . [F]aith is for the most part performative rather than propositional."[20] And later: "faith articulates a loving commitment before it counts as a description of the way things are."[21] Fergusson, contra those "critics who tend to assume that religion is more or less equivalent to a collection of beliefs about the supernatural," claims that "the act of faith requires a comprehensive intellectual and practical reshaping of the self."[22] In other words, the propositional truth claims of the Christian tradition (from the perspective of which each of these authors is writing) cannot be separated from the way they take hold in the lives of those who profess them. The character of their truth is inseparable from their lived manifestation. While none of these authors denies all propositional content (and nor do I in what follows), they do deny that this content can stand on its own. Extricated from its lived manifestation, we might infer, the belief that God exists degenerates precisely into the belief the new atheists understand it to be, namely, belief in a supernatural agent—and it is thereby falsified. As Eagleton says, "God does not 'exist' as an entity in the world. Atheist and believer can at least concur on that."[23]

In the face of these gemlike insights into the problem with the atheists' tendency to separate truth from transformation, many of the theologians structurally replicate the separation. Fergusson does so by the very fact that he responds point by point to the atheist critiques. On the one hand, he considers critiques of the arguments for the existence of God (chapter 3) while, on the other hand, he considers the claim that religion is bad for our health (chapter 6).[24] On the one hand, truth; on the other hand, effect. Hart's argument is largely taken up with the question of effect, but less with the logical question of the Christian truth's transformative impetus, and more with the empirical (and comparative) question of whether Christianity has in fact brought about more good than its rivals.[25] But the empirical question is almost entirely beside the point in respect of the intrinsic inseparability of Christian truth from transformation: that Christians have in fact caused more harm than good may be a result of the fact that they are bad Christians, not that Christian truth is intrinsically harmful. The latter is a logical not an empirical matter. (Hart does not foreclose the logical investigation, and indeed gestures toward it in some of his argumentation, but in its heated polemic his argument degenerates into an empirical-historical showdown with the atheists.)

Turner's argument, with its focus on the question of what is being denied by atheists, deals almost entirely in the propositional. It elegantly (and to my mind conclusively) exposes the fact that most atheists simply do not go far enough in their denials, denying only what the properly apophatic Christian will also want to deny but failing to understand the radical incomprehensibility and transcendence of the God of Christian belief. It then seeks to tease out the difference between the (real) atheist who outdenies the Christian (in denying the possibility of asking the question, Why is there something rather than nothing?) and the Christian (for whom the question is legitimate).[26] To this extent it pushes beyond the propositional to the transformative, for here the nature of the Christian affirmation goes together with a certain ("childish") disposition.[27] In brief, the Christian, like the child who asks the "Why?" question once too often, is willing to ask a question (Why something rather than nothing?) to which there is no conceivable answer, and thus to refuse the conclusion that the universe is just dull fact, regarding it instead, in awe, as gift.[28] But on its own—without fleshing it out, for example, from what we already know from the riches and rigors of Christian discipleship—this is arguably a most attenuated form of transformation. Resolutely staying with the logic of affirmation and denial, Turner leaves to one side the world of Christian discipleship and the sacramental life of the church. His reasons for doing so may have something to do with the distinction between reason and revelation—or so he implies.[29] Nevertheless, I argue in the following that by doing so he misses something crucial about "what is at stake between the theist and the atheist"[30]—something that can be accessed only via the thicker connection between truth and transformation at the heart of the Christian life.[31]

The atheists for their part have taken note of the apophaticist's argument. But they are notably unconvinced. For example, Dennett is impatient with theologians who insist that even the experts do not understand what they are talking about when they talk about God.[32] His impatience seems to come down to the fact that while both may contain mystery, the claims of theologians, unlike those of physicists, do not have "a place where the rubber meets the road."[33] For example, if matter has become a mystery to physicists, that does not prevent predictions being made and confirmed on the basis of their quantum theoretical hypotheses, in such a way that the latter in turn become grounds for action. The assumption seems to be that apophatic theologians do not act on the basis of their belief in God (or at least do not have a warrant for specific action). The weakness of Turner's argument in the face of Dennett's skepticism is that it does not (or does not sufficiently) connect belief with action, truth with transformation.

If Turner and Hart lie at the opposite ends of the spectrum of truth and transformation, then Beattie and Eagleton fall in between, if in slightly different ways. Beattie's ideological critique of the rise of science and othering of religion by definition relates the ideological construction of truth with its harmful effects. The focus of her critique and repair is the construction of religion as irrational, in response to which she offers an account of the much more complex history of the relation between faith and reason within Catholic Christianity.[34] As a response to the atheist charge that "religion is bad for you," her argument (to oversimplify) is that science can and has been worse, and that one of the key reasons given by atheists for why religion is bad for you (that it is irrational) is not true of Catholicism. What she does not do is to show positively how Christian truth claims entail (positive) transformation of life. Her own task is a different, and important, one. But like others, she misses the opportunity to respond to the atheist where the atheist arguably most cries out for response.

Eagleton does connect Christian truth and transformation. His book interweaves theology and politics in such a way that their intrinsic connection is made manifest. However, Eagleton moves from fine-grained observations about the performative character of Christian truth claims to broad-brush revolutionary politics in such a way that it is easy to mistake his argument for a political manifesto in which he outdoes the atheists as a political theorist (thus mimicking the showdown character of Hart's book). In his words: "The antagonism between Ditchkins and those like myself, then, is quite as much political as theological. Where Richard Dawkins and I differ most fundamentally . . . is not on the question of God, science, superstition, evolution, or the origins of the universe. . . . The difference between Ditchkins and radicals like myself also hinges on whether it is true that the ultimate signifier of the human condition is the tortured and murdered body of a political criminal, and what the implications of this are for living."[35] This has all the ingredients for an argument about how Christian truth is fundamentally transformative. But it moves so hastily from narrowly defined theological questions to Christologically based politics that the connection is hardly spelled out. Moreover, the polemical cast of the book prevents Eagleton from acknowledging that his ethical and political disagreement with the new atheists can get off the ground only because of a shared ethical concern. To acknowledge this would be, in an important respect, to join forces with his opponents and to offer his specifically Christian argument as a response to their common concern. While this may not result in agreement, it would nevertheless pave the way for constructive disagreement about what is more than a red herring for both sides.

In this essay I seek, therefore, to tone the polemic down in order to offer, as a considered response to the new atheists' ethical concern, a constructive Christian account of the relation between truth and transformation.[36] My main dialogue partner is Denys Turner, since his case against the new atheists is, on the level of truth claims, the most compelling, while in terms of an ethics of transformation, it is the most in need of repair.

TRUTH AND TRANSFORMATION IN 1 CORINTHIANS 1:18–25

> For the word of the cross is folly (μωρία) to those who are perishing, but to us who are being saved it is the power of God. For it is written,
>
> "I will destroy the wisdom of the wise,
>   and the discernment of the discerning I will thwart."
>
> Where is the one who is wise? Where is the scribe? Where is the debater of this age? Has not God made foolish the wisdom of the world? For since, in the wisdom of God, the world did not know God through wisdom, it pleased God through the folly of preaching to save those who believe. For Jews demand signs and Greeks seek wisdom, but we preach Christ crucified, a stumbling block (σκάνδαλον) to Jews and folly (μωρία) to Gentiles, but to those who are called, both Jews and Greeks, Christ the power of God and the wisdom of God. For the foolishness of God is wiser than men, and the weakness of God is stronger than men.
>
> 1 Corinthians 1:18–25[37]

In 1 Corinthians 1 we move from the world of affirmations and negations into a world of wisdom and foolishness, in which it is not just truth and falsity that are at stake, but life and death. Let us look at how. The contrast of verse 18 (folly to the perishing, the power of God to those being saved) might easily be read according to a new atheist hermeneutic of suspicion so as to support a sharp fideism, in which Christians insulate themselves from atheist arguments by writing them off as so much "worldly wisdom" that is doomed to perish. According to such fideism, it is only to be expected that arguments from evolution expose the word of the cross to be "folly," that is, implausible or absurd. Christians, by contrast, have been vouchsafed the true, divine wisdom, and thus can see through shallow appearances. Such a fideist reading operates on the level of affirmations and denials, treating "the word of the cross" propositionally. For it to be folly is for it to seem implausible as a truth claim.

But whatever else the word (λόγος) of the cross is, it is surely not mere proposition. The word λόγος contains the ambiguity of both "word" and "deed." Even as word, it is not merely stated but preached (see verses 17 and 21). The word of the cross, we might infer, involves a call to action. Rather than a truth claim in the indicative, it might thus better be understood as an imperative: "Take up your cross!" In this case, to consider it "folly" would not be to judge it an implausible truth claim, but to regard it as inviting a crass course of action. This certainly rings true. Of course it's crass—it leads to death! From the perspective of any worldly calculus (which is the perspective of those who are perishing), the way of the cross is ruinous. Specifically, it will be the ruin of the worldly person in her worldly ambition.

However, if the propositional rendering fell short, the imperatival rendering is also shown not to be enough when we look at the contrasting term: "folly" is contrastively paired in verse 18 not with "wisdom" but with "the power of God." The way of the cross is something brought about by God, not a "wise" course of action chosen by the human being who has seen through worldly wisdom, or who works with an alternative calculus. There is no alternative calculus. Moreover, if God has "made foolish [ἐμώρανεν] the wisdom of the world" (verse 20b), then we can infer that the word of the cross does not just *appear* foolish to those who are perishing but *renders* them foolish. What does this mean?

To shed light on its connotations here, I consider the wider usage of the term μωρός (foolish) and associated terms across both testaments. It is a near synonym of ἄφρων, and both are used in very similar contexts in the New Testament. Not much need be made of the distinction. The foolish man (ἀνὴρ μωρός) is the one who builds his house on sand (Matthew 7:26). The rich man who lays up treasure for himself is called a fool (ἄφρων; Luke 12:20). In 2 Timothy 2:23 and Titus 3:9, μωρός is used in description of fractious social behavior. Ephesians 5:17, in the context of instruction about ordered communal life, exhorts the recipients not to be foolish (ἄφρονες). Μωρός is rare in the Septuagint (LXX hereafter; except for Sirach, where it is used abundantly), ἄφρων being much more common, and the word most often used for the well-known fool of Proverbs (usually translating כסיל in the Hebrew). כסיל and נבל are synonyms for the fool in Proverbs, but while כסיל is used exclusively in the Wisdom literature, נבל is used in the Pentateuch and Prophets (frequently in the nominative: "a sacrilege [נבלה] in Israel") to denounce Israel for deeds or words that breach the social order (e.g., Genesis 34:7, Joshua 7:15, Isaiah 32:6).[38]

More clearly in some of these contexts than others, but arguably in all of them, folly brings ruin; it is the fool's undoing. What the fool builds cannot stand (Matthew 7:26, cf. Proverbs 14:1). A fool has no hope (Proverbs 26:12 and 29:20). In Proverbs 9:13–18, the house of the woman Folly turns out to be the abode of death. A pervasive concern in both testaments is the maintenance of social order. Folly is that which undermines it. By analogy with the other uses, we might say that folly is the ruin of life in community. Folly, in sum, is death dealing. To be rendered foolish by God is to be brought to one's fall, to be undone.

From the perspective of the perishing, the cross is folly, I hypothesize, because it is the undoing of worldly social order; and in worldly terms this is simply death. But what about those being saved? As I have already remarked, they are not—as one might have expected on a fideist reading—ascribed a wisdom that contrasts with the folly of the perishing (1 Corinthians 1:18). Moreover, they are not spared folly; on the contrary, they are exhorted to become fools that they may become wise (3:18). The next few verses in our passage (1:19–21) serve to banish wisdom entirely from the creaturely sphere and ascribe it entirely to God. The contrast, in other words, is not between human folly and human wisdom, but between all human wisdom-made-folly on the one hand and the wisdom of God on the other hand. This has two important consequences. First, "the perishing" and "the being saved" do not necessarily refer to two mutually exclusive groups, but they may be complementary descriptions of human beings who are at once perishing and being saved. There is no way to salvation other than through the folly of death. Second, "those being saved" do not inhabit a privileged perspective in which the folly of the world has been left behind.

To return to the debate with the new atheist: far from having a special knowledge, there is no privileged human wisdom the Christian has that the atheist lacks. They find themselves in the same boat, the other side of divine wisdom, having been rendered foolish by it. Turner is right to conclude that there is nothing the theist understands that the atheist does not. But is he right to press the difference in terms of a different kind of affirmation—that of the legitimacy of a question? Where Turner remains within the realm of affirmations and denials (even if, when pushed to its limit, it breaks through to the transformative), 1 Corinthians, as I have already begun to show, considers truth squarely in the context of transformation, where it is a matter of life and death.

To sum up where we have got so far: folly is not about denying the word of the cross as a truth claim (the propositional reading), or about judging it a crass course of action (the imperatival reading), but is about living a life to which the word of the cross deals a death blow (a reading, as we will see, that holds the propositional and the performative together). So far I have focused only on the dynamics of folly. To find a way through to the dynamics of being saved, I turn to the other pivotal term in the above passage: σκάνδαλον (stumbling block). For the purposes of argument, I will treat "folly" and "stumbling block" as parallel rather than contrasting terms. This means forgoing exploration of potential differences between Jewish and gentile reception of the cross. Although this might be important and fruitful on another occasion, it would distract from the particular focus of the present essay: the debate with the new atheists.

Σκάνδαλον is an important and richly connotative word in the New Testament and the LXX, translating two different Hebrew words. It technically means the stick in a trap, but synecdochally it comes to mean trap, and metaphorically, an occasion for or cause of ruin, an entrapment which draws one into sin. The two Hebrew words are מוקש (trap or snare, from יקש, "to strike") and מכשול (stumbling block, from כשל, "to stumble"). Both meet metaphorically in "cause of ruin," but they are different base metaphors.[39] And it is the stumbling metaphor from the Hebrew that has led σκάνδαλον in the Greek to be associated with a stumbling block. Let us trace some of its intertextual uses.

Romans 9:33 is a good place to start, since it is multiply allusive:

> as it is written,
> "Behold, I am laying in Zion a stone of stumbling [λίθον προσκόμματος], and a rock of offense [πέτραν σκανδάλου];
> and whoever believes in him will not be put to shame."

The framework of the citation comes from Isaiah 28:16 LXX: "I will lay for the foundations of Sion a precious, choice stone, a highly valued cornerstone for its foundations, and the one who believes in him will not be put to shame." But the center of the verse—that which is being laid—is substituted for in Romans by a quotation from Isaiah 8:14. In Isaiah 8:14 (Hebrew), the Lord becomes for the houses of Israel "a stone of offense [אבן נגף] and a rock of stumbling [צור מכשול]." Isaiah 8:14 LXX departs significantly from the Hebrew, but it keeps the key noun pair: "you will not encounter him as a stumbling caused by a stone [λίθου προσκόμματι] nor as a fall caused by a rock [πέτρας πτώματι]" (Isaiah 8:14b). Otherwise following the LXX lexically at these key points, Romans 9:33 substitutes σκάνδαλον for πτώμα. Its use of σκάνδαλον to qualify "rock," and in parallel with προσκόμματα, serves to bring σκάνδαλον into the orbit of the stumbling-stone metaphor.

In 1 Peter 2:6, Isaiah 28:16 LXX is cited without the substitution (i.e., with "cornerstone" instead of "stumbling stone"), but alongside a citation (in 1 Peter 2:8) of Isaiah 8:14, "a stone of stumbling, a rock of offense" (exactly as it appears in Romans 9:33). In the context of 1 Peter, σκάνδαλον is thus not only brought into the stumbling-stone orbit but is also closely juxtaposed with the positive "cornerstone" (ἀκρογωνιαῖος). Both are (more or less explicitly) predicated of Christ. Christ is both the one over whom people stumble, and their cornerstone.

Returning to 1 Corinthians, this positive side of Christ's stoniness is developed through the metaphor of believers as God's building (1 Corinthians 3:9), of which Christ is the foundation (1 Corinthians 3:11). The shift from the negative to the positive opens up a new way of looking at the folly of 1 Corinthians 1, understood in parallel with stumbling stone. Might it be the case that to receive the folly of preaching as divine wisdom, one must first stumble over the stumbling stone? Or rather, might Christ become a cornerstone precisely to those who stumble over him? Romans 9:33, by way of its substitution, links the stumbling stone with those who believe. Thus, its substitution of stumbling stone for cornerstone can be read as an overlay rather than a straight replacement. It is not the case, on this hypothesis, that Christ is a stumbling stone to some and a cornerstone to others (creating the insider-outsider dichotomy again), just as he is not folly to some and wisdom to others. Rather, Christ is both simultaneously to those who are (simultaneously) perishing and being saved. (Incidentally, this fits with the Hebrew version of Isaiah 8:14, which names God both a sanctuary and a stone of stumbling for the houses of Israel.)

But why might stumbling be the prerequisite of belief? This is where the building metaphor comes in. The other members of the building are upheld by Christ rather than being the ones who uphold him. Factions have broken out in the community because other stones in the building are being treated as the foundation stone: "One says, 'I follow Paul,' and another, 'I follow Apollos'" (1 Corinthians 3:4), when they are merely servants of a building that upholds them (1 Corinthians 3:5). But to learn to be upheld means to let go of upholding, which in practice means to be made to stumble. One falls over Christ in order to be upheld by him. This, I hypothesize, is what it means to become foolish in order to become wise (1 Corinthians 3:18).

Later in 1 Corinthians, Paul is advising those who know that idols do not have real existence and thus know that meat sacrificed to them can legitimately be eaten. But he continues: "take care that this right of yours does not somehow become a stumbling block [πρόσκομμα] to the weak. . . . Therefore, if food makes my brother stumble [σκανδαλίζει], I will never eat meat, lest I make my brother stumble [σκανδαλίσω]" (1 Corinthians 8:9, 13). To do so, he says in the intervening verse, is to "sin against Christ" (1 Corinthians 8:12). To profess Christ while "scandalizing" one's neighbor is to continue to encounter Christ only as a stumbling block. But to build up the neighbor in love (1 Corinthians 8:1) is also to be built up: to find in Christ one's foundation (cf. 1 Corinthians 8:3). Christ as foundation stone upholds an economy of mutual upbuilding (which will entail both upholding others and being upheld by them).

In other words, therefore, the transformative context in which folly comes to be experienced not just as folly but as the power of God is an economy of mutual upbuilding, in which community members, rather than being their own foundation, discover themselves to be upheld by Christ. This is to be contrasted with a worldly social order, in which the "rulers of this world" (1 Corinthians 2:6) compete for social success as their own foundation stones. To be made foolish is to topple as one's own foundation, finding wisdom rather in being upheld, or more precisely, in the discovery that all upholding of one's own is preceded by a more fundamental being upheld.

TRUTH AND TRANSFORMATION IN THE GOD DEBATE

The transformational dynamic is clear. But what has happened to truth? To pursue this question (with a view eventually to returning to what is at stake in the God debate), I draw on a conceptual apparatus developed by Nicholas Adams in a study on receptive ecumenism and scriptural reasoning.[40] Adams distinguishes between two forms of claim making, which he names "binary" and "triadic," respectively. He offers, as an exemplary binary form, "X is true; not-X is false." The corresponding triadic form is "I affirm X; you deny X." He gives the concrete example: "Jesus is divine and human," which can be rendered triadically as follows: "Christians affirm 'Jesus is divine and human'; Muslims deny 'Jesus is divine and human.'"[41]

The triadic form has the potential to display (in a way in that the binary form does not) the conditions under which the claim is being made. When a Christian affirms the Chalcedonian Definition, she may be doing so under the conditions of a training in the doctrinal disputes surrounding the Definition. A Muslim is likely to come to the proposition with a rather different training. To clarify, what the distinction between forms draws attention to is a distinction between the content of a claim (its what) and the conditions under which it is made (its how). And the latter distinction broadly maps onto what I have been trying to get at in my distinction between truth and transformation.

With the help of Adams's distinction between content and conditions, then, I explore the relation between truth and transformation in the context of 1 Corinthians 1. Let us take as a test case what is arguably the central truth claim implicit in the latter: "Christ crucified is the savior of the world." If this were to be uttered by someone in the understanding that Christ will bring political triumph to Christians, thus licensing the violence of Christians against those of other faiths (as indeed it has been[42]), the claim would surely be falsified. It would be to utter it under the conditions of "those who are perishing," of worldly social order, and thus—one might suppose—to utter folly. There is some mileage in this line of reasoning. However, it would seem to be going too far to say that the claim is simply false when so uttered. One would be more likely to respond by saying, "That is true, but not in the way that you understand." Only so does there remain the potential for irony, as when Caiaphas advises that "one man should die for the people" (John 18:14). For this reason, J. L. Austin's analysis, in which truth is predicated not of a sentence but of an utterance made "by a certain person on a certain occasion," seems overly reductive.[43]

As a further example, consider Peter's declaration (in the Markan version), "You are the Christ" (Mark 8:29). Despite the fact that he proceeds to exhibit complete misunderstanding of what this means, one would hesitate to say that his declaration was simply untrue or false. Instead, one might say that the declaration is vague, and that while Peter goes on to determine its vagueness in a false way, it is nevertheless open to more truthful determinations, ones that will unfold for Peter as the story continues. We might hypothesize, however, that for an utterance to be true in any sense means for it to have *conceivable* truthful determinations. And this is where the conditions of utterance come into play.

To return to 1 Corinthians 1, if the truth of the claim "Christ crucified is the savior of the world" is obscured under the conditions of "those who are perishing," then it begins to come to light under the conditions of mutual upbuilding—the conditions under which folly is experienced as the power of God. These conditions do not have to be realized for the claim to have truth; they merely have to be conceivable. To require otherwise would amount to an impossible perfectionism, quite incompatible with the vision of 1 Corinthians 1, in which the conditions of "being saved" are inextricable from the conditions of "perishing."

To sum up, in the case of the truth claim "Christ crucified is the savior of the world," while the content can be distinguished from the conditions (even when uttered under "falsifying" conditions, the content can still be said, in a broader sense, to be "true"), content cannot be separated from conditions (the truth of the content depends on there being conditions under which that truth is displayed).

Turner's pursuit of an affirmation beyond denials stays in the register of content while hovering free of conditions. In our earlier language, it concerns truth in abstraction from transformation. If we were to transpose the apophaticist's argument with the atheist into the key of conditions, they would ask each other, not "How far do you go with your denials?," but rather, "Under what conditions would you want to affirm that God exists?"

If the claim "Christ crucified is the savior of the world" exhibits a vagueness that requires determination by particular conditions of utterance, then the claim "God exists" does so all the more. Its truth is radically bound up with its conditions of utterance. Certain conditions, as Dawkins rightly points out, falsify it. For example, if God is envisaged as a supernatural agent who interferes with the universe, in particular making an evolutionary explanation of its emergence impossible, then the claim "God exists" is given a sense that robs the universe of its integrity and autonomy (and the claim is thereby falsified). Alternatively, if God is envisaged by analogy with Dawkins's invisible celestial teapot, then the claim "God exists," rather than inviting radical transformation, makes the kind of difference to one's picture of the universe that one can practically ignore (and the claim is likewise falsified).

Anyone familiar with Aquinas's "doctrine" of analogy (at least on an apophatic reading) will realize how deep the problem goes.[44] We get our meaning of "exists" from its creaturely uses. But in the creaturely sphere the meaning of "exists" depends on what it is predicated of. What it is for a book to exist is different from what it is for a person to exist (as different as a book is from a person). The flexibility of "exists" in the creaturely sphere, in which it crosses diverse genera, is what licenses us to predicate it of God truly. However, our understanding of the term's meaning is inseparable from our (creaturely) use of it. We understand the way a book exists from understanding what a book is. Thus, without prior understanding of what God is (which Aquinas definitively rules out), we cannot know the way in which God exists, and thus what we mean when we say "God exists." Even worse, insofar as there is no "way" in which God exists (for God is not a kind of thing), the grammar of the analogical phrase "God exists" breaks down, belying the simpleness of its "referent."

It is just this that gets the new atheists so frustrated. Where, as Dennett asks, does the rubber meet the road? What difference does it make (truly) to affirm "God exists"? For Turner, to reiterate, the answer lies in the affirmation of the possibility of asking the question, Why something rather than nothing?, whose yield is not the content of the answer (which we cannot understand), but the disposition of its asking. This is arguably a rather small yield—at least if not accompanied by other resources that help draw out what is entailed in such childish wonder (one might ask, for example, Are there good and bad forms of it? Are real children always a good model of it? How is it related to the wisdom of experience?). I have hypothesized that this small yield is the result of pursuing the "rubber" question purely in terms of affirmation and denial. While one does reach transformation via the pursuit of the question of affirmations and denials, one can squeeze out only so much transformative yield that way. However, learning from 1 Corinthians 1, if we shift register so to consider "the conditions under which," or the transformational context of utterance of the phrase "God exists," we will find ourselves with a wealth of resources and an enormous yield.

Let me show how this is so, applying our earlier findings to the phrase "God exists." We have seen that "God exists" has no meaning for us when uttered as a proposition analogous to its creaturely counterparts. Under what conditions would it have meaning for us? The meaning of "God exists" is coterminous with the meaning of the claim that the universe is created— that you and me are creatures. This is the upshot of Turner's argument.[45] Thus, the conditions under which the claim "God exists" will display its true meaning are just those conditions under which we live as the creatures God created us to be. In a fallen world in which our primal sinlessness is lost to us, those conditions can only be those of the redemptive transformation to which we are called. And these are just what Paul is articulating in 1 Corinthians—in terms of a community of mutual upbuilding which has Christ as its cornerstone. *This*—just this economy of mutual upbuilding—is the place where the rubber meets the road.[46]

With this shift in register—from truth claims to transformation—the argument with the new atheists can finally be recognized for what it should be: an argument about ethics, in which Dawkins's denial of God's existence is treated less as a philosophical failure (although it may also be that) than as a failure of ethical imagination.[47] To clarify, this is not to do away with propositional truth in favor of ethical transformation; it is to argue, first, for their inseparability, and second, in the case of the logically odd proposition "God exists," whose grammar breaks down, that its "propositional meaning" (if it can still be called that) is indistinguishable from the transformational conditions of its true utterance.

In sum, Dawkins's challenge must be heard by theologians as an ethical challenge: has the church, as morally corrupt, lost hold of any truthful way of uttering "God exists"? That this is a question that must be taken seriously, and indeed must be one that the church continually poses to itself, will become clear if we return, once more, to 1 Corinthians 1. The conditions of mutual upbuilding are not a new social wisdom to be distinguished from the worldly wisdom that has been exposed as folly. These new conditions must themselves continue to be experienced as folly—as that which brings in question the wisdoms that are humanly conceivable. Being "wise" under these new conditions means stumbling again and again over Christ the stumbling stone, to rediscover Christ as cornerstone. The "me" that utters "Christ is my savior" will always also be the perishing self that is dealt a death blow by this very claim. It must be made foolish in order to become wise. As I have shown, the more austere claim "God exists," at least in its Christian rendition, has meaning only insofar as it is caught up in this dynamic. And for this reason, the critiques of the new atheists—however easy it might be to dismiss them on purely propositional grounds—must be heard as another invitation "to become a fool that [one] may become wise" (1 Corinthians 3:18).

CONCLUSION

I have framed my analysis of the debate with the new atheists in terms of the relationship between truth and transformation. I have found that both on the side of the new atheists, and on the side of the theologians, there is a tendency to separate out questions of truth from questions of transformation. However, the theologians simultaneously articulate the theoretical inseparability of truth and transformation, and thus have at their disposal the resources for the repair of the separation in practice. For this reason, my critique has been primarily of the theologians, since—with some exceptions—they fail to follow through on the repair they might have carried out.

Drawing on scriptural resources, I have developed an account of the relationship between the truth and transformative significance of two central theological claims: (1) "Christ crucified is the savior of the world," and (2) "God exists." In summary, I have argued that these two claims display their true meaning under the conditions of an economy of mutual upbuilding, in which stumbling over Christ as stumbling stone leads again and again to the rediscovery of Christ as cornerstone.[48]

In conclusion, I add one further twist to the argument. I have shown that it is quite possible to ask of Peter's declaration "You are the Christ!" whether it is true, but that the answer entails a delicate handling of the relationship between truth and transformation. The saying may be true, but it is by no means straightforwardly so, and its truth can also said to be falsified in Peter's utterance. A more economical and elegant way of approaching the declaration would be to ask whether it is spoken wisely. The answer would then be straightforwardly no but would leave open the possibility that the declaration might be spoken wisely on another occasion. To presuppose that there is a wise way of uttering the same words is to presuppose that they have a conceivable truthful determination. The language of wisdom overlaps both with the language of truth and with the language of transformation. Better, the language of wisdom presupposes the inseparable pairing of truth and transformation. It thus achieves in one move what must be undertaken in several moves when dealing with the distinction. More importantly, framing the question in terms of wisdom precludes the possibility of a false dichotomization of truth and transformation. Instead of asking of those involved in the God debate, Under what conditions would you want to affirm that God exists (thereby transformatively displaying the claim's truth)?, one might simply and more elegantly ask, How might the claim that God exists be uttered wisely?

NOTES

1. This is one of the important upshots of the essay in this volume by Mary-Jane Rubenstein, who, having shown the futility of trying to categorize Einstein's belief in terms of a binary opposition between theism and atheism (with pantheism as an uneasy third category), goes on to investigate the particular contours of his position on its own terms.
2. Terry Eagleton, *Reason, Faith and Revolution: Reflections on the God Debate* (New Haven, CT: Yale University Press, 2009).
3. David Bentley Hart, *Atheist Delusions: The Christian Revolution and Its Fashionable Enemies* (New Haven, CT: Yale University Press, 2009).
4. Denys Turner, "How to Be an Atheist," *New Blackfriars* 83, nos. 977–78 (2002): 317–35.
5. Tina Beattie, *The New Atheists: The Twilight of Reason and the War on Religion* (London: Darton, Longman & Todd, 2007), see esp. 7–8 and 12.
6. David Fergusson, *Faith and Its Critics: A Conversation* (Oxford: Oxford University Press, 2009), esp. 1, 54 and 179.
7. E.g., Fergusson, 69–70.

8. Daniel C. Dennett, *Breaking the Spell: Religion as a Natural Phenomenon* (New York: Penguin Books, 2006), see esp. 246.
9. Dennett, 339.
10. Sam Harris, *The End of Faith: Religion, Terror and the Future of Reason* (London: Free Press, 2005), see esp. 28–35 and chap. 4, "The Problem with Islam." His book begins provocatively with the story of a Muslim suicide bomber. For the quotations, see Harris, 13 and 65 respectively.
11. Harris, 12.
12. Richard Dawkins, *The God Delusion* (London: Bampton Press, 2006), see esp. 317.
13. Dawkins, 31, where he calls it a "pernicious delusion."
14. Dennett, *Breaking*, 272.
15. He does so at the most general level, being concerned with "religion" in general and its "irrationality" in general. In what follows I focus on specific Christian truth claims and the specific forms of transformation they call for.
16. Alain de Botton, *Religion for Atheists: A Non-Believer's Guide to the Uses of Religion* (London: Hamish Hamilton, 2012), 11.
17. Julian Baggini, "Immanent Atheist Religiosity at Babette's Feast" (plenary paper given at the annual conference for the Society for the Study of Theology, April 2018).
18. Julian Baggini, *Atheism: A Very Short Introduction* (Oxford: Oxford University Press, 2003), 91–107.
19. Beattie, *New Atheists*, 150.
20. Eagleton, *Reason*, 111.
21. Eagleton, 119.
22. Fergusson, *Faith*, 36.
23. Eagleton, *Reason*, 111.
24. Fergusson, *Faith*, 34ff. and 120ff., respectively.
25. Hart, *Atheist Delusions*.
26. Turner, "Atheist," 325–31.
27. Turner, 331–32.
28. Turner, 332–34.
29. Turner, 333.
30. Turner, 333.
31. In the following, I am less concerned about what is at stake *between* the theist and the atheist, and more concerned about what is at stake, on a Christian account of belief in God, *for* both theist and atheist alike. This sets my essay apart from the essay in this volume by Henning Tegtmeyer, which presents the potential collapse of apophaticism into atheism as a danger that must be avoided if apophaticism is to be defended. First, I eschew Tegtmeyer's apparent assumption that "atheism" is ultimately univocal (to be contrasted with any theism that does not collapse into it). Second, although I argue that much is at stake, on a Christian account, in belief in God, I do not equate what is at stake with what distinguishes the Christian from the atheist. I merely claim, to anticipate, that belief in God has ethically transformative implications. If an atheist interlocutor is found to embrace those implications without their Christian grounding, I would welcome the convergence rather than seek further ways to distinguish Christian from atheist. In short, I hold that there need be no anxiety about maintaining the distinction between theist and atheist.

32. Dennett, *Breaking*, 220.
33. Dennett, 233.
34. Beattie, *New Atheists*, esp. chaps. 2–3 and 6, respectively.
35. Eagleton, *Reason*, 36–37. "Dithckins" is Eagleton's hybrid name for Richard Dawkins and Christopher Hitchens.
36. To reiterate, although I show (in response to Dennett's "rubber" question) how belief in the Christian God makes a difference, I do not frame this difference as one that necessarily distinguishes Christian from atheist. Indeed, at the root of the argument is a common concern. Whether and how the Christian and atheist diverge beyond that concern is a matter for further investigation, and clearly depends on the particular atheist in question.
37. English Standard Version, slightly modified. In what follows, I use the English Standard Version unless otherwise stated. Translations of the Septuagint are from the New English Translation of the Septuagint.
38. Willem A. VanGemeren, ed., *New International Dictionary of Old Testament Theology and Exegesis*, 5 vols. (Carlisle, UK: Paternoster Press, 1997), no. 5571.
39. G. Kittel and G. Friedrich, eds., *Theological Dictionary of the New Testament*, trans. and ed. G. W. Bromiley, 10 vols. (Grand Rapids, MI: Eerdmans, 1964–1976), s.v. σκάνδαλον.
40. Nicholas Adams, "Long-Term Disagreement: Philosophical Models in Scriptural Reasoning and Receptive Ecumenism," *Modern Theology* 29, no. 4 (2013): 154–71.
41. Adams, "Disagreement," 165.
42. See George Lindbeck's frequently cited example of the crusader who cries "Christus est Dominus" while cleaving the skull of an infidel. George A. Lindbeck, *The Nature of Doctrine: Religion and Theology in a Postliberal Age* (Louisville, KY: Westminster John Knox Press, 1984), 64.
43. J. L. Austin, "Truth," in *Philosophical Papers*, ed. J. O. Urmson and G. J. Warnock, 3rd ed. (Oxford: Oxford University Press, 1979), 117–33, at 119.
44. Thomas Aquinas, *Summa Theologiae* 1a q13 a5. For apophatic readings, both of which inform the following summary, see Denys Turner, *Faith, Reason and the Existence of God* (Cambridge: Cambridge University Press, 2004), 177–90; David Burrell, *Aquinas: God and Action* (London: Routledge and Kegan Paul, 1979), 62–67.
45. Turner, "Atheist," 331.
46. It follows—and this is where I part company with Tegtmeyer as well as Turner—that the difference made is not necessarily that between the Christian and the atheist. By the same token, if there is something at stake between them, it will be in their respective ethical visions.
47. As Eagleton fully recognizes. In his words (to recall), "The antagonism between Ditchkins and those like myself, then, is quite as much political as theological" (*Reason*, 36).
48. It may be fruitful to compare my argument for this conclusion to the argument offered by Vittorio Montemaggi in the present volume. Montemaggi also pushes beyond a purely propositional account of belief to one that involves a more holistic dynamic (of which hope is at the center). But in the course of doing so, he also redefines atheism in terms of this dynamic, as life lived without hope. In the process atheism becomes detached from professing atheists, as a dynamic that can be found among believers and unbelievers alike (and which is—importantly—

internal to the Christian life). In my own argument, by contrast, "atheist" remains a self-designation, not an ideal type. Whether and how the atheist differs from the Christian remains, therefore, a matter for empirical investigation. Nevertheless, my account of the life of mutual upbuilding holds an analogous place in my argument to Montemaggi's account of the life of hope in his. A question for further exploration is whether Pauline "stumbling" has analogies with the lack of hope internal to Dante's journey.

REFERENCES

Adams, Nicholas. "Long-Term Disagreement: Philosophical Models in Scriptural Reasoning and Receptive Ecumenism." *Modern Theology* 29, no. 4 (2013): 154–71.

Aquinas, Thomas. *Summa Theologiae*. London: Blackfriars, 1964–1981.

Austin, J. L. "Truth." In *Philosophical Papers,* edited by J. O. Urmson and G. J. Warnock, 117–33. 3rd ed. Oxford: Oxford University Press, 1979.

Baggini, Julian. *Atheism: A Very Short Introduction*. Oxford: Oxford University Press, 2003.

———. "Immanent Atheist Religiosity at Babette's Feast." Plenary paper given at the annual conference for the Society for the Study of Theology, April 2018.

Beattie, Tina. *The New Atheists: The Twilight of Reason and the War on Religion*. London: Darton, Longman & Todd, 2007.

Burrell, David. *Aquinas: God and Action*. London: Routledge and Kegan Paul, 1979.

Dawkins, Richard. *The God Delusion*. London: Bampton Press, 2006.

de Botton, Alain. *Religion for Atheists: A Non-Believer's Guide to the Uses of Religion*. London: Hamish Hamilton, 2012.

Dennett, Daniel C. *Breaking the Spell: Religion as a Natural Phenomenon*. New York: Penguin Books, 2006.

Eagleton, Terry. *Reason, Faith and Revolution: Reflections on the God Debate*. New Haven, CT: Yale University Press, 2009.

Fergusson, David. *Faith and Its Critics: A Conversation*. Oxford: Oxford University Press, 2009.

Harris, Sam. *The End of Faith: Religion, Terror and the Future of Reason*. London: Free Press, 2005.

Hart, David Bentley. *Atheist Delusions: The Christian Revolution and Its Fashionable Enemies*. New Haven, CT: Yale University Press, 2009.

Kittel, G., and G. Friedrich, eds. *Theological Dictionary of the New Testament*. Translated and edited by G. W. Bromiley. 10 vols. Grand Rapids, MI: Eerdmans, 1964–1976.

Lindbeck, George A. *The Nature of Doctrine: Religion and Theology in a Postliberal Age*. Louisville, KY: Westminster John Knox Press, 1984.

Turner, Denys. *Faith, Reason and the Existence of God*. Cambridge: Cambridge University Press, 2004.

———. "How to Be an Atheist." *New Blackfriars* (2002): 317–35.

VanGemeren, Willem A., ed. *New International Dictionary of Old Testament Theology and Exegesis*. 5 vols. Carlisle, UK: Paternoster Press, 1997.

5

ATHEISM AND METAPHYSICS

A Problem of Apophatic Theology

Henning Tegtmeyer

It is a widespread view that apophatic theology is a superior alternative to more kataphatic modes of theological discourse, especially in the (post) modern age. Hume's, Kant's, and Nietzsche's rejection of metaphysics in general, and of natural theology in particular, still has an enormous impact on philosophical and theological discourse, not to mention Feuerbach's and Freud's subversive reinterpretations of faith. In a way, Heidegger's attack on ontotheology synthesizes the essential motives of Humean, Kantian, Nietzschean, Feuerbachian, and Freudian critiques of theology in one overarching narrative, notwithstanding the fact that of all these thinkers, it was Nietzsche who had the strongest impact on Heidegger's views of theology. Nevertheless, it is precisely the synthetic character of Heidegger's deconstruction of metaphysics and kataphatic theology that has rendered it so influential, especially in "continental" philosophy.

Even though Heidegger himself takes over the term "ontotheology" from Kant,[1] he gives it a much broader meaning than it has in the *Critique of Pure Reason*. According to Heidegger, traditional metaphysics in all its varieties, including Schopenhauer's and Nietzsche's atheism, is bound up with ontotheology. Traditional metaphysics is the attempt to answer the ultimate question of philosophy—that is, What is Being?—by grounding Being in the Being of a supreme entity. There are different ways of doing so, such as "ontological" arguments that exploit the conceptual link between being and perfection, and "cosmological" arguments that inquire into the grounds of Being in causal and modal terms, that is, in terms of first causes and of linking contingency with necessity. Heidegger himself, however, has no patience for these differences because he sees a general pattern at work in all versions of metaphysical thinking: it tends to answer ontological questions theologically, and this is why he characterizes it as ontotheology. For Heidegger, the metaphysical approach to ontology is entirely mistaken. The metaphysical answer to the ultimate question of philosophy is nothing but a pseudo-answer, as it merely reduces (finite) Being to (infinite) Being without telling us what Being is in the first place. Ultimately, Heidegger claims that metaphysics rests on one huge *petitio principii*. Moreover, replacing God with some other entity, such as Nature (Spinozism), the Will (Schopenhauer and Nietzsche), matter, or cosmic energy, does not help to escape this criticism because atheistic metaphysics is still committed to the ontotheological pattern of reasoning.[2] This is why Schopenhauer and Nietzsche, dialectical materialism, and process metaphysics are all equally vulnerable to Heidegger's critique.[3]

Many philosophers and theologians accept Heidegger's rejection of ontotheology, yet they argue that apophatic theology is a radical alternative to, rather than another variety of, metaphysical (onto)theology. This is because apophatic theology emphasizes the radical otherness of God, a move that apparently renders any metaphysical argument theologically obsolete. If God is so immeasurably different from any other entity, there simply cannot be a point in inferring statements about God's essence and existence from statements about the essence and existence of other entities, no matter whether this is done on conceptual grounds alone or in causal or modal terms. If apophatic theology is correct, we do not even know whether the terms "essence" and "existence" apply to God in any way that resembles the familiar logic of those terms. According to apophatic theology, theological discourse cannot have an ontological foundation, except for a purely negative one, based on the claim that God is completely unlike any object of ontology. This entails that apophatic theology is not only not committed to any metaphysical view in particular but also does not depend on metaphysics at all. Thus, it seems that apophaticism is a way of developing a radically non-metaphysical theology. Even though this does not hold for the best-known historical proponents of apophatic theology (e.g., Plato, Plotinus, Pseudo-Dionysius, Eckhart, Nicholas of Cusa), it appears to be at least a viable reinterpretation of apophatic theology that makes it attractive for post-Heideggerian theology.

A different but related claim is that apophatic theology is in a better position to engage in a fruitful dialogue with atheism than other, more kataphatic modes of theological reasoning. Starting from Heidegger's critique of ontotheology, one could argue for this claim as follows: Heidegger has convinced us that metaphysical atheism is just another metaphysical view and therefore vulnerable to the very same objection as metaphysical theism. This shows that it would be incoherent to defend metaphysical atheism while rejecting metaphysics. Yet there are other, less metaphysical versions of atheism, and of agnosticism, for that matter. What both metaphysical and non-metaphysical atheism presuppose, however, is a sufficiently clear understanding of the very meaning of the term "God" in order to meaningfully deny that the term denotes anything in the first place. Atheists have to make sure that they understand what they are talking about, and they definitely *think* they know what is meant by "God."[4] And here apophatic theology comes in by teaching them how difficult, if not virtually impossible it is to determine what "God" is (supposed to mean). But if that is so it is far from clear what an atheist denies in the first place. It would be strange indeed to argue that one knows that a certain term N does not denote anything while admitting that the meaning of N is incredibly hard to determine. How can one know that nothing exists that satisfies all the criteria of being N if one is ignorant of those very criteria? (In addition, an apophatic theologian will add the question, What exactly do you mean by "exists"?) For apophatic theology, the point of such a conversation is certainly not to convert atheists into theists but rather to shake the firm self-confidence of many contemporary atheists, to wake them from their dogmatic slumber.

In what follows, I do not directly address Heidegger's criticism of ontotheology but rather focus on the complex interplay between atheism and apophatic theology. Eventually, however, this will shed some light on the relation between metaphysics and theology in general and hence on Heideggerian worries about ontotheology in particular. These points are briefly sketched in the conclusion. My principal claim is, however, that apophatic theology runs into a dilemma that considerably weakens its position vis-à-vis atheism. The first section that follows is devoted to presenting this dilemma; the following ones to an examination of different strategies to escape it.

THE DILEMMA: APOPHATICISM AND ATHEISM

In its most basic, least sophisticated form, apophatic theology is a set of negative propositions which state what God is *not*. Familiar examples are "God is not visible," "God is not a body," "God is not material," "God is not multiple," "God is not the universe," "God does not have emotions," "God is not evil," "God is not temporal," and so on. A first question that can be raised at this point is, however, whether apophatic theology has to impose restrictions on such a list of negative propositions. In other words, is it possible to negate any conceivable predicate whatsoever? Let us briefly consider a few more contentious negations to illustrate this point: is it really acceptable for apophatic theology to say that God is not the creator of the universe, that God is not almighty, or that God is neither benign nor merciful? I guess that at least some proponents of apophatic theology will hesitate to accept propositions like these without any apologies. Most apophaticists will rather argue that propositions such as "God is almighty" or "In the beginning, God created heaven and earth" are to be read as negations. I return to this move below.

But if hard-boiled apophaticists are prepared to bite the bullet of thoroughgoing negativity a further problem emerges, which has to do with the fact that, in many cases, negative propositions seem to entail affirmative ones. For example, "God is not material" seems more or less synonymous with "God is immaterial," which is an affirmative proposition about God. In other cases, negative propositions at least suggest complementary affirmative statements. For example, it seems quite natural to state that God is not evil but good, or that God is not temporal but eternal. In cases like these, negative propositions pave the way for affirmations, which runs counter to the basic idea of apophatic theology. To block the complete collapse of apophatic theology into kataphaticism, apophaticists have to negate all pairs of contrary predicates that cause the problem. That is, apophaticism is committed to stating that God is neither material nor immaterial, neither good nor evil, neither temporal nor atemporal. As Plotinus has it, the essence of the supreme principle is inexpressible (*arrheton*).[5] Does this commit apophaticism to accepting the proposition that God does neither exist nor not exist? How about contradictions? And how close does apophaticism come to atheism here?

With these considerations, we have already entered the field of paradoxical theology, which is the more sophisticated version of apophatic theology. The transition from simple negative discourse to paradox is unavoidable for apophatic theology because the simple negation of a predicate goes hand in hand with affirmation in the case of binary oppositions since these do not leave room for a middle option. For example, suppose that there is something of which it is true that it is not material. This entails, in and of itself, that the thing in question is immaterial, *tertium non datur*. Conversely, if the thing in question is not immaterial, it is material. Other conceptual oppositions do leave logical space for a neutral middle ground. For example, if a person is not virtuous, this does not entail that she is vicious. She might be somewhere between virtue and vice in a morally mediocre state. Still, one of the three things has to hold of her nonetheless. She has to be either more or less virtuous, or more or less vicious, or more or less mediocre. Virtue admits of degrees, but not anything can be attributed to anything at the same time and in the same respect.

However, paradoxical theology urges us to accept that this familiar piece of logic does not apply to theological discourse. According to Nicholas of Cusa, bivalent logic is the logic of finite predication which must be overcome if we try to understand God's infinity. This infinity is precisely the unity of opposites (*coincidentia oppositorum*).[6] According to this idea, God is both great and small, material and immaterial, good and evil, temporal and atemporal. But since nothing great is small and nothing material is immaterial, and vice versa, we can also state that God is neither great nor small, neither material nor immaterial, neither good nor evil.

Paradoxical discourse is a hallmark of apophatic theology in its received form. It requires us to affirm and deny one and the same divine predicate and to see the relative truth and falsity of both moves to understand how inadequate human language and human thought are in theological matters. Apophaticism both accepts and rejects theological discourse in both the affirmative and the negative mode. Still, there is a slight preference for negation since negation seems to make the inappropriateness of theological language more explicit than affirmation. This is why Pseudo-Dionysius says that, in theology, negations are true whereas affirmations are not fitting.[7] All this shows, however, that predication fails, no matter how sublime the predicates are. Moreover, paradoxical theology argues that sublime predicates must be read as very sophisticated forms of negation, as has already been suggested . For example, the predicate "almighty" is interpreted as a negation of the ordinary usage of the term "mighty." Attributing almightiness to something means to express that that thing which possesses it is more than mighty or, say, "hypermighty." Apophaticism interprets this as a negation that removes both the predicate "mighty" and its contrary. The predicate "creation" is treated similarly: according to apophaticism, the primary meaning of "creation" is to negate both "causation" and "production." Hence to say that God created the universe means, first and foremost, that God neither brought the universe into existence in a causal way nor produced it as a designer or artisan designs and produces an artifact. According to this view, there is no affirmative reading of the claim that God is the ultimate ground of the universe. Saying this rather amounts to saying that God is the unfathomable abyss that traditional metaphysics has called Being itself.[8] At the same time, paradoxical theology warns us not to think that we know what almightiness means. Along these and similar lines, apophatic theology leads us to the mystical silence which accompanies the nonconceptual insight into God's sheer inaccessibility, which is the culmination of apophatic theology.

And here is the dilemma: Everything that has been said about paradoxical theology so far is compatible with atheism. This might sound like good news for the dialogue between theology and atheism but in fact it is not, since it marks the danger of apophaticism simply collapsing into atheism. This already holds for simple theological negation, at least in traditional, Aristotelian logic. According to this view, a proposition of the form "It is not the case that *N* is *F*" is true if *N* either does not exist or does not possess the property *F*.[9] Frege holds a different view of presupposition and argues, on that basis, that "It is not the case that *N* is *F*" would not be false, but rather meaningless, if *N* does not exist.[10] However, if we add contradictory predication to the picture both Aristotle and Frege are in the same boat again: If truly contradictory predicates are ascribed to one and the same subject, this is a license to infer that the subject term does not refer.[11]

If we consider, by contrast, how apophaticism handles predicates with a complex and inscrutable meaning such as "almighty" or "create," we might be prima facie less inclined to suspect hidden atheism. Yet adding semantic inscrutability is not a suitable way to escape atheism. To see this, suppose that an atheist asks an apophatic theologian what the latter means when she says that God created the universe. The apophatic theologian will reply that this means neither that God has caused the universe nor that the universe was produced by an artisan or demiurge called God. Besides that, the apophatic theologian will add, it is incredibly hard to say what creation means in the first place, which is why we all should be happy not to talk about the matter any further. Can one really blame an atheist for thinking that the short and honest version of such an answer would be a blunt confession of unbelief?

If apophatic theology wants to avoid this collapse into atheism, it must add affirmative propositions to the list of acceptable theological statements, and this exposes it to the opposed danger—that is, of turning into kataphatic theology, and thereby into metaphysics. These are the two horns of the dilemma: apophaticism runs the constant risk of sliding either into straightforward atheism or into kataphatic, metaphysical theology, and the avoidance of the one goes hand in hand with a move toward the other.

STRATEGIES TO ESCAPE THE DILEMMA

Most defenders of apophatic theology are not prepared to accept this conclusion readily. Several strategies to save apophaticism as a middle position between atheism and kataphatic theology suggest themselves.[12] It should be noted, however, that the options are limited. To save apophaticism from collapsing into either atheism or metaphysics, its proponents can choose between a strategy of expansion and a strategy of separation. An expanded apophatic theology bases itself on the claim that apophaticism in theology is but one instance of a universal pattern of subversive thinking according to which dichotomies are to be deconstructed and indeterminacy is to be established. This strategy is called "generalized apophatics." It argues that the dilemma dissolves because neither atheism nor metaphysics are available alternatives, and that this can be shown by a general rejection of conceptual oppositions. Generalized apophatics pays a price for this move because it must deprive theology of the special status that many theologians and philosophers ascribe to it, but the best-known defenders of generalized apophatics are prepared to pay this prize. According to them, there is nothing special about theological discourse since they regard apophatic logic as a universally valid pattern of reasoning.

Strategies of separation move in the opposite direction by setting theology strictly apart from any form of "ordinary" philosophical, scientific, or everyday discourse, including the debate between metaphysical atheism and metaphysical theism. There are linguistic and nonlinguistic strategies of separation. Among the proponents of linguistic strategies, some argue for a shift of focus, away from theological assertions and toward other types of religious speech acts such as prayer. I call this strategy "invocationalism." Another linguistic strategy is to reinterpret religious assertions in a way that sets them entirely apart from nonreligious assertions. According to this strategy, which I call "scripturalism," the assertions that one finds in holy texts such as the Bible and that one mentions or uses in religious life, are governed by a special religious semantics that is incommensurable with the semantics of nonreligious assertions, including the semantics of atheistic and theistic metaphysics. A further, very peculiar linguistic strategy to escape the dilemma is fictionalism. According to this view, the seemingly kataphatic assertions that one finds in texts such as the Bible do not refer to real objects in the real, historical world but rather to fictional worlds. They are as-if assertions that do not actually have truth values. Fictionalists therefore argue that it would be misplaced to confront religious language with metaphysical issues in general or with atheism in particular. This fits into the overall pattern of linguistic defenses of apophaticism to immunize apophatic theology against the intrusion of metaphysics.

Regarding nonlinguistic strategies, the currently best-known strategy is to prioritize religious practice rather than religious language. For simplicity's sake, I call this strategy pars pro toto "sacramentalism" because its most prominent version has been developed with a focus on the sacrament of the Eucharist. Unsurprisingly, therefore, the most nuanced versions of sacramentalism have been developed in Catholic thought and in the Orthodox tradition, but there are also Jewish versions. In general, sacramentalism is a powerful response to the dilemma because it supplements apophatic theology not on the level of language but on the level of nonlinguistic expressions of faith. Therefore, it appears to be a very promising strategy to escape the dilemma.

In what follows, I examine these strategies more closely, starting from the best-known ones and continuing with those that are less frequent in the current discussion. Therefore, I start with generalized apophatics, sacramentalism, and invocationalism and close with a brief discussion of scripturalism and fictionalism.

FIRST ESCAPE STRATEGY: GENERALIZED APOPHATICS

The first strategy to save apophaticism from collapsing into either atheism or kataphaticism is what John Caputo calls "generalized apophatics."[13] The underlying idea is to view theology not as a sui generis field of discourse that is governed by a peculiar logic but as continuous with other, more mundane forms of conversation. A central intuition of generalized apophaticism, which is foundational for deconstructive philosophy in general, is that the boundaries between literal and figurative speech, and hence between predication proper and metaphor, cannot be drawn with precision, which means that there are always borderline cases. This entails that there cannot be a sharp distinction between univocal and equivocal predication, hence also not between affirmation and negation, between consistent and inconsistent language use, and ultimately also not between logic and rhetoric. Consider the ambiguous predicate F.[14] If there are cases in which it cannot be determined whether F is used literally or metaphorically, it can also not be determined whether "A is both F and non-F" is consistent or inconsistent, because it is an open question as to whether "A is non-F" is the negation of "A is F." The very idea of kataphatic thinking is built on the distinction between univocal and equivocal language use; so if this distinction turns out to be unfounded, apophaticism haunts language and thought in general.

In and of itself, however, that consideration does not suffice to establish the intended conclusion. Fair enough, one might object, predicate use is full of borderline cases. For example, there are people who are called bald even though they have not lost all of their scalp hair. From this, however, it simply does not follow that there is no real difference between being hairy and being bald. Analogously, the distinction between the literal and the metaphorical use of predicates such as "cultivated" is often hard to draw. We might find it hard to determine whether to call Joan "a cultivated person" is an instance of metaphorical predication. This holds for many so-called frozen metaphors. However, the existence of gray zones like these in between extremes does not speak against the existence of the extremes as such, nor does it destroy their opposition. Similarly, the fact that equivocal language use is sometimes hard to distinguish from univocal language use does not render language as a whole ambiguous. Hence proponents of the first strategy must do more to bring home their point.

The move that apophaticists usually make at this point is known from ancient skepticism and consists in employing the *sorites* paradox. Adapted to the case of ambiguous predicates, the argument runs like this: Suppose that there is a gray zone within the use of a certain term F so that it is impossible to determine whether F is predicated of objects univocally or equivocally within the zone. If that is the case, however, the borderline between using F ambiguously and using it clearly univocally, or clearly equivocally, for that matter, cannot be drawn sharply. That is, if "x_1 is F" and "y_1 is F" are both ambiguous, there is no good reason to believe that "x_2 is F" is clearly univocal whereas "y_2 is F" is clearly equivocal. This same consideration, however, applies to every further element $x_3, \ldots, x_n$ and $y_3, \ldots, y_n$. In short, if there are predicates with some gray zone between univocal and equivocal applications, it follows that these predicates are ambiguous throughout.

This, however, is a sophism, albeit a nice one. Equivocation can be removed very easily by stipulation, that is, by introducing new terms. Instead of having a partly or completely ambiguous term F we might prefer to have two terms F and G so that F univocally denotes $x_1, \ldots, x_n$, whereas G univocally denotes $y_1, \ldots, y_n$. F and G can be artificial terms, but very often expressions from ordinary language will do the same job. For example, we might wish to reserve the term "cultivated" for the agricultural sphere, which is why we decide to replace this term by other terms such as "very well-educated," *gebildet*, "refined," and so on, in case we talk about persons. There might be cases in which short and concise terms must be replaced by lengthy descriptions to preserve roughly the same connotations that the original term has, but that is irrelevant for the argument. The point of this argument is that ambiguity can be made explicit by using different expressions for the univocal and the equivocal applications of a certain predicate. If that is the case, however, it is possible to reverse the *sorites* argument. That is, if we can clearly identify the extremes of the univocal and the equivocal use of a certain predicate, we can work ourselves through to the allegedly ambiguous cases as well by testing which of the newly introduced univocal terms fits best. The result will always be clear, so the argument goes. Even if the outcome of the test were that both predicates F and G apply, this would not be a counterexample. What we have in such cases is not an inscrutable semantic ambiguity but an instance of double predication which ought to be analyzed as two distinct propositions that replace the opaque initial expression.

Note that the underlying idea is not the dream of a radical reform of language, with the goal of imposing a purely univocal language on us all.[15] There is no imperative to replace all equivocal and ambiguous predicates. The idea is rather that such a replacement is possible on a case-by-case basis and just for the sake of making equivocations and semantic ambiguities explicit if necessary. This is based on the assumption that semantic clarifications that make equivocations explicit are possible without destroying the meaning of the original expression. Replacements of certain terms by other terms ought to be semantically conservative.

Yet apophaticists will not be ready to accept the notion of a semantically conservative replacement of equivocal and ambiguous terms by univocal terms. For them, such a replacement inevitably alters language use; in other words, it is an act of linguistic violence that imposes a regime of univocal logic on a hitherto "wild" and opaque language use, ignoring otherness or "the nonidentical," as Adorno used to put it in his critique of Hegelian dialectics.

This move, however, is slightly at odds with the overall tendency of generalized apophaticism to regard concepts and categories as arbitrary stipulations, a tendency rooted in the antiessentialism or "generalized nominalism" that governs this view.[16] According to general nominalism, any general term and any description impose an order that is foreign to its elements because these terms do not reflect the nature of the things themselves. This does not mean to suggest that we better stop talking but rather that we stop pretending to know what we are talking about, and that we begin "to treat each name as a *nomen negativum*," as Caputo puts it.[17] In line with this overall nominalism, he presents his generalized apophatics not as an already-established point of view but rather as a project that one can subscribe to: "So to the *theologia negativa*, one could add a *anthropologia negativa*, an *ethica negativa, politica negativa*, where of the humanity, or the ethics, or the political, or the democracy to come we cannot say a thing, except that they want to twist free from the regimes of presence, from the historically restricted concepts of humanity, ethics, and democracy under which we presently labor."[18] This raises the question what enables "us" to say this about the humanity, the ethics, and politics to come. Is this something that we know on the basis of an insight into what humanity really is? But generalized nominalism holds that the term "humanity" is nothing but a *flatus vocis* that does not refer to anything in things themselves. Or is it rather something that "we universal apophaticists" *want* the future to be? Then generalized apophaticism is every bit as arbitrary, aggressive, and violent as it accuses its essentialist opponent to be because it tries to impose its own preferred order of thinking onto people and things.

To sum up the discussion of the first escape strategy: to escape the dilemma of apophatic theology, some of its proponents suggest to generalize apophatics. Ultimately, however, this move merely runs into another version of the same dilemma that we have started with. That is, either generalized apophatics claims that any conceptual framework that is used to represent reality in thought is arbitrary and violent—such a claim, however, can be defended only on the basis of a robust metaphysical view (i.e., on a radical nominalism that states that reality is made up of particulars each of which is entirely unique)—or generalized apophatics withdraws to voluntarism, claiming that the apophatic vision of reality has to be adopted on the basis of a sheer decision to do so. The problem with such a move is that it fails to be rationally compelling for the addressee. Authors such as Caputo invest a lot of rhetoric into making generalized apophaticism appealing, but they fail to offer good reasons why a general apophatic attitude toward reality is preferable to an overall kataphaticism.[19] Regarding atheism, this strategy does not bring theology one step closer to a fruitful dialogue because general apophaticism is virtually indistinguishable from atheism.

A diametrically opposed strategy would be to use this discussion as an argument for the reverse claim, that is, that radical atheism runs the constant risk of collapsing into general apophaticism and to try a reductio ad absurdum of radical atheism along these lines. This, however, would certainly not work as a defense of apophatic theology.

SECOND ESCAPE STRATEGY: SACRAMENTALISM

Another escape strategy is to combine apophaticism in theological discourse with a strong emphasis on the experience of religious practice. Proponents of this strategy resist the temptation to generalize apophaticism; they confine themselves to theological discourse. Within this field, authors such as Marion insist that God is strictly "unthinkable."[20] If one does not accept this, one turns God into a being, or into an idol, as Marion also puts it. At the same time, thinking keeps being challenged to think about God precisely because of God's resistance against being thought about. God is without Being since God is not grounded in Being, and therefore God does not fall under the universal concept of Being. In other words, God is more than Being, or beyond Being, as Plato puts it. It is precisely this thought about God's radical otherness and transcendence—which even transcends Being—that condemns us to apophatic silence in theology.[21] Of course, this is paradoxical, given that theology is a form of discourse.[22]

Yet apophatic silence is not complete because there is another, nonphilosophical source of theological inspiration: divine revelation.[23] Based on revelation, it becomes possible to assert God's supreme goodness, which is prior to Being, as Marion argues, following Pseudo-Dionysius.[24] At the same time, an apophatic theologian has to insist that goodness is not a divine attribute in the kataphatic sense because it does not determine what God is at all. It merely indicates supreme venerability; it expresses highest respect, and hence extreme distance.[25] Again through revelation, however, Divine goodness can be experienced as charity. This is the point at which religious practice comes into play. For Marion, the unsurpassable experience of divine goodness as charity takes place in the sacrament of the Eucharist. Unlike other religious practices, Christian or non-Christian, the Eucharist is not a merely human celebration of divine goodness but an immediate manifestation of divine charity itself, because the sacrament has not been invented by sinful human beings but instituted by Christ himself. It does not merely symbolize divine charity but is, in and of itself, an immediate gift of charity that allows us to participate in the paschal event. It goes without saying that this whole analysis rests on a robustly Catholic understanding of the sacraments.[26] At the same time, however, any trace of traditional metaphysics has to be removed from this apophatic sacramentalism, which is why traditional doctrines such as transubstantiation are rejected, whereas the doctrine of the real presence of Christ in the sacrament of bread and wine is retained.[27] This turns the Eucharist itself into authentic theology.[28] Every other form of theology, especially theological discourse as a research activity, is of secondary importance for sacramentalism.[29]

At first sight, it might seem that this second strategy is more successful than the first, because it seems to steer clear of both metaphysics and atheism. It does not collapse into metaphysics with its persistent refusal to ascribe any affirmative attribute to God; it even interprets Divine goodness in an apophatic manner. At the same time, its robust insistence on eucharistic practice as the experience of real divine presence sets it apart from any form of atheism.

At a closer look, however, this balance appears to be rather unstable. That is, sacramentalism comes closer to metaphysics than its proponents are prepared to acknowledge. This is the case because the Eucharist is not a mute rite at all; on the contrary, it is governed by well-defined speech acts whose performance in the right order structures this core part of liturgical service. Of course, these speech acts need to be embedded in the appropriate liturgical context and performed by persons who are entitled to do so, as Marion repeatedly emphasizes.[30] Yet the whole liturgical setting of the Eucharist would be entirely devoid of meaning without the biblical narrative and the way Christian theology confirms the link between the life, death, and resurrection of Jesus of Nazareth and Christian liturgy in general, and between the Last Supper and the Eucharist in particular. From the church fathers onward, Christian theology usually assumed that this confirmation involves a very complex and demanding metaphysics which contains strange and unusual concepts such as trinity, incarnation, resurrection, and at least some functional equivalent to transubstantiation. In this respect, metaphysics was taken to be useful for theology in two ways, by explicating these concepts very precisely and by thereby showing why it is that these concepts are so demanding and paradoxical but not incoherent. Neither of those tends to reduce theology to metaphysics. In other words, the task of metaphysics was traditionally seen as a clarification of faith, not as a full (reductive) explanation of its content. Traditional Christian theology would not allow metaphysics to explain the birth, life, death, and resurrection of Christ in general metaphysical terms, neither in terms of causation nor in terms of emanation, and to thereby reduce it to some general explanatory pattern. In spite of this reservation, mainstream Catholic theology used to consider metaphysics indispensable for the articulation of Christian faith.[31]

Yet apophatic sacramentalists refuse to accept metaphysical aid. Marion, for instance, fully recognizes the need for further reflection and contemplation of the meaning of the Eucharist and of eucharistic presence. At the same time, he wholeheartedly rejects the idea that the Eucharist needs an "explanation," let alone in metaphysical terms. I take him to use the term "explanation" in a broad sense here, which includes conceptual clarification. This is why Marion insists, "A gift, and this one above all, does not require first that one explain it, but indeed that one receive it."[32] This being granted, it needs to be added that receiving a gift and recognizing it as a gift have to take place in good faith, which presupposes, among other things, at least an inchoate understanding of what the whole event is supposed to mean. This is nothing that Marion would deny. Yet he insists that faith can express itself without any aid from the standpoint of metaphysics.

This refusal to engage metaphysics turns sacramentalism into a variety of fideism, that is, the view that faith unaided by reason is, or rather ought to be, cognitively autonomous, and that it does not need any additional support beyond the authority of scripture and of the church. It ought to be *fides ex auditu*, and nothing but that.[33] What fideism rejects is the idea that faith needs to be supported, justified, or defended on nonfideistic grounds.[34]

This is not the right place to discuss fideism in general and its problems. Regarding sacramentalism, however, the following conclusion seems in order: if sacramentalism chooses to be a variety of fideism, this clearly disqualifies it as a suitable partner for a fruitful dialogue with atheism. Again, this is something that Marion openly acknowledges by simply calling atheism "impossible."[35] Between sacramentalism and atheism, there is no common ground that would make a conversation possible.

THIRD ESCAPE STRATEGY: INVOCATIONALISM

Another strategy to escape the dilemma of apophatic theology can be called *invocationalism*. This strategy is also present in Marion, especially in his thoughts on confession and prayer.[36] However, it has its origins in ordinary-language philosophy in general and in speech-act theory and Wittgenstein in particular. The core idea is to analyze religious language as a system of speech acts that belong to different types. Traditional philosophy of religion has focused on assertions because it takes faith to be based on the belief in the truth of a certain set of propositions. According to invocationalism, however, this focus on religious assertions is a serious distortion of religious life in general and religious experience in particular because other types of speech acts play a much more dominant role in religious practice than traditional philosophy of religion is prepared to recognize. The most prominent example is prayer.[37] Prayer does not assert anything about God, at least not explicitly, but rather invokes God, appeals to God's mercy in petitionary prayer and praises his goodness in thanksgiving. Similarly, invocationalism analyses confession not in terms of its propositional content but in terms of its performative character, that is, as expressing self-accusation and remorse. Even confessing one's faith—for example, publicly during the Mass—is not seen primarily as an expression of belief but as an expression of belonging to the community of believers. This, invocationalists argue, is a general fact about religious language whose dominant character is not assertoric but expressive and appellative. Such an interpretation of religious language use can go hand in hand with apophatic theology because the latter helps invocationalism to steer clear of metaphysics whereas its own nonassertoric, expressivist understanding of religious language keeps atheism at bay.

It is often considered an additional merit of invocationalism that it seems compatible with agnosticism. Anthony Kenny famously argued that even for an agnostic, it can make sense to pray: "It is surely not more unreasonable than the act of a man adrift in the ocean, trapped in a cave, or stranded on a mountainside, who cries for help though he may never be heard or fires a signal which may never be seen."[38] This consideration also suggests that believers and nonbelievers can engage in the same religious practice jointly. Religious practice leaves room for agnosticism and even for atheism, at least if we agree with Marion that agnosticism just is a form of atheism.[39] And surely this is what really and even frequently happens in everyday religious life. Believers and agnostics kneel down side by side and utter the same prayers. On the basis of such experiences, invocationalism encourages us to hope that shared religious practice might become the common ground on which a dialogue between faith and atheism can eventually take place.

It does not seem entirely unreasonable to adopt this hope. Yet there is a problem with the invocationalist's understanding of religious language and religious practice. Ultimately, this understanding is based on the assumption that the propositional content of religious assertions does not matter for those religious speech acts and practices that the invocationalist takes to be essential. But this hardly seems credible. Consider Kenny's examples from the previous quote: Kenny seems correct when he argues that it can be reasonable to call for help for someone who is in need even if this person has no firm beliefs whatsoever about the availability of potential helpers. Yet this does not show that such a person does no need to have any further beliefs at all that render cries for help reasonable in the first place. There are two kinds of beliefs in particular that make cries for help in these and similar situations reasonable. First, the person in need must believe that it is at least possible that there is someone out there who might hear her crying or see her signaling, however small she might take the chance to be. Second, she must have certain beliefs about the nature of potential helpers, for example, that they understand language or signs in the right way and that they are potentially willing to lend a helping hand. One does not call sharks, bears, and wolves for help but rather human beings, angels, or God. If one of these two kinds of beliefs is absent, a cry in the wilderness is not a cry for help but something else, perhaps a sheer expression of fear or despair or something like that. Moreover, it is certainly not the case that crying for help somehow creates such beliefs; having the latter is rather a precondition of doing the former.

Analogously, if an agnostic honestly kneels down to pray to God this can make sense to herself on two conditions: First, she has to believe that it is at least possible that there is an addressee, some being that is able to receive her prayer (i.e., that God exists), no matter how unlikely she takes God's existence to be. Second, she has to believe that this being, whatever it is, is good and admirable rather than evil and horrible, at least with respect to her situation.[40] Otherwise, the agnostic will not be able to understand her own speech act as reasonable and sincere. Arguably, it can even be reasonable for agnostics or atheists to pray to God that he turn them into believers, and on the basis of this option, Tim Mawson argues that they are epistemically obliged to do so.[41] Even in such a case, however, both rational requirements must be met, as Mawson himself recognizes.[42] Hence it is not the case that the act of praying produces or causes the belief that there might be a being "out there" that listens to one's prayers. If the agnostic or atheist fails to have beliefs of this kind but utters "prayers" nonetheless, she will not take herself to be praying but rather to be engaging in something else, perhaps in soliloquy or in playing a game.

All in all, invocationalism fails to show that religious speech acts such as petitionary prayer and related religious practices are autonomous and not in need of concomitant religious beliefs. If that is so, apophatic theology does not have the conceptual resources to supply invocationalism with the account of religious beliefs that it needs either. This means, conversely, that invocationalism cannot help apophaticism to escape atheism. In fact, invocationalism itself presupposes certain at least weakly nonatheistic beliefs that it cannot account for by itself. Hence, it will simply not do to say that "predication must yield to praise."[43] It cannot yield to praise entirely since praise presupposes affirmative predication.

FURTHER ESCAPE STRATEGIES: SCRIPTURALISM, FICTIONALISM

There are further escape strategies for apophatic theology, some of which are well known, whereas others are more extravagant. One of the oldest strategies of theology to distance itself from metaphysics is to choose an entirely revelation-based faith that refuses to accept any form of philosophical justification in kataphatic terms. Ultimately, this leads to scripturalism, a view according to which holy, divinely inspired texts are the only legitimate source of kataphatic claims about God.[44] These kataphatic claims, however, have a very peculiar, "scriptural" meaning that resists any easy translation into "mundane" language and thought in general and into the language of metaphysics in particular. Scripturalism is very common in the Jewish, Christian, and Islamic tradition. Within Christianity, it has been dominant in Protestantism in all of its varieties from the outset, including both "orthodox" and "liberal" approaches.

Some scholars take scripturalism to be opposed to apophatic theology as well,[45] but that is a misunderstanding. Nothing in apophaticism is incompatible with scripturalism as such. On the contrary, scripturalism can make use of apophatic theology to keep metaphysics out of its way, whereas apophatic theology can choose scripturalism as a faith-based way out of atheism. One key example of such an alliance between apophaticism and scripturalism is Karl Barth's reading of Anselm's *Proslogion*.[46] Barth takes Anselm himself to bring about this synthesis of apophaticism with scripturalism, which also means that *Proslogion* is read not as a piece of natural theology at all but rather as a piece of religious prose. In this vein, Barth even wants us to read Anselm's famous "one argument" not as a refutation of atheism but rather as a clarification of why atheism is not an option *for a believer*. Barth himself does not appear to be interested in the broader tradition of apophatic theology and its roots in Greek philosophy, but his own kerygmatic theology shows many traces of apophaticism nevertheless.

It is its underlying fideism, however, which brings scripturalism very close to sacramentalism and makes it vulnerable to the same kind of critique. This is not meant to suggest, however, that the differences between scripturalism and sacramentalism are minor. The contrary is true. For example, sacramentalism relies on divine presence in the sacraments, something that scripturalism is deeply suspicious of. But this does not matter for the critique, which focuses on fideism as a common element in both. Hence if sacramentalism is not a suitable candidate for a dialogue with atheism then scripturalism is neither.

Other potential strategies are much more extravagant and rarely tried. Let me just mention one strategy that has regained some popularity recently and that is fictionalism.[47] Fictionalism urges us to treat religious narratives such as the book of Genesis or the Gospels as depictions of fictional worlds that are potentially worthwhile to engage with, just like good novels, thrilling movies, or the mythological tales of foreign cultures. Engaging with them does not commit one to believing in the existence of the agents and events that are represented within these fictional universes; one can become a "follower" without being a "believer." What is so interesting about following these fictional narratives, fictionalists argue, is not so much the question whether these fictional characters really exist but the question what our world would be like if they did and if we encountered them. Along these lines, fictionalism tries to offer an alternative account of what religious commitment can consist in, not in terms of truth but in terms of absorption.[48]

While fictionalism as such is strongly committed to an anti-metaphysical and antirealist agenda within philosophy of religion, potential relations to apophatic theology have hardly ever been discussed. This is a bit surprising, given the fact that current defenders of fictionalism often claim to be defenders of religious commitment and religious practice but opponents of metaphysical theology. Therefore, it would seem quite natural to refer to apophatic theology as a non-metaphysical form of theology that criticizes metaphysical approaches to theological discourse. Moreover, fictionalism could use apophatic aid to defend itself against the accusation of arbitrariness that it frequently provokes. At the same time, it cannot be accused of kataphaticism because it insists that any kataphatic language that we find in religious discourse can and ought to be interpreted as merely fictional, and this is what might be taken to render it potentially acceptable for apophatic theology.

Whatever the merits of such a potential alliance might be, however, it cannot solve the problem that we discuss here. That is, if apophatic theology runs the risk of collapsing into atheism, fictionalism has already taken a few more steps in the same direction. In fact, it can be regarded as a sophisticated form of atheism that invites atheists to open themselves to religious language and religious imagery precisely by taking its content less seriously than atheists usually do. Of course, this might result in an interesting dialogue within atheism, but it is not the potential dialogue between atheists and believers that we have been looking for because fictionalism simply cannot be a living option for faith.

This is certainly not the last word on fictionalism and apophatic theology since further, more nuanced versions of fictionalism are conceivable which are not committed to a thoroughgoing antirealism with respect to religious language. Such a qualified fictionalism, however, would probably run into similar difficulties as apophatic theology.

CONCLUSION: APOPHATICISM, METAPHYSICS, AND ONTOTHEOLOGY

In this chapter, the dilemmatic position of apophatic theology between kataphaticism and atheism has been discussed. We have examined several strategies of contemporary apophaticism to escape this dilemma, some of which admit of being combined (sacramentalism and invocationalism, for example) whereas others mutually exclude each other (generalized apophatics and sacramentalism, for example, or scripturalism and fictionalism). None of these escape strategies, however, succeeds in solving the initial dilemma because each tends to lead apophaticism back to either the one or the other of its horns.

This cannot be more than a provisional result because further escape strategies might be there to be tried out. Nevertheless, it seems to raise doubts about the stability of apophatic theology, at least about its non-metaphysical versions. One way out could be to take more seriously the genuinely metaphysical aspirations of traditional apophatic theology—as in Plotinus, Eckhart, or Nicholas of Cusa—much more than current apophaticism does, and hence to examine the complex interplay between kataphatic and apophatic metaphysics that these thinkers build their theology on. Another option could be to reconsider Heidegger's rejection of ontotheology as such. Perhaps Heidegger has led contemporary theological discourse into a dead end, and perhaps it is our task to find our way back to the open road again.

NOTES

1. Immanuel Kant, *Critique of Pure Reason*, ed. and trans. Paul Guyer and Allan W. Wood (Cambridge: Cambridge University Press, 1999), B660.
2. This cannot be more than a rough sketch of the role of Schopenhauer's and Nietzsche's metaphysical atheism in Heidegger's argument. For a subtle and multilayered reconstruction of Nietzsche's metaphysical commitments, see Ryan Coyne's chapter in this volume.
3. See Martin Heidegger, *Identität und Differenz*, Gesamtausgabe 11 (Frankfurt: Klostermann, 2006); Jean-Luc Marion, *God without Being: Hors-Texte*, trans. T. A. Carlson, 2nd ed. (Chicago: University of Chicago Press, 2012), 33–34.
4. To be sure, atheism in the proper sense of the term cannot rely on just one particular definition of *God* because it is a rejection of each and every kind of theism, notwithstanding the fact that most atheists take some versions of theism to be more relevant than others. Still, they believe that the term *God* does not refer at all no matter how theism defines its meaning, be that in monotheistic, polytheistic, pantheistic, or panentheistic terms. It is perhaps needless to say that this is a bold move, as it presupposes a sufficient understanding of those definitions and of what follows from them. Agnosticism is a moderate alternative to atheism both conceptually and with respect to its own ontological commitments. I thank George Pattison for pressing me on this point.
5. See Plotinus, *Enneads*, trans. Arthur H. Armstrong, 7 vols., Loeb Classical Library (Cambridge, MA: Harvard University Press, 1966–1988), 3:13, 1–2.
6. This conception is developed in Nicholas of Cusa, *De docta ignorantia—On Learned Ignorance*, trans. Jasper Hopkins (Minneapolis: Arthur J. Banning Press, 1981), bk. I, chap. 22–24, 36–43.
7. This is often quoted in the apophatic literature, sometimes without even mentioning the well-known source, for example, in *De docta ignorantia*, I chap. 26, 46.
8. Such an apophatic reading of creation is nowadays often attributed to Schelling's *Freedom* essay. I think that this rests on a misreading of Schelling, but this claim cannot be argued for here. See Friedrich Wilhelm Joseph Schelling, *Philosophical Investigations into the Essence of Human Freedom*, trans. Jeff Love and Johannes Schmidt (New York: SUNY Press, 2007).
9. See Aristotle, *De interpretatione—On Interpretation*, trans. Harold P. Cook (Cambridge, MA: Harvard University Press, 1962), 16a, ll. 16–18; Michael Wolff, *Abhandlung über die Prinzipien der Logik* (Frankfurt: Klostermann, 2009), § 9.

10. That is, a proposition that contains an empty name can have a sense but no truth value. See Gottlob Frege, "Über Sinn und Bedeutung" (1892), reprinted in Günther Patzig, *Funktion, Begriff, Bedeutung* (Göttingen: Vandenhoeck & Ruprecht, 1962), 42.
11. "*N* is not *F*" negates *F(N)* in "*N* is *F*" if, and only if, *F* is used in the same sense in both propositions. Only then are *F* and *non-F* truly contradictory predicates.
12. I thank Stephan van Erp for raising this issue.
13. See John Caputo, *The Prayers and Tears of Jacques Derrida: Religion without Religion* (Bloomington: Indiana University Press, 1997), 41.
14. For the sake of the argument, *ambiguity* is not taken to be a synonym for *equivocation* here but rather as referring to the indeterminate middle ground between univocal and equivocal meaning.
15. Within the confines of this chapter, I leave the whole problem of analogous language to one side.
16. Caputo, *Prayers and Tears*, 56.
17. Caputo, 56.
18. Caputo, 56.
19. An indispensable ingredient of this rhetoric are the terms *freedom* and *liberation*, going hand in hand with a staunch refusal to discuss the question what these terms mean in theoretical contexts such as theology.
20. Marion, *God without Being*, 46. He stresses this by crossing out the term *God* in the same way that Heidegger crosses out *Being* (*Seyn*), not to eradicate the term but rather to keep it from being handled metaphysically.
21. See Marion, 53.
22. "Theology can reach its authentic *theo*logical status only if it does not cease to break with all theo*logy*." Marion, 139, emphasis in original.
23. See Marion, 52, 143.
24. See Marion, 74.
25. See Marion, 76, 107.
26. See Marion, 262n5, where Marion distances himself from Protestant interpretations which stress the radical absence of Christ from the Eucharist.
27. See Marion, 165.
28. See Marion, 153. Later we read: "A theology is celebrated before it is written" (157).
29. See Marion, 158.
30. See, e.g., Marion, 153.
31. An argument for the indispensability of metaphysics for Christian faith is presented in my "Why Christianity Needs Metaphysics," *Tijdschrift voor Filosofie* 80, no. 3 (2018): 443–66.
32. See Marion, *God without Being*, 162.
33. Marion, 144.
34. Regarding Marion, the accusation of fideism might seem unfair, given the huge amount of philosophical erudition and argument that he invests into his apophatic theology. It would be ridiculous to say that he rejects philosophy as part of his theological thought. Yet his philosophy focuses on the phenomenology of the gift, hence on the experience of the believer and the practice of faith. His explication of the *content* of faith, by contrast, is openly nonphilosophical. Therefore, he deserves to be called a fideist in my view.

35. Marion, 107.
36. See Marion, 186–97.
37. See D. Z. Phillips, *The Concept of Prayer* (London: Routledge, 1965). Even though Phillips does not follow an apophatic agenda in his philosophy of religion, he favors mysticism, which expresses itself in apophatic theology, among other things. Sometimes, however, Phillips's Wittgensteinianism brings him very close to apophatic thought. See, for example, his "Wittgensteinianism: Logic, Reality, and God," in *The Oxford Handbook of Philosophy of Religion*, ed. W. J. Wainwright (Oxford: Oxford University Press, 2005), esp. 460–62.
38. Anthony Kenny, *The God of the Philosophers* (Oxford, UK: Clarendon, 1979), 129.
39. See Marion, *God without Being*, 107. On this point, however, I rather agree with Kenny, who holds that atheism and agnosticism differ in principle. See Kenny, *Faith and Reason* (New York: Columbia University Press, 1983). Andre C. Willis's chapter in this volume approaches this topic from a different angle.
40. Satanism is a complex issue that cannot be discussed here. I presume, however, that even Satanists worship the devil not as an evil being but as a being with the power to help them and to satisfy their desires.
41. See Tim J. Mawson, "Praying to Stop Being an Atheist," *International Journal for Philosophy of Religion* 67, no. 3 (2010): 173–86.
42. See Mawson, 173–74.
43. See Marion, *God without Being*, 106.
44. Note that scripturalism is not necessarily committed to a literal reading of holy texts. *Sola scriptura* does not entail, in and of itself, that figurative readings are illegitimate, even though many scripturalists also happen to be literalists.
45. See, e.g., M. Striet, *Offenbares Geheimnis: Zur Kritik der negativen Theologie* (Regensburg, Germany: Pustet, 2003).
46. Karl Barth, *Fides quaerens intellectum. Anselms Beweis der Existenz Gottes im Zusammenhang seines theologischen Programms*, 2nd ed. (Darmstadt, Germany: WBG, 1958). See also J. Burton Fulmer, "Anselm and the Apophatic: 'Something Greater Than Can Be Thought,'" *New Blackfriars* 89, no. 1020 (2008): 177–93.
47. See Amber Griffioen, "Religious Experience without Belief? Toward an Imaginative Account of Religious Engagement," in *Religious Experience Revisited: Expressing the Inexpressible?*, ed. Thomas Hardtke, Ulrich Schmiedel, and Tobias Tan (Leiden, Netherlands: Brill 2016), 73–88; "Prolegomena zu einer jeden künftigen '(Nicht-)Metaphysik der Religion—(Anti-)Realismus, (Non-)Kognitivismus und die religiöse Imagination," in *Gott ohne Theismus? Neue Positionen zu einer zeitlosen Frage*, ed. R. Gutschmidt and T. Rentsch (Münster: Mentis, 2016), 127–47. H. J. Schneider's pragmatist theory of religious belief contains important fictionalist ingredients as well. A powerful source of inspiration for fictionalism is Hans Vaihinger's *Philosophy of the As-If*, trans. Charles K. Ogden (London: Routledge, 1968).
48. Some versions of Nietzscheanism come very close to fictionalism. See, for example, Richard Schacht's vision of the religion of the future: "the religion of the future will look much more like the arts, sciences, philosophy and literature of the present—at their best, to be sure—than it will look like religions of the past." Richard Schacht, "After Transcendence: The Death of God and the Future of Religion," in *Religion without Transcendence?*, ed. D. Z. Phillips and Timothy Tessin (London: Macmillan, 1997), 73–92, at 92.

REFERENCES

Aristotle. *De interpretatione—On Interpretation*. Translated by Harold P. Cook. Loeb Classical Library. Cambridge, MA: Harvard University Press, 1962.
Barth, Karl. *Fides quaerens intellectum: Anselms Beweis der Existenz Gottes im Zusammenhang seines theologischen Programms*. 2nd ed. Darmstadt, Germany: Wissenschaftliche Buchgesellschaft, 1958.
Caputo, John. *The Prayers and Tears of Jacques Derrida: Religion without Religion*. Bloomington: Indiana University Press, 1997.
Frege, Gottlob. "Über Sinn und Bedeutung." Reprinted in *Funktion, Begriff, Bedeutung*. Edited by Günther Patzig. Göttingen, Germany: Vandenhoeck & Ruprecht, 1962.
Fulmer, J. Burton. "Anselm and the Apophatic: 'Something Greater Than Can Be Thought.'" *New Blackfriars* 89, no. 1020 (2008):177–93.
Griffioen, Amber. "Religious Experience without Belief? Toward an Imaginative Account of Religious Engagement." In *Religious Experience Revisited: Expressing the Inexpressible?*, edited by Thomas Hardtke, Ulrich Schmiedel, and Tobias Tan, 73–88. Leiden, Netherlands: Brill, 2016.
———. "Prolegomena zu einer jeden künftigen '(Nicht-)Metaphysik der Religion—(Anti-)Realismus, (Non-)Kognitivismus und die religiöse Imagination." In *Gott ohne Theismus? Neue Positionen zu einer zeitlosen Frage*, edited by Rico Gutschmidt and Thomas Rentsch, 127–47. Münster: Mentis, 2016.
Heidegger, Martin. *Identität und Differenz*. Gesamtausgabe 11. Frankfurt: Klostermann, 2006.
Kant, Immanuel. *Critique of Pure Reason*. Translated and edited by Paul Guyer and Allan W. Wood. Cambridge: Cambridge University Press, 1999.
Kenny, Anthony. *The God of the Philosophers*. Oxford, UK: Clarendon, 1979.
Kenny, Anthony. *Faith and Reason*. New York: Columbia University Press, 1983.
Marion, Jean-Luc. *God without Being: Hors-Texte*. Translated by T. A. Carlson. 2nd ed. Chicago: University of Chicago Press, 2012.
Mawson, Tim J. "Praying to Stop Being an Atheist." *International Journal for Philosophy of Religion* 67, no. 3 (2010): 173–86.
Nicholas of Cusa. *De docta ignorantia—On Learned Ignorance*. Translated by Jasper Hopkins. Minneapolis: Arthur J. Banning Press, 1981.
Phillips, D. Z. *The Concept of Prayer*. London: Routledge, 1965.
———. "Wittgensteinianism: Logic, Reality, and God." In *The Oxford Handbook of Philosophy of Religion*, edited by W. J. Wainwright, 447–71. Oxford: Oxford University Press, 2005.
Plotinus. *Enneads*. Translated by Arthur H. Armstrong. 7 vols. Loeb Classical Library, Cambridge, MA: Harvard University Press, 1966–1988.
Schacht, Richard. "After Transcendence: The Death of God and the Future of Religion." In *Religion without Transcendence?*, edited by D. Z. Phillips and Timothy Tessin, 73–92. London: Macmillan, 1997.
Schelling, Friedrich Wilhelm Joseph. *Philosophical Investigations into the Essence of Human Freedom*. Translated by Jeff Love and Johannes Schmidt. New York: SUNY Press, 2007.

Striet, Magnus. *Offenbares Geheimnis: Zur Kritik der negativen Theologie.* Regensburg, Germany: Pustet, 2003.

Tegtmeyer, Henning. "Why Christianity Needs Metaphysics." *Tijdschrift voor Filosofie* 80, no. 3 (2018): 443–66.

Vaihinger, Hans. *Philosophy of the As-If.* Translated by Charles K. Ogden. London: Routledge, 1968.

Wolff, Michael. *Abhandlung über die Prinzipien der Logik.* Frankfurt: Klostermann, 2009.

6

ATHEISM AND POLITICS

Abandonment, Absence, and the Empty Throne

Devin Singh

While atheism has often been portrayed as a facet of secular modernity, it has always been intertwined with Christianity. Not only does Christian liturgy celebrate the death of God on the cross, but the history of the Christian church proceeds in light of the ascension of Christ. Ascension itself, I argue, reveals an atheistic kernel at the heart of Christian tradition. Often grafted together as an afterthought to or extension of the resurrection, or grouped vaguely with discussion of eschatology and Christ's return (parousia), the ascension instead marks a distinct and significant step in the Christological drama set forth in Christian scripture and tradition. By "ascension" I mean the depiction of Christ being taken up into heaven before the disciples (Luke 24:51; Acts 1:9). This stage in the narrative of Christ has been mostly overlooked and given short shrift in theology, despite it marking the entire phase of history in which the church exists.[1] I suggest that part of this neglect is bound up with the challenge of what ascension itself marks out: the abandonment by Christ of the church and the emptiness, lack, and void that reside within ensuing Christian tradition. Scant attention to the ascension in scripture, and its various minimalist developments as a doctrinal locus, stand in stark contrast to the towering and blatant reality for which it is a signifier: the absence of Christ.

That Christ is nowhere to be found may seem a rather obvious point, and yet it requires delineation and sustained interrogation. For the primary reality known by the church and Christian history is that of the missing and absentee Christ. Only the first disciples and purported eyewitnesses to Jesus's life, death, and resurrection enjoyed the unique relationship with Jesus characterized by bodily presence. The actuality of the church and all theological reflection operate instead in light of his absence. This sustained operation is significant in light of the very disavowal of absence that is the norm for Christian thought and practice, proceeding as they do under the signs of resurrection, victory, and presence, despite realities of ascension, abandonment, and absence.

This chapter explores this broad topic selectively by considering the legacy of political theology in ascension's wake. This is a question of the politics generated by the atheism at the heart of Christian thought. What is the politics that is engendered, a politics of the empty throne that upholds a sovereignty marked by the void? For it is not that the king's head has been "cut off" or that the "royal remains" have been distributed among the body politic.[2] In this case, the king is not merely lacking a head but a body, for the corpse is nowhere to be found.

The church's disavowal of such absence, however, has not ceased to generate haunting presences, accumulating across history in various concepts of sovereign legitimacy as well as in various forms of institutionality that endeavor to instantiate and materialize the reign of an absent lord. It may be that the alternative, radical challenge of Christian thought, one that much theology misses and appears unable to see, is the undoing of all claims to founding and authoritative presence. Rather than the declaration "no Caesar except Christ" and a replacement of the earthly king with the King of Kings, which is a kind of enforced presence, ascension might instead allow the recognition that the king is dead and all kings are dead.[3] Sovereignty is empty and vacant.[4] Beyond simply an unmasking that reveals that the emperor has no clothes, the insight of the empty throne, abandonment, and atheistic void is that there is no emperor at all.[5] While atheistic claims to divine absence and political assertions of empty sovereignty are certainly not new, my contention is that the ascension has signaled such realities all along. It thus subsists as an unacknowledged theological source of Christian atheism.

ASCENSION AND/AS ABANDONMENT

Certainly most, if not all, living religious traditions that identify a founder or determinative figure deal with the problem of loss, for these figures are no longer present. Yet Christianity creates a unique set of problems for itself in this regard, ones that may not attend other traditions. Christianity is predicated on the immortality and, indeed, divinity of its founder (leaving aside here assertions that Paul is the true founder). It proclaims its founder as continuing to live and acclaims its founder as a risen lord who holds authority and exerts ongoing influence over individual lives, communities, nations, world history, and the cosmos itself.

Comparing Christianity to its Abrahamic cousins is useful in this regard: in Judaism, Abraham and Moses died mortal deaths. Leaving aside Enoch and Elijah, Judaism recognizes the mortality and mundane, earthly deaths of its patriarchs and prophets. Islam, too, acknowledges the death of Mohammed. While both traditions include doctrines of resurrection, neither of these traditions proclaims the contemporaneous, risen presence of these founding figures (leaving aside, again, the Passover chair for Elijah). More to the point, neither of these traditions *needs* these founding figures to be alive and immortally present. Furthermore, in terms of our conversation, neither of these traditions proclaims such founding figures as establishing kingdoms and exerting forms of rule and governance that persist in the present.

Most forms of Christian thought, however, make central the ongoing, living presence of Christ as founder, savior, and lord. Christ reigns over a contemporaneous divine kingdom, one that, while not of this world, is taken to exert decisive earthly and historical influence. These central tenets, combined with the obvious and embarrassing contrast of Christ's death and absence, generate a variety of creative coping strategies. Based on the conceptual requirements of Christianity to enshrine its founder as divine, living, reigning, and as somehow near and at hand (spatially and temporally), Christian thought has produced a variety of innovative tactics of presence. These strategies open up novel lines of thought and generate certain institutions and patterns of community. Such thought and practice have been significant for the development of the West.

The doctrine of the ascension, therefore, is a marker and placeholder for the trauma of abandonment and horror of the void that persist as a centerpiece to Christianity. The ascension is the attempt to figure and represent this trauma, as a primary response and coping strategy by the church. Further coping strategies that elaborate upon this founding trauma and its repression include depictions of the church as the body of Christ (*corpus mysticum*), presentations of the eucharist as various types of presence (real, spiritual, figurative) of Christ, and theorizations of the Holy Spirit as comforter and consoler for such abandonment and as the reification of Christ's absence. Each set of ideas and ensuing edifices of thought and practice are built around attempts to foster presence in the midst of absence, whether to paper over and elide the embarrassment of abandonment or reconfigure and provide an apologia for this void.

Christian thought and practice also present a number of symptoms of this repression of founding trauma. Such symptoms emerge around the aforementioned coping strategies for loss and the disavowal of abandonment. A first set of symptoms arise from positing the church as the body of Christ, the institutional history of which has frequently combined with Christian empire, with its political theologies of domination and permanence. Ecclesial merger with state institutions is one symptomatic grasping for presence, as the anxious, enforced assertion of the reign of a risen king, despite obvious and ongoing evidence to the contrary. Vexations around the possibilities and parameters of political theology stem in the first place from the need to correlate this absent lord to concurrent worldly powers.

A second set of symptoms emerge around the various theoretical permutations of the eucharist, which do not, of course, occur in a vacuum but are everywhere correlated to these agonistic definitions of the church vis-à-vis wider society and the state. Reflection on eucharist grounds an increasingly expansive set of claims around sacramentality and eventually theories of representation itself. Thus, the figures of presence enjoined in eucharist engender a range of possibilities of authoritative representation claimed by the roles and offices of church and state.[6] It is no coincidence that debates over eucharistic presence during the Reformation correlate to new definitions of the church in relation to society, with political anxieties kindled as the Holy Roman Empire transitions to the modern nation-state.[7] But even earlier medieval migrations in ideas of the body of Christ from the church to the bread and beyond can be understood in light of larger political battles being waged within Christendom, including the Investiture Controversy and pope-emperor rivalries.[8] Thus, the eucharist represents one central attempt to figure presence, specifically Christ's bodily presence despite his absence. Deliberation on the eucharist modulates within a larger network of claims that depict the church and society as modes of presence of the once and future king who is nowhere to be found.

These explorations around the ways the eucharist becomes, instantiates, signifies, or represents the body of Christ also engender a highly charged and generative site of reflection for philosophies of presence, representation, and signification.[9] A legacy of thought around metaphysics and semiotics thus emerges in part motivated by the anxieties of the missing body of the lord.[10] Certainly, philosophies of presence preexist Christianity, as evidenced in the ways Christian thinkers retrieved Greek reflection as a tool to aid in fashioning a mask for the void. Yet Christian legacy provides its own anxious twist to such reflection by wedding the necessity of presence to matters of salvation and communal survival.

Finally, the third cluster of strategies around the Holy Spirit show symptoms such as a focus on the miraculous, on charisma, and gifts of power as markers of the divine. Such events are framed as irruptions of an invisible lord into history and serve to reassure the abandoned church of the risen king's ongoing presence and secure reign despite, again, much evidence to the contrary. Carl Schmitt employs the miracle as a site of reflection for political theology: "the exception in jurisprudence is analogous to the miracle in theology."[11] As a divine disruption or momentary suspension of the laws of nature, the miracle marks the theological correlate to the sovereign exception in the suspension of constitutional law. Thus, the assertion of an interruption and irruption, as an in-breaking of the absent yet supposedly present and reigning lord, finds its shadow side in serving to authenticate sovereignty as the power to found and legitimate an order. In both theological and political cases, the needs of power and presence assert themselves to quell concerns about absence.

It may thus be worthwhile to think Pentecost as another symptomatic legacy of the abandonment marked by ascension. The Spirit is construed as an outpouring of power and presence that seeks to render invisible its underlying reason for being: comfort and consolation in the face of abandonment and hence as an underscoring and even instantiation of absence. Focus on the Holy Spirit as plenitude, superabundance, and presence appears to neglect Jesus's depictions in the Upper Room Discourse (John 13–17) of the Spirit as consolation for his absence and hence as supplement. The Spirit in no way overcomes the lack but rather highlights and sacralizes it. Ignoring this pneumatological dynamic skews interpretations of the Spirit toward power and triumph, where miracles and charismatic gifts provide arguments for victory and authority despite evidence instead of loss and absence. Subsequent trinitarian doctrinal casuistry, contending with Jesus's claim that the Spirit cannot come until Jesus is gone, will make its uneasy, paradoxical attempts to assert Christ's presence through the Spirit despite maintaining the distinction of persons.[12]

In pursuing a line of inquiry that posits ascension as a coping strategy for abandonment, I do not intend to take up the approach, popularized in historical-critical scholarship on the resurrection, that depicts such narratives as hallucinations of grief or other group psychological attempts to revise the empirical facticity of Jesus's death with Christian mythology.[13] I am not interested in evaluating the historicity of ascension, except to the extent that a historical claim to the ascension is central to Christian self-understanding and resultant doctrinal formulation and institution building. In other words, I accept and work within the assertions of the tradition that Christ was somehow "taken up" into heaven in full view of the disciples (Luke 24:51; Acts 1:9), and find little value in vindicating "real" or "brute" history over against such interpretive testimony.[14] I am thus also positing a fundamental kind of unity, if not identity, between the Jesus of history and Christ of faith, rejecting any easy bifurcation that allows one to circumvent the problems raised by ascension.

Just as I have little interest in approaches that "prove" that the resurrection "could not have happened," to belabor the rather obvious claim that ascension violates all physical laws and is hence impossible is beside the point. Whether one believes in the ascension of Christ historically as a point of faith, accepts it figuratively as a fruitfully generative metaphor, or denies it on grounds of absurdity, one cannot avoid, it seems to me, the resultant historical legacy set into motion by the construction of a system of thought and practice around the doctrine itself. It is this legacy that interests me, in all its theoretical, social, and political implications.

THE GLORIOUS VOID

My route into this topic arose in part through engaging Giorgio Agamben's reflections on glory in relation to political theology in Western tradition.[15] Glory emerges as a central site of reflection for him because it helps explain the substantive role of ritual, pomp, and adulation that attend both political acclamation and religious liturgy around divine kingship. Since religion and politics regularly coincide around the tropes of kingdom and government, the mechanisms of glory prove a useful glimpse into this intersection, revealing at the same time why glory is not ancillary but central to the function of politics and political theologies. Glory serves to cover and obfuscate, and, through this, to fill the void and provide substance to overlay certain underlying concerns in Christian theology.

For Agamben, glory masks at least two anxieties: the vicariousness of power in the trinitarian Godhead and the inoperativity at the heart of the divine life. For the former, Agamben follows certain approaches to the Trinity (Augustine and Aquinas, primarily) that emphasize the mutual deputizing, authorizing, and glorifying of the three persons. The Son's identity cannot be understood without reference to the Father, and vice versa, for the Son is not a son without the Father, as the Father is no father without the Son. This relational deputizing of identity has political correlates, wherein "the intra-Trinitarian relation between the Father and the Son can be considered to be the theological paradigm of every *potestas vicaria*, in which every act of the vicar is considered to be a manifestation of the will of the one who is represented by him."[16] Here the vicarious representation of the Father by the Son doubles back upon the Father within the trinitarian economy. For, "the Trinitarian economy is the expression of an anarchic power and being that circulates among the three persons according to an essentially vicarious paradigm."[17] In Agamben's reading, the eternal and mutual deputizing of identity among Father, Son, and Spirit reveals an eternal deferral of authority in the Godhead, as each member vicariously represents and glorifies the other. Indeed, the Trinity subsists as a kind of eternal glorification among the persons, a glorification that is its only substance, he will say, masking the anarchic (as in foundationless, lacking an *archê*) absence of power. There is nowhere where the "buck stops" and thus no site of actual sovereignty as final authority. Power is without foundation.

The mutual, endless, obfuscating deputation and glorification of the Father and Son emerge correlatively between kingdom and government, since Father and Son mark such sites, respectively, both in conceptual form and in earthly echoes. Kingdom refers to the center of sovereign authority while government marks out the administrative edifice that implements sovereign will and manages its territory and subjects. Yet the distinction blurs in the cycle of mutual legitimation, for "Government glorifies the Kingdom, and the Kingdom glorifies Government. But the center of the machine is empty, and glory is nothing but the splendor that emanates from this emptiness, the inexhaustible *kabhod* that at once reveals and veils the central vacuity of the machine."[18] There is no actual center and seat of power in kingdom or government, since power proves anarchic and hence groundless, and glory masks this lack and provides a kind of substance to the void. The governmental machine that Agamben critiques and seeks to unmask is this work of glorification that exists ultimately for itself in stultifying circularity.

The other anxiety addressed and covered by glory is that of a fundamental inoperativity that characterizes the divine life. Questions about God's immanent identity, as God in Godself, outside of the economic activities of creation and redemption, ultimately lead to depictions of an inactive God that are problematic for Christian thought. As Agamben claims, traditional Christian theology certainly wants to uphold some notion of Sabbath rest for God, in keeping with the creation narrative and eschatological imagery. But the centrality of labor and economy in Christian understandings of God and the appropriation of Aristotelian preferences for actuality over potentiality mean that depictions of the inactive God subsisting prior to creation or of God resting in posteschatological consummation are embarrassments for the tradition.

Agamben notes that the question "What was God doing before He made heaven and earth? . . . Why did He not continue to do nothing forever as He did before?" which posed no problems for pagans or Gnostics, was met not with reasoned explanation but with admonishment by the likes of Augustine and Luther, for instance. The question "was particularly embarrassing for Christians, precisely because the Trinitarian economy was essentially a figure of action and government."[19] As a result, "glory is what must cover with its splendor the unaccountable figure of divine inoperativity."[20] Agamben concludes that what is masked is a basic inoperativity of power in the divine life, the notion that power in the Godhead is fundamentally one of inactivity and rest.

Glory emerges as one means to distract from this embarrassment. Glorification as such contributes to the governmental machine, lending its own presence, structure, and activity to the absence, void, and inactivity that threaten to reveal themselves:

> At the beginning and the end of the highest power there stands, according to Christian theology, a figure not of action and government but of inoperativity. The indescribable mystery that glory, with its blinding light, must hide from the gaze of the *scrutatores maiestatis* is that of divine inoperativity, of what God does before creating the world and after the providential government of the world is complete. . . . Glory, both in theology and in politics, is precisely what takes the place of that unthinkable emptiness that amounts to the inoperativity of power . . . That means that the center of the governmental apparatus, the threshold at which Kingdom and Government ceaselessly communicate and ceaselessly distinguish themselves from one another is, in reality, empty; it is only the Sabbath and *katapausis*—and, nevertheless, this inoperativity is so essential for the machine that it must at all costs be adopted and maintained at its center in the form of glory.[21]

Thus, for Agamben, the heart of divine life is marked by a void that signifies the groundlessness of power, that power has no source or ultimate fount of legitimacy. This reality is exemplified in a baseline inoperativity or inactivity that can be construed most simply as powerlessness or as *potentia* that, because it is not actualized, is read as *impotentia*.

What interests me about turning to the ascension in light of this exploration is that it attends to the economic, historical, and material sides of these issues. It also addresses existential, experiential, and, dare I say, empirical reality. Agamben's provocative speculations about an ultimately vacuous Godhead remain unresolvable in the sense that they are *theologia* and address God in Godself, outside of human observation. Grappling with the legacy of ascension, however, represents *oikonomia* in the sense of the purported outworkings of God in creation and history, the incarnational engagement with material realities and bodies, and matters of the human senses and phenomenology. In other words, while the issues Agamben raises can remain only conceptual problems, for they deal with how one might *think* about the Godhead, addressing the ascension as abandonment and void deals with the actual reality that the risen and exalted Christ is nowhere to be found even though the church continually proclaims his victory, reign, and presence and carries on accordingly. I seek an approach that takes on the historical debris and wreckage left in the wake of the church and its vision and politics of ascension.

Furthermore, Agamben's interpretation—at least in terms of the eternal deferral of authority in the Godhead—depends upon a particular exposition of the Trinity, one that could be countered with a stronger emphasis on the monarchy of the Father as the fount of authority in the Godhead, as emphasized by Gregory of Nazianzus, for instance.[22] This would resolve the challenge of power's vacuity and lack of foundation by locating it in the Father—if, still, deferring the problem by positing the Father as the groundless ground of power. It is more difficult, however, to counter a reading of ascension as absence—except with more strident assertions of presence and protestations that ascension means exaltation, sacramentality, and the like, which are simply more words to fill the glaring and obvious void that stares Christian tradition in the face.

The work of glorification that emerges in liturgy is one of attending to and interacting with a departed founder and ruler as if he were still there. Such liturgy, Agamben claims, following Erik Peterson, also founds a politics.[23] Agamben has highlighted the theological object of glory—that is, the vacuous Trinitarian Godhead—with its void of power. Alternatively, my interest is in the ascension as the context, experience, and history of the void, coupled with simultaneous denial and disavowal of the absence that ascension reveals. Not only are the absence and void marked by the ascension a much more obvious reality and starting point than speculation about trinitarian vacuity, but they signify the inception of the church as an institution predicated on this disavowal, an institution that has gone on to leave its indelible imprint upon politics, philosophy, and culture in the West and beyond.

THE EMPTY THRONE

Agamben invokes Christian iconography of the empty throne (*hetoimasia*) as evocative of this void and absence in the Godhead and of the inoperativity of divine power:

> In the iconography of power, profane and religious, this central vacuity of glory, this intimacy of majesty and inoperativity, found its exemplary symbol in the *hetoimasia tou thronou*, that is, in the image of the empty throne ... *The empty throne is not, therefore, a symbol of regality but of glory.*

Glory precedes the creation of the world and survives its end. The throne is empty not only because glory, though coinciding with the divine essence is not identified with it, but also because it is in its innermost self-inoperativity and sabbatism. The void is the sovereign figure of glory.[24]

For Agamben, then, this iconography reveals that the Godhead is devoid of power just as the throne is empty. The pomp and circumstance of glory form a mystifying cloud that blinds the adoring onlooker to the reality of this vacant seat. In such imagery of the empty throne, Christians unwittingly betray the anarchic, that is groundless, power of God.

What Agamben provides is, of course, a revisionist reading. Most Christians do not interpret such iconography as proof of an empty Godhead. The dominant interpretation, rather, is that of the deferral of judgment until Christ's return and of a longing for such parousia. *Hetoimasia* means "preparation" and signifies the preparation of the judgment seat of Christ as well as the preparation of all things for the eschaton. Often, in such imagery, the empty throne is accompanied by a closed book, which may symbolize the ledger of accounts by which all shall be judged when it is opened on the Last Day (Revelation 20:12). As Thomas Cattoi recounts, in his comparative reading of Christian and Buddhist iconography of the empty throne, the image reflects the belief that "The resurrected Christ is gone, 'he is not here'" (Matthew 28:6); he will return at the end of times to judge the living and the dead. The empty throne is a reminder that we now live in the end times, but also in a time of respite; the judgment will come, the angels appear to say, and yet Christ is deferring the moment when there will be no more mercy, but only justice."[25] The empty throne suggests anticipation and as such marks historical time as the time of sojourn and waiting. History is the time between ascension and parousia, as the church trudges anxiously under the sign of absence and abandonment, awaiting the return of the king.[26]

More than an emptiness and void at the heart of the Trinity or a hidden inoperativity in God, the empty throne attests to ascension as the absence of Christ and the church's anxious wait for his manifestation and return. In a way, such iconography comes closest to an honest reckoning with ascension as abandonment, representing the missing king. Granted, dwelling with such absence may be truncated by the liturgical work of a proclamation that insists on imminent return: "In the iconography of Torcello, the very absence from our sight of Christ's bodily frame is presented to the onlooker as a provisional reality, a transient phase of human history, which will cease on the day when emptiness will be replaced by glory. On that day, the throne will no longer be empty."[27] The emptiness of the throne is liturgically interpreted as provisionary and, as such, the potential significance of such absence is muted.

Agamben comes close to recognizing the centrality of ascension for the problematics of the empty throne and the vacuous and vicarious circulations of power that it signifies. He notes that the basis of ecclesial authority and sacramental power is predicated upon the absent Christ:

> The vicariousness of pontifical power with regard to Christ was theologically founded on the delay of the *parousia*. "Given that Christ had to subtract his carnal presence from the Church . . . it was necessary to institute ministers who would administer sacraments to men. These are called priests. . . . And after the subtraction of Christ's corporeal presence, given that questions concerning faith were going to occur, which would have divided the Church, whose unity requires the unity of faith . . . the one who has this power is Peter, and his successors."[28]

Such theology reveals that, *pace* Agamben, it is not delay of parousia per se but more fundamentally the absent Christ that prompts the issue of sacramental power and the unification of sovereign decision in the pontifical seat. The absence of Christ's body means the insinuation of priestly bodies into the void, to govern the abandoned community and administer power in a vacuum. The cycle of disavowal and legitimation that arises here is critical to note: such priestly representatives will deny the absence of Christ while simultaneously relying on such absence as the source of their authority. Vicarious and deputized power emerge in the aftermath of abandonment.

The long tradition of Christian political theology that has developed in the wake of ascension recognizes the threat of fragility and vulnerability brought on by absence. The problem is not merely what to do with the royal remains, but their lack. There is no corpse over which to grieve. There is no body of the king to serve as signifier for the body politic of the commonwealth. There is no flesh to be divided among the people. The empty throne troubles the confident assertions of political theology that speak of divine sovereignty over history, politics, and community.

THE IMPOSSIBILITIES OF POLITICAL THEOLOGY

Erik Peterson's influential essay "Monotheism as a Political Problem" makes its own contribution to Christian reflection on theology's relationship to politics and on the role of the church in society.[29] As such, it also interacts with the fraught legacy of absence generated by ascension. Most of

Peterson's essay is devoted to recounting a litany of early Christian thinkers who, erroneously, claims Peterson, make correlations between the solitary monarchy of God and the monarchy of a political ruler. Eusebius serves as the chief defendant in this account, guilty of his apparently unequivocal exaltation of Constantine and his moves to draw parallels between God and Emperor.[30] Peterson also impugns Tertullian and a number of other patristic theologians who, Peterson claims, are beholden to pagan, Hellenistic philosophies of kingship or strict Judaic monotheisms, and so fall prey to a correspondence between earthly and heavenly singular authorities. The Christian difference, serving as a refrain throughout his text, is trinitarianism. The Trinity disrupts and undermines the tendency to draw such parallels between God and political rulers.

We would be misled, however, if we concluded that it was the specific triunity of the Godhead that somehow avoided earthly parallels. Although this is the arc of Peterson's argument, mounting up evidence of the persistent and problematic monotheisms of many early Christian thinkers, led astray as they apparently were by Jewish and pagan ideals, the point is not that triunity on its own is the solution. As Peterson and commentators have noted, there have been attempts to create—perhaps laughably—triumvirate kingships and other tripartite forms of rule in the history of Christian empire in an effort to imitate the Trinity. The Trinity alone does not preclude attempts at Christian political theology. What is needed, rather, is a hermeneutical principle to disrupt such correlations.

What I consider Peterson's sleight of hand and disingenuousness appear briefly in the concluding paragraphs of his long and ponderous essay. After making the case, page after page, that strict monotheism is not true Christian theology and lends itself to political theology, while trinitarianism is authentic Christian theology and prevents falling into the trap of political theology, he turns to Gregory of Nazianzus's *Third Theological Oration*. He cites Gregory's claim that there is no earthly correlate to divine triunity: "the Monarchy of the triune God . . . [was a] conception of unity [that] had no correspondence in the created order."[31] Peterson concludes, with maddening swiftness and simplification, "With such arguments, monotheism is laid to rest as a political problem." And further: " With this [Trinitarian doctrine] . . . the linkage of the Christian proclamation to the Roman Empire was *theologically* dissolved."[32]

The problem is that the operative principle invoked here by Gregory of Nazianzus is that of divine transcendence and hence radical difference from creation. An attribute of God "had no correspondence in the created order." Peterson's essay should not have been about vindicating the trinity over against strict monotheisms, since even versions of monotheism could just as rightfully embrace such a notion of transcendence and thus sever any link to creation and to earthly political regimes. His essay should have been about divine difference, which undercuts any attempts at legitimating earthly institutions with divine models. In an odd attempt to claim triumph for Christian trinitarian uniqueness, which works out to be something of a red herring, Peterson mounts up evidence to praise the Trinity as special and anti-political-theological, but then then switches gears dramatically in his final two pages to assert without argument or further evidence a hermeneutical claim about divine transcendence as the actual antagonism of political theology.

What is remarkable is the stature and legacy of Peterson's essay and the absence of any critique pointing out Peterson's poor argumentation in this central regard. Yet the ambiguity of his essay is borne out in the genealogy it bequeaths. One can draw a line of influence from Peterson to Jürgen Moltmann to a legacy of social trinitarian theologians who mobilize Peterson's principles while doing precisely what Peterson says is impossible, that is, constructing a politics based on the Trinity.[33] This is because they follow the thrust of his essay that celebrates Christian trinitarian uniqueness while apparently missing or at least sidelining the brief yet operative crux, the central role played by divine transcendence and difference, which are in fact the only conceptual basis for undercutting political theology on Peterson's terms. The Trinity alone, without further qualification, makes no difference for or against political theology. Because of this, not only can these contemporary theologians construct a variety of trinitarian political theologies, but almost the *entire history* of Christendom provides empirical evidence against Peterson's wishful claims—for, heterodox emperors and regimes notwithstanding, most rulers and administrations upheld a doctrinally orthodox Trinity while simultaneously enforcing political theology and empire. In other words, their trinitarian commitments did nothing to prevent their political theologies of imperial rule.

The line of thought that mobilizes divine difference, the repressed but pivotal theme in Peterson's essay, is apophatic theology and mystical traditions associated with the *via negativa*.[34] Ultimately, Peterson's implicit claim is one of apophasis with regard to political theology: just as linguistic statements about God cannot find a firm referent in the God they attempt to figure, because divine difference exceeds the created capacities of language to signify, so earthly political constructs can claim no anchor or legitimation in God, whose reign and lordship are so utterly different that correspondence is absurd—even idolatrous.

Peterson's essay trades on divine transcendence and difference and hence at some level deals fundamentally with divine absence. To be sure, we do not need to construe transcendence as absence. Arguments about radical divine difference that exceeds creaturely difference and allows God to escape opposition and relate noncompetitively with creation might support claims of radical divine proximity and presence.[35] Yet reflection on transcendence emerges from the experience of absence and sense of distance and otherness from God, for at stake is God's nonidentity with creation and the infinite qualitative distinction and gulf—however proximate—between the two. Apophatic theology acknowledges the hidden or missing *Deus absconditus* who escapes linguistic predication and indeed human conceptualization. In my view, the specter of ascension is therefore here important to note.

Questions about whether and how to model earthly kingships after the heavenly one emerge because Christ the risen, exalted, and eternal king is not present. Had he been, his kingdom would be instituted, rendering such debates moot. Political theology thus emerges as a discourse of legitimation and legitimacy.[36] At its heart is a struggle to legitimate the authority and proclamation of an institution whose legitimacy is continually called into question given its failure to make good on its central claim about a reigning lord. The echo of such political theology across the ages transfers these founding struggles for legitimation, as ensuing political regimes assert legitimacy as representatives and stand-ins for this absent lord and ground of their authority. In so doing, they inherit and redeploy a structure of acclamation and disavowal, denying the absence of power at the center of the regime while simultaneously claiming legitimacy through its lack. Just as priests and bishops require Christ's absence for their claims as vicarious representatives, Christian emperors learn to rule in the name of the divine king who never comes. This raises the possibility that the political theology of secular sovereignty, claiming its legitimacy as representative of the people, similarly requires their absence or even erasure.

The problematic temptation to correlate earthly and heavenly monarchies arises in the first place with the Christian insistence of acclamation, asserting the royal kingship of the absentee Christ. Had Christ been construed only as servant or slave, for instance, with no moves toward royal exaltation, the basis of correlation would have been undercut. Yet the assertion of Christ as actively reigning king in the face of ascension and abandonment raises the conundrum of how earthly regimes may carry out their governance in deferential cooperation. Ascension as marking the absent yet somehow reigning lord and king thus gives rise to foundational quandaries of political theology.

ANTICHRIST AND *KATECHON*

Peterson's essay was part of series of exchanges with Carl Schmitt around the challenge of political theology. As observers have noted, what appears truly at stake in this debate is not the possibility of political theology but its nature and terms. For Peterson went on to write extensively about the Christian church's relationship to secular politics, and about the forms of politics that the church founds. Trinitarian difference notwithstanding, Christian theology had much to say about the shape politics should take and about the nature of Christian engagement with the worldly sphere. What was Peterson and Schmitt's debate really about, then?

In Agamben's own idiosyncratic reading and revisionist interpretation, the more significant site of commonality and contention between Schmitt and Peterson concerns the delay of the return of Christ and the historical time that has resulted in the interim. For Schmitt, the source of this delay, the so-called restrainer or *katechon* (2 Thessalonians 2:6–7), was Christian empire itself. For Peterson, it was the failure of the Jews to accept the Messiah and convert. According to Schmitt, empire subdues the lawlessness that marks the time of Antichrist that must occur before parousia. According to Peterson, God's merciful patience with the unbelief of the Jews, "until the full number of Gentiles" are saved (Romans 11:25), explains the delay of the parousia. As Agamben claims: "Thus, what is really at stake in the debate is not the admissibility of political theology, but the nature and identity of the *katechon,* the power that defers and eliminates 'concrete eschatology.' But this implies that what is crucial for both Schmitt and Peterson is ultimately the very neutralization of a philosophy of history oriented toward salvation. At the point where the divine plan of *oikonomia* had reached completion with the coming of Christ, an event (the failed conversion of the Jews, the Christian empire) that had the power to suspend the eschaton took place."[37] For Agamben, the different nuances placed on the underlying cause of the delay and resultant historical time produced different theological and political projects in these thinkers.

The problem of the *katechon* or restrainer speaks to the reality of the interim, the delay between ascension and return. More specifically, it signals the anxieties raised by Christ's abandonment of the church and failure to return, and points to the various explanatory mechanisms marshaled to address this baseline embarrassment. Why hasn't the ascended Christ returned? What if he never returns? What if ascension is all that remains?

The solutions embraced by these thinkers show two major trends that ascension bequeaths: the formation of Christian empire to fill the void, constructing an edifice of roles, offices, and institutions to provide the substance to the missing king's reign; or the correlative displacement and supersession of the Jews, as the anxious jockeying by the church to assert Christ's presence and authority where there is none. In symbolic retaliation for the purported Jewish rejection of the lordship of Jesus: "We have no king but Caesar!" (John 19:15), the Jews are in turn forced to acknowledge an absent king and empty throne or to suffer the consequences. The two trends—Christian empire and antisemitic displacement—work in tandem to facilitate the erasure of bodies in the name of the absent king whose presence must be asserted and enforced. Such strategies of displacement and domination continue in transmuted form across history as Christian empire encounters various non-European and religious others and initiates its colonial project.[38]

Thus, the dilemma of the *katechon* is really a problem of ascension. Without Christ's desertion and absence, and without proclamations of the central necessity of his ongoing lordship and reign, this question of what is delaying his return would not arise. Explanations for the *katechon* turn out to be coping strategies for the void. As such, they generate their own legacy of theoretical, social, and political consequences, exacerbating and inflicting the founding trauma of abandonment upon others.

ATHEISTIC PROTEST AT THE VOID

In distinction from, for instance, scientific atheism, which typically denies theological claims from the vantage point of an external, scientific discourse, protest atheism takes the claims of Christian theology about the justice and goodness of God on their own terms and turns them against the tradition.[39] Jürgen Moltmann has praised protest atheism as one of atheism's most intellectually astute and theologically honest forms.[40] Such unbelief, captured for Moltmann in Dostoyevsky's Ivan Karamazov, rages against the realities of evil and suffering in the world and against a notion of God who has the power to stop it.[41] For Moltmann, it is theologically virtuous to accuse and confront God in this regard. God can handle such assaults since the crucified God, who experiences the depths of such suffering completely and meets humanity there in profound solidarity, provides for Moltmann the answer.

Moltmann's willingness to sustain the challenge of protest atheism and not sidestep the problems of theodicy is laudable. Yet his solution to the abandonment, isolation, and silence that give rise to protest atheism, raging as it rightfully does at the absence of a king who promises mercy and justice for all, is to assert the hidden presence of the crucified God. The solution to the absurdity of suffering under a righteous, merciful, and all powerful God is to claim that God suffers too and meets the broken in their brokenness. Such a vision has been tremendously generative, and I do not want to minimize the consolation it has brought to many.

Yet what if we sustain the initial impulse of protest a little while longer? What if we tarry in the reality of absence and accept this lack as both the starting point and telos of Christian theology, grappling with the silence and void left by the ascended and absconded Christ? This is to confront the unsettling reality that despite Jesus's promises to be present among the poor and marginalized (Matthew 25:31–46), their poverty and suffering persist. Such longed for presence of Christ among the downtrodden is rendered even more tenuous when considered in light of the temporal contrast between Christ and the poor that Jesus himself proclaims: "for you always have the poor with you, but you will not always have me" (Matthew 26:11). In apparent foreshadowing of his death and absence—and its historical extension in his ascension—Jesus inserts a temporal disjunction between his presence and that of the poor. Whatever glimpses one may catch of Christ among the poor, his actual presence will not be there, and this is justifiable grounds for protest and mourning.

This means that despite figurations of the church as Christ's presence among the poor, however laudable when such views engender solidarity and protest, the church simply is not Christ.[42] The church of and for the poor does not fully compensate for the absent Christ. Thus, there should be no swift moves to assert hidden presence, as if the church historical has misrecognized the departure of its lord and needlessly awaits the return of one who never left. For if Christ's current presence is full and substantive and provides a real solution to absence, then the interim of ecclesial history, questions of the *katechonic* delay, and longing for parousia are spurred by unfounded concerns.

If presence is real and actual, then the deputized role played by the pontiff, priests, and the sacraments—their representational power as a stand-ins for the absent lord—are unnecessary and even erroneous. In other words, their basis of vicarious authority and efficacy are meaningless since the one they vicariously represent has been here all along. Remarkably, the Protestant rejection of the pope's role as divine representative, and the—particularly Calvinist—rejection of real presence, sacramentality, and iconic imagery served to banish God even more profoundly from the world.[43] Carried out under the auspices of direct communion with God and the circumvention of "idolatrous" representational mediators, Reformed Protestantism in effect radicalized—or at least more fully attested to—the ascension and Christ's withdrawal, and in so doing underscored divine absence. In asserting a kind of immediacy—apprehending the ascended Christ "by faith alone"—such thought postulated that rather than accessing the omnipresence of the body of Christ on earth, believers were drawn up and out of the world during worship and communion to encounter the ascended body of Christ localized in heaven with God (*extra Calvinisticum*). Debates about the Protestant disenchantment of the world, therefore, a legacy of discussion initiated in part by Max Weber's work, are struggles with the fallout from varying stances on ascension.[44]

This means that protest atheism reveals the true kernel for Christian theology after ascension. It is a theology that must assert and embrace the absent and missing Christ, and as such accepts its theological operation as an empty, broken fragment of a lost dream. In this sense it does not remain as protest, for it recognizes that the protest emerges from an expectation of arrival, a desire for manifestation. Protest atheism, on the one hand, believes too faithfully in the hiddenness of the righteous king, and shakes its fist at the absent God who refuses to appear, particularly among the poor and excluded.

Ascension atheism, on the other hand, moves past this righteous, justified, and understandable protest to a form of contrite acceptance. Facing the trauma of abandonment, it acknowledges the absurdity of the denial and cover up that is the very history of Christian theology and ecclesial tradition. Accepting unbelief, absence, and loss, it begins to conceive of the work of mourning such loss and of reconstituting an always fractured wholeness in its wake. Rather than reinflicting the void unawares in a host of new contexts, as Christian empire and political theology have done throughout the history of the West, it keeps awareness of absence and loss front and center.

According to the political terms explored in this chapter, what might emerge from the recognition of the ascension and loss of the king who was promised? As suggested at the outset and underscored by the empty throne, the suppressed transcript of ascension may be the exposure of absence lurking behind all claims to kingship and to sovereignty more broadly. More radical than critiques that point out the various supports marshaled by sovereign power to exalt itself and protect its position, ascension atheism suggests that there is no sovereign at all. It exposes the tendency to seek, await, and act as if the sovereign is present and real, thus providing space to interrogate why such moves appear necessary in human community at all.[45] It may also help explain the tendency to correlate sovereignty with loss and expenditure, where sovereign assertions of supremacy, inasmuch as they emerge in contexts influenced by Christian thought, display the need to reenact this founding loss that marks visions of community in Christian tradition and in its secular wake.[46] It raises the watchful warning that when such models of sovereignty claim to represent the people, their own absence and invisibility may be required. It may also expose the problems inherent in Christian political critiques of sovereign power that assert an even more sovereign and exalted Christ in its place. Rather than relativizing earthly power under the supreme lordship of the King of Kings, accepting the abandoned and empty throne means proceeding with the proclamation that all kings are dead and gone and that we have kept their myths alive too long.

NOTES

1. Among the few, direct, sustained theological engagements with ascension are Douglas Farrow, *Ascension and Ecclesia: On the Significance of the Doctrine of the Ascension for Ecclesiology and Christian Cosmology* (Grand Rapids, MI: Eerdmans, 1999); and Douglas Farrow, *Ascension Theology* (London: T&T Clark, 2011).
2. Michel Foucault, *Power/Knowledge: Selected Interviews and Other Writings, 1972–1977*, ed. Colin Gordon (New York: Pantheon Books, 1980); Eric L. Santner, *The Royal Remains: The People's Two Bodies and the Endgames of Sovereignty* (Chicago: University of Chicago Press, 2011).
3. I explore one prominent and influential attempt to outdo earthly sovereignties with a more exalted divine sovereignty in Devin Singh, "A Tale of Two Sovereignties: Karl Barth and Carl Schmitt in Dialogue," in *Theo-Politics? Conversing with Barth in Western and Asian Contexts*, ed. Markus Höfner (Lanham, MD: Lexington Books/Fortress Academic, 2021).
4. This would be to invert the important concerns raised about a vacuous God-concept that remains a placeholder for sovereignty in Claude Lefort, "The Permanence of the Theologico-Political?," in *Political Theologies: Public Religions in a Post-Secular World*, ed. Hent de Vries and Lawrence Eugene Sullivan (New York: Fordham University Press, 2006). See also Paulina Ochoa Espejo, "On Political Theology and the Possibility of Superseding it," *Critical Review of International Social and Political Philosophy* 13, no. 4 (2010): 475–94.
5. For important reflections on the nudities of sovereignty, see Marie-José Mondzain, *Le commerce des regards* (Paris: Seuil, 2003).
6. Carl Schmitt, *Roman Catholicism and Political Form*, trans. G. L. Ulmen (Westport, CT: Greenwood Press, 1996).
7. Christopher Elwood, *The Body Broken: The Calvinist Doctrine of the Eucharist and the Symbolization of Power in Sixteenth-Century France* (New York: Oxford University Press, 1999).
8. Ernst Kantorowicz, *The King's Two Bodies: A Study in Medieval Political Theology* (Princeton, NJ: Princeton University Press, 1957). See also Devin Singh, "Until We Are One? Biopolitics and the United Body," in *"In Christ" in Paul: Explorations in Paul's Theology of Union and Participation*, ed. Kevin J. Vanhoozer, Constantine R. Campbell, and Michael J. Thate, WUNT/II (Tübingen, Germany: Mohr Siebeck, 2014).
9. See the chapter by Vittorio Montemaggi in this volume for Dante's struggle with

divine absence and its influence on Western literary tradition. Among thousands of possible exemplars of Western philosophy's grappling with presence, absence, and representation in the shadow of theology, see, e.g., Erich Auerbach, *Mimesis: The Representation of Reality in Western Literature* (Princeton, NJ: Princeton University Press, 2013); Hans Belting, *Likeness and Presence: A History of the Image Before the Era of Art* (Chicago: University of Chicago Press, 1994); Jacques Derrida, *Of Grammatology*, trans. Gayatri Chakravorty Spivak, 40th anniversary ed. (Baltimore: Johns Hopkins University Press, 2016); Martin Heidegger, *Being and Time*, trans. John MacQuarrie and Edward Robinson (London: SCM Press, 1962); Marie-José Mondzain, *Image, Icon, Economy: The Byzantine Origins of the Contemporary Imaginary*, trans. Rico Franses (Stanford, CA: Stanford University Press, 2005); George Steiner, *Real Presences*, Leslie Stephen Memorial Lecture (New York: Cambridge University Press, 1986).

10. It is no coincidence, for instance, that Jean-Luc Marion's attempt to grapple with metaphysics, sign systems, and ontotheology ends with a celebration of the eucharist. See Jean-Luc Marion, *God without Being: Hors-Texte*, trans. Thomas A. Carlson (Chicago: University of Chicago Press, 1991).

11. Carl Schmitt, *Political Theology: Four Chapters on the Concept of Sovereignty*, trans. George Schwab (Cambridge, MA: MIT Press, 1985), 36.

12. Linn Marie Tonstad departs from such tradition and opens up promising lines of trinitarian inquiry by embracing the absence signaled by ascension. Insights that arise from the loss of the body of Christ include an undoing of ecclesial claims to being or controlling access to that body, as well as a decentering of notions of "personhood" deemed so essential to trinitarian conceptualizations. See Linn Marie Tonstad, *God and Difference: The Trinity, Sexuality, and the Transformation of Finitude* (New York: Routledge, 2016).

13. Of many examples of this approach, consider Gerd Lüdemann, *What Really Happened to Jesus: A Historical Approach to the Resurrection*, trans. John Bowden (Louisville, KY: Westminster John Knox Press, 1995).

14. One laudable biblical studies approach that embraces the realities of absence and founding trauma for early Christian tradition is found in Michael J. Thate, *The Godman and the Sea: The Empty Tomb, the Trauma of the Jews, and the Gospel of Mark* (Philadelphia: University of Pennsylvania Press, 2019).

15. Giorgio Agamben, *The Kingdom and the Glory: For a Theological Genealogy of Economy and Government*, trans. Lorenzo Chiesa and Matteo Mandarini (Stanford, CA: Stanford University Press, 2011); Devin Singh, "Anarchy, Void, Signature: Agamben's Trinity among Orthodoxy's Remains," *Political Theology* 17, no. 1 (2016): 27–46.

16. Agamben, *Kingdom and the Glory*, 138.
17. Agamben, 138.
18. Agamben, 211.
19. Agamben, 162.
20. Agamben, 163.
21. Agamben, 242.
22. E.g., Gregory of Nazianzus, *Or* 42.15.
23. On the politics of liturgy, see esp. "Christ as *Imperator*" in *Theological Tractates*, by Erik Peterson, trans. Michael J. Hollerich (Stanford, CA: Stanford University Press, 2011), 143–50.

24. Agamben, *Kingdom and the Glory*, 243, 245.
25. Thomas Cattoi, "The Empty Throne: Religious Imagery and Presence in Byzantine and Buddhist Art," *Journal of Inter-Religious Dialogue* 10 (2012): 15.
26. It goes without saying that imagery of the empty throne operates alongside contravening theological claims that Christ has not simply ascended to heaven but has also ascended to and taken a seat on his throne "at the right hand of the Father" (Col 3:1; Heb 1:3; Nicene Creed). Thus, the throne is not empty but is occupied by the risen and ascended Christ. I do not treat this separately here because this is precisely the very theme I am exploring in this chapter, that is, the Christian concept of the ascended and reigning Christ despite his obvious absence. The imagery of the empty throne is more interesting as a minority report that suggests a suppressed acknowledgment of such absence despite proclamations of triumph and presence.
27. Cattoi, "Empty Throne," 16.
28. Agamben, *Kingdom and the Glory*, 138. Quoting John Quidort, *Fratris Johannis de Parisiis . . . de potestate regia et papali* (1614), in Melchior Goldast, *Monarchiae sacri Romani imperii, sive Tractatuum de iurisdictione imperiali seu regia et pontificia seu sacerdotalis* (Frankfurt: Zunnerum, 1668), 111.
29. Erik Peterson, "Monotheism as a Political Problem: A Contribution to the History of Political Theology in the Roman Empire," in *Theological Tractates*, ed. Michael J. Hollerich (Stanford, CA: Stanford University Press, 2011), 68–105.
30. I evaluate Peterson's claims and his caricature of Eusebius in greater detail in Devin Singh, "Eusebius as Political Theologian: The Legend Continues," *Harvard Theological Review* 108, no. 1 (2015): 129–54.
31. Peterson, "Monotheism as a Political Problem," 103.
32. Peterson, 103.
33. Moltmann expresses great admiration for Peterson and acknowledges his debt to him, calling the essay a "magnificent treatise." See Jürgen Moltmann, "Political Theology," *Theology Today* 28, no. 1 (April 1971): 6–23. Of the many examples of social trinitarianism that interact with Moltmann's and (usually implicitly) Peterson's claims, consider Leonardo Boff, *Holy Trinity, Perfect Community* (Maryknoll, NY: Orbis, 2000); Catherine Mowry LaCugna, *God for Us: The Trinity and Christian life* (San Francisco: Harper, 1991); Miroslav Volf, *After Our Likeness: The Church as the Image of the Trinity* (Grand Rapids, MI: Eerdmans, 1998).
34. On apophatic theology, see Henning Tegtmeyer's chapter in this volume.
35. Two representative arguments in this regard are Kathryn Tanner, *Jesus, Humanity and the Trinity: A Brief Systematic Theology* (Minneapolis, MN: Fortress Press, 2001); Denys Turner, *Faith, Reason, and the Existence of God* (Cambridge: Cambridge University Press, 2004).
36. Themes of legitimation and legitimacy are explored well in Adam Kotsko, *Neoliberalism's Demons: On the Political Theology of Late Capital* (Stanford, CA: Stanford University Press, 2018). See now also Clifford B. Anderson, "Constitutional Theology: Karl Barth and Carl Schmitt on Legitimacy and the Rule of Law," in *Theo-Politics? Conversing with Barth in Western and Asian Contexts*, ed. Markus Höfner (Lanham, MD: Lexington Books/Fortress Academic, 2021).
37. Agamben, *Kingdom and the Glory*, 7–8.
38. A variety of studies have emerged about the role that foundational Christian supersessionism and antisemitism have played in later European theorizations

of racial and colonial others. See, e.g., J. Kameron Carter, *Race: A Theological Account* (New York: Oxford University Press, 2008); M. Lindsay Kaplan, *Figuring Racism in Medieval Christianity* (New York: Oxford University Press, 2019).

39. See the chapter by Susannah Ticciati in this volume for assessment of the scientific and "new" atheists.
40. Jürgen Moltmann, "Godless Theology," *Christian Century*, December 20–27, 2007, 1328–29.
41. See the chapter by George Pattison in this volume for Dostoevsky on atheism.
42. I have in mind here inspiring visions of ecclesial poverty as "solidarity and protest" as set forth in Gustavo Gutiérrez, *A Theology of Liberation: History, Politics, and Salvation*, trans. Sister Caridad Inda, rev. ed. (Maryknoll, NY: Orbis Books, 1988), 163–72.
43. On this theme, see, e.g., Carlos Eire, *War against the Idols: The Reformation of Worship from Erasmus to Calvin* (Cambridge: Cambridge University Press, 1986).
44. See Max Weber, *The Protestant Ethic and the Spirit of Capitalism*, trans. Stephen Kalberg, rev. and updated ed. (New York: Oxford University Press, 2011). Against a view of Calvinist disenchantment, explored instead as "resignification," see now Michelle Chaplin Sanchez, *Calvin and the Resignification of the World: Creation, Incarnation, and the Problem of Political Theology in the 1559 Institutes* (Cambridge: Cambridge University Press, 2019).
45. These perennial and yet episodic human proclivities toward hierarchy and centralized rule have been explored anthropologically and archaeologically, respectively, in David Graeber and Marshall Sahlins, *On Kings* (Chicago: Hau Books, 2017); Kent V. Flannery and Joyce Marcus, *The Creation of Inequality: How Our Prehistoric Ancestors Set the Stage for Monarchy, Slavery, and Empire* (Cambridge, MA: Harvard University Press, 2012).
46. Here the project connects with Bataille's studies of sovereignty, excess, sacrifice, and expenditure, and with the theories of community developed in light of his reflections, those that deal in different ways with the problem of absence at the heart of Western political traditions. See Georges Bataille, *The Accursed Share: An Essay on General Economy*, trans. Robert Hurley, 3 vols. (New York: Zone Books, 1988); Giorgio Agamben, *The Coming Community*, trans. Michael Hardt (Minneapolis: University of Minnesota Press, 1993); Maurice Blanchot, *The Unavowable Community*, trans. Pierre Joris (Barrytown, NY: Station Hill Press, 1988); Jean-Luc Nancy, *The Inoperative Community*, trans. Peter Connor et al. (Minneapolis: University of Minnesota Press, 1991); Jean-Luc Nancy, *The Disavowed Community*, trans. Philip Armstrong (New York: Fordham University Press, 2016).

REFERENCES

Agamben, Giorgio. *The Coming Community*. Translated by Michael Hardt. Minneapolis: University of Minnesota Press, 1993.

———. *The Kingdom and the Glory: For a Theological Genealogy of Economy and Government*. Translated by Lorenzo Chiesa and Matteo Mandarini. Stanford, CA: Stanford University Press, 2011.

Anderson, Clifford B. "Constitutional Theology: Karl Barth and Carl Schmitt on Legitimacy and the Rule of Law." In *Theo-Politics? Conversing with Barth in*

Western and Asian Contexts, edited by Markus Höfner, 131–46. Lanham, MD: Lexington Books/Fortress Academic, 2021.

Auerbach, Erich. *Mimesis: The Representation of Reality in Western Literature.* Princeton, NJ: Princeton University Press, 2013.

Bataille, Georges. *The Accursed Share: An Essay on General Economy.* Translated by Robert Hurley. 3 vols. New York: Zone Books, 1988.

Belting, Hans. *Likeness and Presence: A History of the Image Before the Era of Art.* Chicago: University of Chicago Press, 1994.

Blanchot, Maurice. *The Unavowable Community.* Translated by Pierre Joris. Barrytown, NY: Station Hill Press, 1988.

Boff, Leonardo. *Holy Trinity, Perfect Community.* Maryknoll, NY: Orbis, 2000.

Carter, J. Kameron. *Race: A Theological Account.* New York: Oxford University Press, 2008.

Cattoi, Thomas. "The Empty Throne: Religious Imagery and Presence in Byzantine and Buddhist Art." *Journal of Inter-Religious Dialogue* 10 (2012): 10–22.

Derrida, Jacques. *Of Grammatology.* Translated by Gayatri Chakravorty Spivak. 40th anniversary ed. Baltimore: Johns Hopkins University Press, 2016.

Eire, Carlos. *War against the Idols: The Reformation of Worship from Erasmus to Calvin.* Cambridge: Cambridge University Press, 1986.

Elwood, Christopher. *The Body Broken: The Calvinist Doctrine of the Eucharist and the Symbolization of Power in Sixteenth-Century France.* New York: Oxford University Press, 1999.

Espejo, Paulina Ochoa. "On Political Theology and the Possibility of Superseding it." *Critical Review of International Social and Political Philosophy* 13, no. 4 (2010): 475–94.

Farrow, Douglas. *Ascension and Ecclesia: On the Significance of the Doctrine of the Ascension for Ecclesiology and Christian Cosmology.* Grand Rapids, MI: Eerdmans, 1999.

———. *Ascension Theology.* London: T&T Clark, 2011.

Flannery, Kent V., and Joyce Marcus. *The Creation of Inequality: How our Prehistoric Ancestors Set the Stage for Monarchy, Slavery, and Empire.* Cambridge, MA: Harvard University Press, 2012.

Foucault, Michel. *Power/Knowledge: Selected Interviews and Other Writings, 1972–1977.* Edited by Colin Gordon. New York: Pantheon Books, 1980.

Graeber, David, and Marshall Sahlins. *On Kings.* Chicago: Hau Books, 2017.

Gutiérrez, Gustavo. *A Theology of Liberation: History, Politics, and Salvation.* Translated by Sister Caridad Inda. Rev. ed. Maryknoll, NY: Orbis Books, 1988.

Heidegger, Martin. *Being and Time.* Translated by John MacQuarrie and Edward Robinson. London: SCM Press, 1962.

Kantorowicz, Ernst. *The King's Two Bodies: A Study in Medieval Political Theology.* Princeton, NJ: Princeton University Press, 1957.

Kaplan, M. Lindsay. *Figuring Racism in Medieval Christianity.* New York: Oxford University Press, 2019.

Kotsko, Adam. *Neoliberalism's Demons: On the Political Theology of Late Capital.* Stanford, CA: Stanford University Press, 2018.

LaCugna, Catherine Mowry. *God for Us: The Trinity and Christian life.* San Francisco: Harper, 1991.

Lefort, Claude. "The Permanence of the Theologico-Political?" In *Political Theologies: Public Religions in a Post-Secular World*, edited by Hent de Vries and Lawrence Eugene Sullivan, 148–87. New York: Fordham University Press, 2006.

Lüdemann, Gerd. *What Really Happened to Jesus: A Historical Approach to the Resurrection*. Translated by John Bowden. Louisville, KY: Westminster John Knox Press, 1995.

Marion, Jean-Luc. *God without Being: Hors-Texte*. Translated by Thomas A. Carlson. Chicago: University of Chicago Press, 1991.

Moltmann, Jürgen. "Political Theology." *Theology Today* 28, no. 1 (April 1971): 6–23.

———. "Godless Theology." *Christian Century*, December 20–27, 2007, 1328–29.

Mondzain, Marie-José. *Image, Icon, Economy: The Byzantine Origins of the Contemporary Imaginary*. Translated by Rico Franses. Stanford, CA: Stanford University Press, 2005.

———. *Le commerce des regards*. Paris: Seuil, 2003.

Nancy, Jean-Luc. *The Disavowed Community*. Translated by Philip Armstrong. New York: Fordham University Press, 2016.

———. *The Inoperative Community*. Translated by Peter Connor, Lisa Garbus, Michael Holland and Simona Sawhney. Minneapolis: University of Minnesota Press, 1991.

Peterson, Erik. "Monotheism as a Political Problem: A Contribution to the History of Political Theology in the Roman Empire." Translated by Michael J. Hollerich. In *Theological Tractates*, edited by Michael J. Hollerich, 68–105. Stanford, CA: Stanford University Press, 2011.

———. *Theological Tractates*. Translated by Michael J. Hollerich. Stanford, CA: Stanford University Press, 2011.

Sanchez, Michelle Chaplin. *Calvin and the Resignification of the World: Creation, Incarnation, and the Problem of Political Theology in the 1559 Institutes*. Cambridge: Cambridge University Press, 2019.

Santner, Eric L. *The Royal Remains: The People's Two Bodies and the Endgames of Sovereignty*. Chicago: University of Chicago Press, 2011.

Schmitt, Carl. *Political Theology: Four Chapters on the Concept of Sovereignty*. Translated by George Schwab. Cambridge, MA: MIT Press, 1985.

———. *Roman Catholicism and Political Form*. Translated by G. L. Ulmen. Westport, CT: Greenwood Press, 1996.

Singh, Devin. "Anarchy, Void, Signature: Agamben's Trinity Among Orthodoxy's Remains." *Political Theology* 17, no. 1 (2016): 27–46.

———. "Eusebius as Political Theologian: The Legend Continues." *Harvard Theological Review* 108, no. 1 (2015): 129–54.

———. "A Tale of Two Sovereignties: Karl Barth and Carl Schmitt in Dialogue." In *Theo-Politics? Conversing with Barth in Western and Asian Contexts*, edited by Markus Höfner, 147–68. Lanham, MD: Lexington Books/Fortress Academic, 2021.

———. "Until We Are One? Biopolitics and the United Body." In *"In Christ" in Paul: Explorations in Paul's Theology of Union and Participation*, edited by Kevin J. Vanhoozer, Constantine R. Campbell, and Michael J. Thate, 529–56. WUNT/II. Tübingen, Germany: Mohr Siebeck, 2014.

Steiner, George. *Real Presences*. Leslie Stephen Memorial Lecture. New York: Cambridge University Press, 1986.
Tanner, Kathryn. *Jesus, Humanity and the Trinity: A Brief Systematic Theology*. Minneapolis: Fortress Press, 2001.
Thate, Michael J. *The Godman and the Sea: The Empty Tomb, the Trauma of the Jews, and the Gospel of Mark*. Philadelphia: University of Pennsylvania Press, 2019.
Tonstad, Linn Marie. *God and Difference: The Trinity, Sexuality, and the Transformation of Finitude*. New York: Routledge, 2016.
Turner, Denys. *Faith, Reason, and the Existence of God*. Cambridge: Cambridge University Press, 2004.
Volf, Miroslav. *After Our Likeness: The Church as the Image of the Trinity*. Grand Rapids, MI: Eerdmans, 1998.
Weber, Max. *The Protestant Ethic and the Spirit of Capitalism*. Translated by Stephen Kalberg. Rev. ed. New York: Oxford University Press, 2011.

7

ATHEISM AND LITERATURE

Living without God in Dante's Comedy

Vittorio Montemaggi

CAN WE SPEAK OF ATHEISM IN DANTE'S *COMEDY*?

In asking whether we can speak of atheism in Dante's *Comedy*, I wish to contribute to the reflections made by contributors to this volume by bringing to them a text that might well appear to be conceptually and historically quite far from modern and contemporary debates on atheism, which are otherwise the main focus of the present volume. My primary aim in doing so is to open up, in the light of Dante's *Comedy*, perspectives that might fruitfully contribute to our discussions but that might otherwise not be so readily available. At the same time I hope that in the light of our discussions, the present chapter might also open up perspectives on Dante's *Comedy* that might otherwise not be so readily available and that merit further study.

The present chapter aims to be suggestive and interrogative, not conclusive. As became apparent in the discussions at the conference on which the present volume is based, reflection on Dante's *Comedy* can indeed be a rich and generative exercise for illuminating important dimensions of collective exploration of varieties of atheism. As also became apparent, however, reflection on Dante's *Comedy* can do this precisely because what it offers does not easily "fit," conceptually and methodologically, with contemporary debates on atheism. Probing questions asked in the space between interpretation of Dante's text and exploration of varieties of atheism can generate fruitful insights for thinking about both.

In an obvious sense, from our contemporary perspective, to speak of atheism in Dante's *Comedy* is of course counterintuitive. There is no such thing, either described in the poem or attributable to the poet's vision underlying it. The closest we seem to get to atheism in the poem's descriptions, is in the circle of the "heretics" in *Inferno* 10, whose inhabitants we are told believe that the soul dies with the body. This is the first circle of Hell proper, immediately following Dante's and Virgil's entry into the city of Dis. There is debate as to what exactly according to Dante is the sin being punished here.[1] Whatever its precise definition, however, it does bear some resemblance to some modern conceptions of atheism: the denial of the immortality of the soul as imagined by Dante seems to resonate with varieties of atheism that emphasize, at the expense of the spiritual, the material constitution of the human being and of reality more generally.[2] But this is not in itself enough to speak of atheism being depicted in the *Comedy*.

Moreover, even as far as the poet's own vision is concerned, atheism does seem very far from the picture. As strong as the pull might have been for Dante of certain aspects of material reality, Dante is no atheist. That said, his *Comedy* is informed by a rich, complex and thorough apophaticism, in and through which we are led to the luminous silence as which the poem ends, once all dualisms are transcended and the human being is, as Dante puts it at the very end of the poem, perfectly at one with the "love that moves the sun and other stars" (*Paradiso* 33.145). It would indeed be rewarding, in the spirit of our collection, to integrate reflection on Dante's apophaticism into broader reflection on the relationship between apophaticism and atheism. This is not, as such, what I propose to do.[3] I do, however, wish to address an aspect of Dante's poetry closely tied to its apophaticism as its underlying energy.

The *Comedy*'s underlying energy is hope.[4] As Beatrice puts it to Saint James in *Paradiso* 25.52–57, no one has more hope than Dante. If love is the poem's end and (as stated in *Purgatorio* 24.52–54) also its beginning or motive force, hope is the energy by which the poem becomes what it is. In what follows, I explore Dante's conception of hope in relation to some of the overarching questions addressed in this collection. In particular, I suggest an interpretation of the beginning of Dante's journey by which the whole of the *Comedy* might be seen as a theological and spiritual journey grounded in questions that resonate with those of our project: In what does the difference between believing and not believing in God consist? To what extent is the difference an intellectual one, in a conceptual sense? To what extent is it a broader matter, encompassing patterns of thought, perception, and action that are not easily reducible to concepts or ideas? As regards the last of these questions, moreover, I hope the present chapter might meaningfully also invite readers to consider what kind of difference can be made to reflection on atheism by the art of literature, which seems to offer rich resources at the level of form and narrative for exploring patterns of thought, perception and action that are not easily reducible to concept or ideas.

On the one hand, the *Comedy* can be read as a powerful statement that there can be no such thing as atheism: the poet's work is animated by deep belief in the participation of all reality in God. In and through its rich, complex and thorough apophaticism—centered on the mystery of the divinity of human personhood and encounter—the *Comedy* aims to draw its readers deeper into recognition of reality as manifestation of divine love. Yet at the same time, the *Comedy*—especially in the *Inferno*—would clearly also seem to display the wish to map out the variety of ways in which human beings choose to live without God.[5] Indeed, the first part of Dante's journey—which by extension can be seen to represent Dante's idea of the first step of any spiritual journey—could be read in a certain sense as an exploration of a particular variety of atheism: the human choice to disregard in thought, perception, and/or action that all reality is manifestation of divine love.[6]

The name usually given to such choice as understood by Dante is "sin." I am not, however, trying to suggest that we should today think that sin as such is atheism or atheism as such is sin. I am simply trying to suggest that reflection on Dante's depiction of sin might enrich debates on atheism by offering us a rich, complex and thorough exploration of what it means to live without God. I am particularly interested, in this regard, in how all living without God is said by Dante to have something in common: the abandonment of hope. The abandonment of hope for Dante is not a difference between believer and nonbeliever. Dante, in any case, does not seem to distinguish between those who believe in God and those who do not. He distinguishes between those who believe in Christ and those who do not, and he is careful to specify that this distinction does not coincide with the distinction between those who explicitly profess faith in Christ and those who do not.[7] As portrayed in the *Comedy*, the abandonment of hope pertains both to those who profess Christian belief and to those who do not, and in either case coincides with Hell. Abandoning hope is not a failure to assert the right belief, idea or concept, it is a failure to be true to one's true being—and ultimately, to love. As Kenelm Foster puts it, the *Inferno* can be read as an account of human wrongdoing that according to Dante would stand in any world that is human at all.[8] As such, what it presents is not so much varieties of human failure to believe in God but rather varieties of human failure to love, and of human failure to acknowledge the human being's own, inherent divinity.

Hope for Dante is the sure expectation of eternal glory, the orientation of one's whole being to eternal at-one-ment with, in and as divine love.

As such it coincides with belief in Christ, insofar as belief in Christ is belief in Resurrection, the eternal unfolding of personal embodied existence with, in and as the love that God is. *Inferno, Purgatorio,* and *Paradiso* can be read, respectively, as exploration of what it means to fail, learn, and succeed to live with God, as oriented toward Resurrection; and the *Comedy* as a whole, as both poetry and theology, one through the other, can be read as animated by hope: expression of sure expectation of the meaningfulness of such orientation.

In the light of these considerations, in what follows I outline Dante's explicit definition of hope in the *Comedy*, reflect on Dante's presentation of the entrance to Hell as key to reading the *Inferno* and the *Comedy* as a whole, and present a key image from *Inferno* 1 as focal point for reflection on the possible significance of the *Comedy* in connection with the overarching questions addressed by the present volume.

DANTE'S HOPE

In *Paradiso* 23–27, the cantos of the Heaven of the Fixed Stars, Dante sees the blessed of the heavenly church in triumph, gathered under the glory of the assumed Mary and illumined by the radiance of the ascended Christ.[9] He is then examined on the three theological virtues—faith, hope, and love—respectively by Saints Peter, James, and John the Evangelist. In the second of the three exams, Dante offers the following definition of hope to James:

"Spene," diss' io, "è uno attender certo	"Hope is that sure expectation," I declared,
de la gloria futura, il qual produce	"of glory that will come. The grace of God
grazia divina e precedente merto.	and precedent good works produce this power.
Da molte stelle mi vien questa luce;	From many stars its light comes down to me.
ma quei la distillò nel mio cor pria	But David first instilled it in my heart,
che fu sommo cantor del sommo duce.	that highest singer of the highest Lord.
'Sperino in te,' ne la sua tëodia	'Let those have hope in you who know His name.'
dice, 'color che sanno il nome tuo':	So David, in his psalmody, sings out.
e chi nol sa, s'elli ha la fede mia?	And who can not know that who shares my faith?
Tu mi stillasti, con lo stillar tuo,	Then you in your epistle—as with drops
ne la pistola poi; sì ch'io son pieno,	of dew—distilled my hopes. So I am full,
e in altrui vostra pioggia repluo."	and rain your cooling shower on other lives."[11]
(*Paradiso* 25.67–78)[10]	

Dante's words are both conventional and original. The first *terzina* translates into Italian the expected textbook definition of hope found in Peter

Lombard's *Sentences* (3.16.1). After this, we immediately find the word *stelle*, which throughout the *Comedy*—from *Inferno* 1.38 to *Paradiso* 33.145— is intimately connected to the particular theological dynamics of Dante's own work. Moreover, in lines 67–69 we find a reference to the confluence of grace and human agency. The significance of this is enhanced upon encountering, in lines 75–78, the letter of James (which Dante believed to have indeed been written by James, son of Zebedee, brother of John the Evangelist) as one of the two sources from which it is said Dante's own hope derives. One of the defining characteristics of the epistle, which in fact does not explicitly or extensively treat of hope, is its foregrounding the importance of works, alongside faith, for a proper unfolding of Christian life. Dante's understanding of hope would thus seem to be importantly tied to the active life of the church. Indeed, in the passage just quoted, James's epistle is given as reason for which Dante is active in communicating to others the hope received from Scripture. The link between Dante's hope and the active life of the church is further confirmed by the way in which, in presenting Dante to James, Beatrice strongly ties Dante's hope to his "militancy" in the earthly church:

La Chiesa militante alcun figliuolo	The Church, at war on earth, has not a child—
non ha con più speranza, com' è scritto	and this is written in that Sun whose rays
nel Sol che raggia tutto nostro stuolo:	here shine upon our ranks—more full of hope.
però li è conceduto che d'Egitto	It has, therefore, been granted him to come,
vegna in Ierusalemme per vedere,	before his term of soldiership is through,
anzi che 'l militar li sia prescritto.	from Egypt to behold Jerusalem.
(*Paradiso* 25.52–57)	

The meaning of the reference to Dante's active life is further enriched by references to the Resurrection. This is the eternal glory spoken of in *Paradiso* 25.68. Dante spells this out a few lines later on:

E io: "Le nove e le scritture antiche	And I: "The Scriptures, both the old and new,
pongon lo segno, ed esso lo mi addita,	define and indicate that goal for me:
de l'anime che Dio s'ha fatte amiche.	the friendship God concludes with certain souls.
Dice Isaia che ciascuna vestita	Isaiah says that each, in his own land,
ne la sua terra fia di doppia vesta:	will be arrayed in two-fold vestiture.
e la sua terra è questa dolce vita;	And 'his own land' is here, this sweetest life.
e 'l tuo fratello assai vie più digesta,	And yet more fully your own brother makes
là dove tratta de le bianche stole,	this revelation clear to us. He speaks
questa revelazion ci manifesta."	(in the Apocalypse) of pure white dress."
(*Paradiso* 25.88–96)	

The word *terra* is used a number of times in the episode of the Fixed Stars to refer quite unambiguously to that which is earthly (most strikingly in John's "In terra è terra il mio corpo" [My body lies as earth in earth] in *Paradiso* 25.124). In this case, however, the word *terra* is used to refer to how, in hope, that which is earthly is revealed as finding its perfect fulfillment in, and as, that which is heavenly. Dante's understanding of hope is thus importantly defined by a strong emphasis not only on individual action but also on the body. Dante's poetry is oriented in and toward the mystery by which human beings can, through both merit and grace, act within earthly community in such a way as to come, in all their physicality, to participate in eternal glory.

Dante's poetry is also informed by hope in another crucial sense. Indeed, hope is a necessary condition of theological discourse, of all speech aiming to speak meaningfully of God and of the relationship between God, the cosmos, and human beings. Ultimately, theological discourse can be uttered only in hope: the hope that, in and through its necessary finitude and vulnerability, human language might speak divine truth, which in itself is necessarily beyond both thought and speech. In this sense, Dante's definition of hope can be seen to be a definition of the *Comedy* itself. Dante writes with hope in the meaningfulness of his theological discourse: a discourse about the divine which is truthful insofar as which is animated by Dante's "attender certo" of eternal glory, his "sure expectation," at once divine and human (*Paradiso* 25.68–69), in the truth of humanity's divinity, which finds its supreme conceptual expression in the doctrine of the Resurrection. A discourse, moreover, which is presented as not self-referential or self-serving but, in embracing its vulnerability in sure expectation of truth, self-giving: "e in altrui vostra pioggia repluo." Dante's examination on hope thus has very important metaliterary, theological implications: what Dante says about hope also defines how Dante speaks, of hope and also more generally.

At the beginning of Dante's examination on hope, in *Paradiso* 25.40–47, the questions set by James are: What is hope? In what measure does Dante possess it? Whence does it come to him? Before Dante begins to speak in response to James's questions, Beatrice answers the second question for him with the words already cited (*Paradiso* 25.52–57). She then explains that Dante can answer the other two questions for himself, because

. . . *non li saran forti*	These won't prove difficult,
né di iattanza; ed elli a ciò risponda,	and yet won't tempt him into mere display.
e la grazia di Dio ciò li comporti.	Let him reply. May God's grace bear him on.
(*Paradiso* 25.61–63)	

These words might at first sight appear formulaic. They are, in fact, among the most significant lines in the *Comedy*. Let us note, first, the exact correspondence between lines 62–63 and line 69, cited earlier. In Dante's speaking of hope, Beatrice says, may there be a confluence of merit and grace—just as in the generation of hope itself. In speaking of hope Dante's speech can display a cooperation of divinity and humanity similar to that out of which flows the theological virtue of hope itself. This is indeed significant. Let us recall that in lines 52–57 Dante had been presented by Beatrice as possessing hope in very high degree, and that it is on account of this that he is allowed to take the extraordinary journey he is on.[12] Dante's hope is, in other words, what makes the journey of the *Comedy* possible. It makes sense, from this point of view, for there to be a coincidence between what Dante says about hope and the way he is presented as speaking in his theological examination—all the more so if we remind ourselves that the *Comedy* is fiction: the journey actually made possible by Dante's hope is the writing of the *Comedy* itself.

As far as his writing is concerned, Dante in the *Comedy* does not only foreground his hope. He also famously foregrounds his pride.[13] Indeed, it is precisely in connection to Dante's pride that Beatrice confidently presents Dante to James.[14] She explains that, for Dante, responding to James's two questions that still go unanswered will be neither exceedingly difficult nor occasion for pride. In speaking of and in hope, Dante can confidently reveal his goodness ("bontà," line 66) and not fall into pride. Hope, as the hallmark of Dante's speech, is what is said to guarantee Dante's humility and therefore poetic and theological authority.[15]

In the latter sense, theology, as hope, cannot bypass the limitations of pride and finitude. It can, however, be eschatologically oriented so as to reveal the promise of their redemption. As George Pattison puts it:

> To speak—to speak simply about anything, not necessarily about love or ontology or God—is to place a stake on the possibility of being listened to, that is, on the good will of the other; to listen is, similarly, to place a stake on the good will of the speaker, trusting s/he is not simply wasting my time, deceiving me, or attempting to suborn me. Speaking and listening in the fullest sense are each possible only if, in principle, we have the possibility of recognizing each other as more than an other-I, of recognizing each other as other. But to the extent that no single exchange can conclusively vindicate our trust in the good will of the other, . . . we may say that this possibility has an essentially futural dimension and may not be absolved from the tension of not yet and now. It is a matter of hope.
>
> Yet it is also a matter of gratitude. . . . [L]ove is not given to us as a

given. In the word of love, love is given to us solely and exclusively as possibility and the now of its being spoken and listened to is fulfillable only in a time still to come. We may think that gratitude is appropriate only in response to the giving of a gift, to what we have been given, what we have received. How might we be grateful for what we might receive but have not yet received? The answer is simple and, I hope, obvious. In the possibility of love, in the hope grounded in the promise of each word spoken in the name of love (and every word, we have noted, may be such a word, even when it is not a word about love but only, let us say, about the weather, so long as it is a word spoken or listened to on the presumption of good will), in this possibility, in this promise we already have quite a lot to be grateful for. Why? Because simply as possibility, simply as promise, the word of love opens a way out of the potential hell that, for many, is their present. Whether or not we, inhabiting a post-Aristotelian universe, can still say that this is the love that moves the sun and other stars, it is this word of promise that, by showing us what we might become shows us also what we are and how we might, even now, be. Love, the word of love, therefore grounds human beings' "to be" and if, at a common sense level, being precedes love in the order of knowing, we may paradoxically say that love precedes being in the order of being itself.[16]

It is extremely significant, here, to recall also that it is in terms of the Resurrection that Dante defines his hope in *Paradiso* 25. If as suggested by *Paradiso* 23 the Ascension and the Assumption theologically ground the possibility of Dante's journey, they do so because they ground hope in the Resurrection: in the futural possibility of eternal, bodily, glory for all human beings. Hope in the Resurrection is what spiritually animates Dante's poetry. In fact, we are already told at the beginning of the *Purgatorio*, precisely, that "resurrected" is what Dante's poetry aspires to be so as truthfully to speak of the realm of salvation: "ma qui la morta poesì resurga" (*Purgatorio* 1.7): the dead poetry of the *Inferno* needs to be resurrected for Dante to be able to speak truthfully in *Purgatorio* and *Paradiso*. From the very beginning of his journey into the realm of salvation, Dante seems programmatically to link his poetry to hope in the Resurrection. As vital part of his active participation in the life of the church, Dante's poetry in the *Purgatorio* and the *Paradiso* not only speaks hope in the Resurrection; it *is* hope in the Resurrection. But what about the *Inferno*?

Hope—defined by the union of humanity and divinity represented by the Resurrection—is what ultimately for Dante marks the distinctive character of the Christian worldview. To share this hope is to live at one with the ground of all being. Not to share it is to alienate oneself from it. It is certainly significant, in this respect, that in the *Inferno* it is as lack of hope that the condition of Hell is described. In other significant respects, however, the poetry of the *Inferno* can be seen as extraordinary expression of hope.

ENTERING HELL

From *Inferno* 4.126 to *Inferno* 33.4–5, the condition of the human beings Dante encounters in the *Inferno* is described with reference to lack of hope. Indeed, lack of hope is famously already inscribed on the gate of Dante's Hell itself:

Per me si va ne la città dolente,	Through me you go to the grief-wracked city.
per me si va ne l'etterno dolore,	Through me to everlasting pain you go.
per me si va tra la perduta gente.	Through me you go and pass among lost souls.
Giustizia mosse il mio alto fattore;	Justice inspired my exalted Creator.
fecemi la divina podestate,	I am a creature of the Holiest Power,
la somma sapïenza e 'l primo amore.	of Wisdom in the Highest and of Primal Love.
Dinanzi a me non fuor cose create	Nothing till I was made was made, only
se non etterne, e io etterna duro.	eternal beings. And I endure eternally.
Lasciate ogne speranza, voi ch'intrate.	Surrender as you enter every hope you have.
(*Inferno* 3.1–9)	

As appalling as these words appear to be, they are also a reminder that for Dante, Hell, too, is manifestation of divine love.[17] The creation of Hell coincides with the creation of all that is eternal; and it is expression of Trinitarian life—divine power, wisdom and love: Father, Son, and Holy Spirit. But what exactly does the inscription on the gate of Hell mean?

The words "Lasciate ogne speranza, voi ch'intrate" are among the most famous of the *Comedy*. And they are all but universally read as imperative—the command to abandon hope upon entering Hell. It is worth considering, though, whether they might not be more ambiguous than generally realized. Grammatically, the words could equally be in the indicative, and thus descriptive: you who enter here abandon hope. On this second reading, hope is not something that the damned have and are asked to give up on entering Hell. Hope is, rather, that the giving up of which makes one enter Hell. On this second reading, moreover, the reference to eternity which on the gate of Hell precedes the reference to hope is not to be read necessarily as a reference just to the eternity of punishment but to the eternity of the possibility of regaining hope. The gate of Hell as Dante depicts it is, after all, open (see also Matthew 16:18).[18] And ultimately, the *Comedy* presents prayer for others that is genuinely offered in love and hope as potentially stronger than Hell and damnation, able to draw others toward the possibility of salvation, beyond what they would be able on their own to recognize.[19]

We saw above that hope for Dante is, as theological virtue, hope in the Resurrection: the orientation of one's being in and toward the mystery of eternal union between the human person and God. All sin, for Dante, is expression of the human person's illusion to live without God, independently of such union. This illusion Dante characterizes primarily as lack of hope: failure to configure one's being in recognition that "to be" is "to be dependent on, and expression of, divine love"; and that therefore human being is future oriented toward eternal realization and fulfillment of our union with God. Such lack of hope is not, for Dante, defined relative to conceptual knowledge of Christ or Resurrection. Dante's Hell (and not just his Limbo) is populated by both Christians and non-Christians, and Dante's Purgatory and Heaven include people who in life had no direct contact with Christian teaching.[20] Lack of hope is not defined as necessarily tied to failure to assent to particular doctrinal propositions, but to failure to be fully true to one's being and to love fully; and Hell is the condition that follows from this.

Not long after passing through the gate of Hell, Dante and Virgil see the damned lining up, ready to be ferried across the river into Hell proper. Here, Virgil explains to Dante that those entering Hell,

. . . *pronti sono a trapassar lo rio,*	are eager to be shipped across.
ché la divina giustizia li sprona,	Justice of God so spurs them all ahead
sì che la tema si volve in disio.	that fear in them becomes that sharp desire.
(*Inferno* 3.124–26)	

These lines suggest that for Dante the condition of Hell is not imposed externally on those entering it, but inhabited freely by them, as their own desire. A crucial, but usually neglected, aspect of Dante's Hell is that none of its inhabitants believes being there does not conform to justice. Some of them curse God, others confront him in anger, but none of them actually protests that being in Hell is not a just unfolding of their existence. Knowledge of divinity and self-knowledge coincide. Relationship with God is not relationship with something external to oneself but the very ground of one's being. As Denys Turner puts it:

> Dante's hell is not just a place of punishment inhabited by sinners. It is a place where sinners, by choice, inhabit their sins and live their lives structured by sin's distorted perceptions of love. That love they have to reject,

as being an invasion of some imagined personal space independent of God, as a violation of their personal freedom and autonomy. But this self-deceived self-affirmation shows up in the refusal of the damned to accept that there can be any narrative other than their own, for they deny that there is, after all, any *divina commedia*. The damned all have their own stories to tell, and Inferno tells them. Each of them, from Francesca da Rimini to Ugolino, know that those stories which they each tell of their fates recount not just why they were sent there to hell in the first place—that is, their specific sin—but also why they are held there without term in a condition of sinfulness, for the grip of hell is but the grip with which they hold onto their stories, without which they cannot imagine for themselves an identity or reality. They need their stories, stories of their own telling, and they need the misrepresentations that those stories tell. Hell is but the condition consequent upon their ultimate refusal to abandon that need. Hell, then, is not the condition of those who have sinned, for many who have sinned more grievously than Francesca and Paolo are not in hell but in a place of Redemption in purgatory. Hell is the condition of those who do not repent of their stories, who refuse the offer of their revision by the divine love, and insist on living by means of the story that sin tells, the story of the attempt to achieve a self-made significance independently of the story of the divine love.[21]

What Turner says about narrative could be inflected by what was said above about hope. The stories told by the sinners of Dante's *Inferno* are stories that reject orientation in and toward full realization of the human person as expression of divine love.

This is all very significant, I think, because it suggests that however we wish to interpret Dante's *Inferno*, we need to acknowledge that what Dante wishes to present in it is not so much a rigid structure of punishment imposed on humanity by divinity but a graphic expression of what the human choice to live in the illusion of independence from God leads to. The *Inferno* can be read along lines similar to those along which the penitent are asked to contemplate the examples of punished vice punctuating the narrative of *Purgatorio*. Like that of the latter, the main purpose of the *Inferno* might ultimately be not judgment but self-reflection. On this view, the purpose of reading the *Inferno* is not finding out who gets punished for what. It is learning about the human—our own—condition. The *Inferno* in this sense represents the sinful recesses of our being, and it displays what the consequences are, in terms of the perversion of human community, if we allow ourselves to live by sin; and Dante invites us to recognize this, as a necessary and constructive process of self-understanding. Without critical self-reflection, we could say, it is impossible to read the *Inferno* as theology. Without critical self-reflection, it is arguably impossible to do any good theology at all.

What Dante says about divine justice at the end of *Inferno* 3—that it manifests in and as human desire, conscience and self-awareness itself—could thus be taken as a key for reading the *Inferno* as a whole. Dante is asking us to read the *Inferno* not simply as a cautionary tale, but as an aid for exploring our inner being and the sinfulness residing therein. Unless we read the *Inferno* in conscious reflection as to how it can help us understand who we are and how we come to be who we are, we will not be engaging with the text in a way that can bring its theology to life. Perhaps, in the latter sense, there is something in the *Inferno* of broader theological relevance. We often see our task as theologians as that of showing others how to think of divinity; and in the process of doing so, we often also thereby try to define what it is to get God "wrong." Perhaps Dante's *Inferno* can help us be more aware of the need to integrate within all this awareness of how *we* get God "wrong."

Whether or not we agree with Dante's specific conceptions of how it is that we can get God "wrong," his poem can be read as a powerful reminder of the importance, in doing theology, not only of the ability to articulate ideas but also of the openness to recognizing how in thought and in action we fail to live by them. We could say that commitment to introspection in action is, in this sense, a necessary spiritual counterpart to commitment to apophaticism in discourse. Hope, from a Dantean perspective, is vital in both: we might say that as hope is the animating energy of apophatic theological discourse, so is hope the animating energy of "infernal" introspection. In both cases, hope is what guards us from presuming that honest recognition of failure is all there is to it. Moreover if, as recognized in the present volume's remit, it might be fruitful to reflect on the relationship between apophaticism and atheism, then it might also be fruitful to reflect on the relationship between atheism and the kind of introspection to which we are invited by Dante's *Inferno*. In this sense, reflecting on varieties of atheism could become also an invitation to reflect more deeply than we are accustomed to on the varieties of ways in which, even in the exercise of theology, we choose to live without God, in a self-centered lack of full hope in the love which gives us being. In this sense, atheism or living without God do coincide with sin, but not as a matter of conceptual definition by which someone who believes in God can judge the atheist as sinful. Rather, atheism or living without God coincides with sin in believers' recognition of their own limitations, and in their awareness that the failure they might wish to call atheism is first and foremost in themselves and needs consciously to be integrated into the dynamic, ongoing and lifelong process that is journeying toward God.[22]

Seen in the latter perspective, the *Inferno* too can indeed be seen as expression of hope. Dante's extraordinary journey through Hell can, from a metaliterary point of view, be seen as his attempt to explore, reflect on, and acknowledge sin while holding on to the hope—for himself and us—that such exploration, reflection, and acknowledgment can coincide with the spiritual goodness that leads toward union with the love that moves the sun and other stars.[23]

ATHEISM AND DANTE'S SPIRITUAL JOURNEY

Nel mezzo del cammin di nostra vita	At one point midway on our path in life,
mi ritrovai per una selva oscura,	I came around and found myself now searching
ché la diritta via era smarrita.	through a dark wood, the right way blurred
(*Inferno* 1.1–3)	and lost.

With this, we are only three lines into the *Commedia*, and no one other than Dante appears to inhabit the scene.[24] Yet the poem already presents us with at least two instances of human encounter. Most sharply, there is the encounter of Dante with himself. "Mi ritrovai": in the dark wood, Dante finds himself again—he (re)awakens to his own humanity. The humanity he finds, though, is not simply his. "Nostra vita": it is in the midst of our life, the life he shares with us, that Dante becomes self-aware. In encountering himself, Dante encounters humanity as a whole.

Dante encounters himself as lost. Not the easiest of beginnings. Yet already, in itself, progress. To know oneself as lost is already to know one could, in principle, be otherwise. Immediately after telling us how deathlike his experience of the dark wood is—even in memory alone (*Inferno* 1.4–7)—Dante informs us that

... per trattar del ben ch'i' vi trovai,	since my theme will be the good I found there,
dirò de l'altre cose ch'i' v'ho scorte.	I mean to speak of other things I saw.
(*Inferno* 1.8–9)	

In the *Comedy* Dante essentially wishes to speak of goodness: not lost humanity, but humanity encountering the good anew. Dante's telling us this refines our perception of the human encounters with which the poem opens. The Dante who finds himself at the beginning of the *Comedy* is not just the character who awakens in the dark wood. It is also the poet, who by fashioning himself as character enters into a journey of conscious self-discovery, toward goodness. And in his wish to invite his readers to share in this journey, the humanity Dante encounters apart from his in doing so is not just a general, abstract one, but the particular one of each individual human being who reads the *Comedy*. It is also my humanity, and yours.

Having awakened to his and our humanity, Dante is able to start journeying out of the dark wood (*Inferno* 1.10–48). He starts ascending a hill, whose summit is illuminated by the rays of the sun. Progress is impeded, however, by the sudden appearance of three beasts. The pilgrim's first encounter with other living creatures in the *Comedy* is not with human beings. He is still with no immediate human company other than his own. Indeed, whatever their particular allegorical meaning, the beasts can be seen as externalizing metaphorically the inner dispositions of character that prevent from Dante making progress on his journey toward divinity, symbolized by the sun.

Next, Dante gives us an image as theologically significant as anything else offered us in the poem. To describe his feelings at the prospect of having to retrace his footsteps toward darkness because of the third beast, Dante tells us:

Ed una lupa, che di tutte brame	And then a wolf. And she who, seemingly,
sembiava carca ne la sua magrezza,	was gaunt yet gorged on every kind of craving—
e molte genti fé già viver grame,	and had already blighted many a life—
questa mi porse tanto di gravezza	so heavily oppressed my thought with fears,
con la paura ch'uscia di sua vista,	which spurted even at the sight of her,
ch'io perdei la speranza de l'altezza.	I lost all hope of reaching to those heights.
E qual è quei che volontieri acquista,	We all so willingly record our gains,
e giugne 'l tempo che perder lo face,	until the hour that leads us into loss.
che 'n tutti suoi pensier piange e s'attrista;	Then every single thought is tears and sadness.
tal mi fece la bestia sanza pace,	So, now, with me. That brute which knows no peace
che, venendomi 'ncontro, a poco a poco	came ever nearer me and, step by step,
mi ripigneva là dove 'l sol tace. (*Inferno* 1.49–60)	drove me back down to where the sun is mute.

The ambiguity of "sanza pace"—is it a reference to Dante or the she-wolf?—enhances the significance of the she-wolf as metaphorical externalization of Dante's inner character. This, in turn, enriches the significance of the image of the greedy man that follows. Dante, here, is doing nothing less than setting out the central theological principle underlying the exploration of the relationship between humanity and divinity presented in the

Comedy. The image reveals the reason Dante is unable to go beyond the beasts is that he does not properly understand how God relates to God's creation. At the beginning of his journey Dante is thinking of the summit of the hill, and the possibility it symbolizes of being at one with the divine, as one would of a material possession: a thing, object, or idea a human being can desire, reach, acquire, and possess—and consequently lose. Dante is thinking of God as part of creation, as being merely one of the things that are. This is not what God is. If it were, God could not have created all there is ex nihilo. And this, as Dante will learn on his journey, would be a contradiction. If one is not thinking of the ground of all existence, itself not existing in any particular way but, as being itself, bringing and sustaining everything into existence, one is simply not thinking of God, no matter whatever else one holds about particular aspects of divinity.

Inferno 1.49–60 offers us a precise diagnosis of Dante's spiritual ills. He is yet to properly configure his self in relation to divinity. The divine is here seen as a possession; and the self is still at the center of the self's own world, in the illusion of self-definition and self-subsistence: it does not conceive of divinity as its own existence.[25] God is there to reach but not to be. Which is to say that the self is still living in pride, yet to undergo the radical decentering of self entailed by humility, whereby one sees what is other than oneself—and ultimately God—not as something to possess but as source of meaning and life. To reach such humility, another kind of journey is needed than that which the pilgrim initially attempts to undertake.

Dante is thus famously rescued by Virgil, who tells him he needs to follow him and later Beatrice, on a journey that will bring him to encounter the damned, the penitent, and the blessed—to consider, that is, how other human beings have either failed or succeeded in living in proper relationship with God (*Inferno* 1.61–136). This is vital: it suggests that ultimately, for Dante, there is an inextricable connection between relating to God and encountering other human beings, and that exploring this interconnection is necessary for understanding human creatureliness. And this, in turn, reveals why Dante might have chosen to do theology in and through a literary text, a narrative poem telling the story of such a journey.

Dante has to be guided and the journey is to be communal—toward increasingly penetrating insight into the dynamics of human interaction as seen in the light of divinity. What I believe to be particularly interesting in the context of the present collection is the extent to which what Dante describes in *Inferno* 1.49–60 can be seen as a variety of atheism. In other words, and in the light of the reflections offered in previous sections of the present chapter, to what extent is the beginning of Dante's spiritual journey in the *Comedy* characterized by lack of hope, or the choice to live without

God? And related to this, to what extent does the *Comedy* thus suggest that reflection on this variety of atheism is a fundamental theological underpinning to reflection on spiritual journeying more broadly conceived?

These questions are not meant to suggest, simplistically, that atheism is something to overcome so as to get spiritual journeying properly under way. They are meant, rather, to suggest that atheism and spiritual journeying might be more intimately connected than we often think.[26] From perspectives offered by Dante's *Comedy*, atheism might be seen not simply as the explicit rejection of belief, but as coinciding with forms of thought, perception, and action that amount to the choice of living without God, whatever one explicitly professes to believe in. Much as a rigorous apophaticism can help theological discourse avoid idolatry, rigorous introspective reflection on the various ways in which we choose to live without God can help us avoid pride in spiritual journeying. In connection to both, reflection on atheism can help sharpen in honesty our understanding of ourselves and our relationship with divinity.

The latter is, of course, a conclusion an atheist might well want to reject. The Dantean focus on hope as the distinctive energy of Christian belief, however, might enrich the debate by offering Christian theologians further resources for recognizing affinities with atheism, and atheists further resources, as the original description of the project on which the present volume is based puts it, for conceiving transcendence within the immanent frame of modernity, especially, perhaps, as regards not conceptual debate but inter-relationality, and the extent to which in our interactions we embody or fail to embody hope, humility, love.

NOTES

I am profoundly grateful to David Newheiser, George Pattison, Regina Schwartz, Susannah Ticciati, and Denys Turner for conversation and inspiration in the preparation of the paper originally prepared for the conference on which the present volume is based. I am equally grateful for the inspiration provided by conversations at the conference itself. I refer explicitly in the present chapter to some aspects of this, but I also wish to acknowledge here a debt that is broader than the space available allows me to explicitly acknowledge. What is presented in this chapter originally grows out of work I have been carrying out for a monograph provisionally entitled *Goodness and Hell: The Theology of Dante's* Inferno. This in turn builds on Vittorio Montemaggi, *Reading Dante's* Commedia *as Theology: Divinity Realized in Human Encounter* (New York: Oxford University Press, 2016). Some portions of the present chapter follow closely prologue 1 and chapter 2.9–10 of the latter; readers can refer to these and the book more broadly for wider bibliographical reference than I am able to provide here. For the questions animating my current project, I am indebted especially to Rowan Williams, "Meet the Author: An Unusually Personal Account of the World View behind Dante's Masterpiece," *Times Literary Supplement*, September 15, 2017, https://www.the-tls.co.uk/articles/dantes-commedia-rowan-williams-theology/.

1. See, e.g., George Corbett, *Dante and Epicurus: A Dualistic Vision of Secular and Spiritual Fulfilment* (Oxford, UK: Legenda, 2013).
2. As far as Dante himself is concerned, what *Inferno* 10 seems to dramatize, in the encounter between the pilgrim and Farinata degli Uberti and Cavalcante dei Cavalcanti, is that it is politics and poetry that most run the risk of generating an attachment to worldly matters so strong as to draw all attention away from spiritual journeying. Later, especially in the encounter between Dante and Beatrice in *Purgatorio* 30–31, we learn also that the attraction of Beatrice's earthly beauty was so strong for Dante as to almost definitively distract him from recognition of her immortality and from belief in Resurrection.
3. For further reflection on Dante's apophaticism, see Vittorio Montemaggi, "In Unknowability as Love: The Theology of Dante's Commedia," in *Dante's Commedia: Theology as Poetry*, ed. Vittorio Montemaggi and Matthew Treherne (Notre Dame, IN: University of Notre Dame Press, 2010), 60–94.
4. For reflection on hope from a contemporary perspective, see David Newheiser, *Hope in a Secular Age: Deconstruction, Negative Theology and the Future of Faith* (Cambridge: Cambridge University Press, 2019).
5. I am especially grateful to Alda Balthrop-Lewis for helping me see, through her response to my paper at the conference, the broader implications of this idea. In particular, Balthrop-Lewis's response highlighted the need for more detailed reflection, on the one hand, on the relationship between "living without God" atheism and sin, and on the other hand, on "living without God" atheism as an integral part of fruitful spiritual journeying. Although I hope that the present chapter already presents an improvement in these respects relative to the paper presented at the conference, these are indeed matters that would deserve further, more detailed reflection.
6. See also the chapter by Susannah Ticciati in the present volume.
7. See especially *Paradiso* 19–20.
8. Kenelm Foster, "The Theology of the *Inferno*," in *God's Tree: Essays on Dante and Other Matters* (London: Blackfriars Publications, 1957), 50–66.
9. See also the essay by Devin Singh in the present volume.
10. The text of the *Commedia* is cited following Dante Alighieri, *Commedia*, ed. Anna Maria Chiavacci Leonardi, 3 vols. (Milan: Mondadori, 1991–1997).
11. Translations are taken from Dante Alighieri, *The Divine Comedy*, trans. Robin Kirkpatrick, 3 vols. (London: Penguin, 2006–2007).
12. It is important to clarify, relative to the question of pride addressed below, that Beatrice is not saying that Dante has more hope than anyone else, but that at the moment, no one has more hope than Dante—in other words, that there could be someone out there now with as much hope as Dante, and that there could be someone at other times with more hope than him.
13. See *Purgatorio* 10–12, especially in the light of *Purgatorio* 13.136–38.
14. It is significant, in connection with the question of pride, to note the use of *esperto*, expert, in *Paradiso* 25.65—a term used elsewhere in the *Comedy* to refer

only either to paradigmatically proud figures (Ulysses and Nembrot—respectively in *Inferno* 26.98 and 31.91) or to the dynamics of Dante's own sacred journey (in *Purgatorio* 1.132 and 2.62).

15. In this sense, hope and humility seem to be presented by Dante as counterbalancing the limitations inherent in his pride, and as related to this in the violence and vengefulness that his poetry, especially in the *Inferno* but also in the *Purgatorio* and the *Paradiso*, seems so strongly to direct against other human beings and against other religious traditions and forms of Christianity different from his own. I am grateful for the advice offered by colleagues on this question in discussions at the conference on which this volume is based. See also Montemaggi, *Reading Dante's* Commedia, chap. 3.

16. George Pattison, "Love, Being and Things to Come," unpublished paper shared with author. See also George Pattison, *A Metaphysics of Love: A Philosophy of Christian Life, Part 3* (Oxford: Oxford University Press, 2021), especially chap. 2.

17. See especially *Inferno* 1.8.

18. It might indeed be possible to read Dante's *Inferno* as evidence of Dante's belief not in the rigidity of hell, but in its provisionality, and certainly in the provisionality of all human statements presuming to see into divine judgment, such as the *Comedy* itself. In this respect, it would be important to consider how *Inferno* 20 might be interpreted in the light of *Purgatorio* 20 and *Paradiso* 20. It would also be important consider the figure of Virgil, the theological significance of which has not yet been studied fully in the depth it deserves. See Montemaggi, *Reading Dante's* Commedia *as Theology*, chap. 3.5–10. See also Thomas Graff, "Virgil the Theologian," *Le tre corone* 7 (2020): 119–32; James Wetzel, "A Meditation on Hell: Lessons from Dante," *Modern Theology* 18, no. 3 (2002): 375–94.

19. See especially *Paradiso* 20.94–117.

20. See especially the figures of Cato (*Purgatorio* 1–2) and Ripheus and Trajan (*Paradiso* 20).

21. Denys Turner, *Julian of Norwich, Theologian* (New Haven, CT: Yale University Press, 2011), 92.

22. A fuller treatment of these questions would need to take into account the important perspectives opened up by *Paradiso* 8–9, which present the view that, from the perspective of beatitude, sins are no longer seen as sins but as part of the goodness that has led one to God. See especially *Paradiso* 9.31–36, 103–8.

23. I am grateful to David Ford, Deborah Ford, and Loraine Gelsthorpe for our ongoing exploration of how in these respects the spiritual journey presented by the *Comedy* might resonate with the psychological journey of therapy.

24. As Nicholas Adams pointed out in discussion of these lines at the conference on which this volume is based, the opening of Dante's *Comedy* can be an illuminating point of reference for theological and metaphysical reflection that values acknowledgment of the importance of recognizing that human reflection always begins "in the middle" and cannot presume to obtain more privileged points of view. See also Nicholas Lash, "Anselm Seeking," in *The Beginning and the End of "Religion"* (Cambridge: Cambridge University Press, 1996), 150–63.

25. Compare *Purgatorio* 17.106–11.

26. For reflection on some of the wider implications of this idea, see Vittorio Montemaggi, "How to Say 'Thank You': Reflecting on the Work of Primo Levi," in *Desire, Faith, and the Darkness of God: Essays in Honor of Denys Turner*, ed. Eric

Bugyis and David Newheiser (Notre Dame, IN: University of Notre Dame Press, 2015), 367–90.

REFERENCES

Alighieri, Dante. *Commedia*. Edited by Anna Maria Chiavacci Leonardi. 3 vols. Milan: Mondadori, 1991–1997.
———. *The Divine Comedy*. Translated by Robin Kirkpatrick. 3 vols. London: Penguin, 2006–2007.
Corbett, George. *Dante and Epicurus: A Dualistic Vision of Secular and Spiritual Fulfilment*. Oxford, UK: Legenda, 2013.
Foster, Kenelm. "The Theology of the *Inferno*." In *God's Tree: Essays on Dante and Other Matters*, 50–66. London: Blackfriars Publications, 1957.
Graff, Thomas. "Virgil the Theologian." *Le tre corone* 7 (2020): 119–32.
Lash, Nicholas. "Anselm Seeking." In *The Beginning and the End of "Religion,"* 150–63. Cambridge: Cambridge University Press, 1996.
Montemaggi, Vittorio. "How to Say 'Thank You': Reflecting on the Work of Primo Levi." In *Desire, Faith, and the Darkness of God: Essays in Honor of Denys Turner*, edited by Eric Bugyis and David Newheiser, 367–90. Notre Dame, IN: University of Notre Dame Press, 2015.
———. "In Unknowability as Love: The Theology of Dante's Commedia." In *Dante's Commedia: Theology as Poetry*, edited by Vittorio Montemaggi and Matthew Treherne, 60–94. Notre Dame, IN: University of Notre Dame Press, 2010.
———. *Reading Dante's* Commedia *as Theology: Divinity Realized in Human Encounter*. New York: Oxford University Press, 2016.
Newheiser, David. *Hope in a Secular Age: Deconstruction, Negative Theology and the Future of Faith*. Cambridge: Cambridge University Press, 2019.
Pattison, George. *A Metaphysics of Love: A Philosophy of Christian Life, Part 3*. Oxford: Oxford University Press, 2021.
Turner, Denys. *Julian of Norwich, Theologian*. New Haven, CT: Yale University Press, 2011.
Wetzel, James. "A Meditation on Hell: Lessons from Dante." *Modern Theology* 18, no. 3 (2002): 375–94.
Williams, Rowan. "Meet the Author: An Unusually Personal Account of the World View behind Dante's Masterpiece." *Times Literary Supplement*, September 15, 2017. https://www.the-tls.co.uk/articles/dantes-commedia-rowan-williams-theology/.

8

ATHEISM AND THE AFFIRMATION OF LIFE

Dostoevsky's Response to Russian Nihilism

George Pattison

"If God does not exist, then everything is permitted." Citing these words from *The Brothers Karamazov*, Jean-Paul Sartre declared them to be "existentialism's point of departure."[1] As he further explained, there is no source of meaning or value apart from human freedom, a situation he referred to as our "abandonment." There is no God and no eternal human nature or essence. Consequently, there is no theological, biological, or historical determinism to prescribe what we should do to ease the burden of having to choose and to accept responsibility for who we are—all of which, in Sartre's view, is integral to the meaning of atheism. However, it is striking that Sartre ascribes these words directly to Dostoevsky, without pausing to note that they are in fact the words of a fictional character, Ivan Karamazov, who is presented in the novel as a morally flawed and mentally unstable personality. Furthermore, in thus making Dostoevsky a spokesman for existentialist atheism, Sartre seems entirely to ignore the critical view, today perhaps the majority critical view, that sees Dostoevsky's writings and, in particular, *The Brothers Karamazov*, as having a strongly Christian tendency.[2]

Yet Sartre's oversight (if that is what it is) is understandable. As a standalone piece of writing, "Rebellion," the chapter from which the quotation comes, could very plausibly serve as an exemplary text for the protest atheism of the twentieth century. Ivan's ruthless presentation of the sufferings inflicted upon children by war, by unjust social conditions, and even by their parents, is painful to read (not least since the examples are all drawn from life), and any merely intellectual response seems not just inadequate but offensive. Who would want to worship a God who allowed such things? The radical 1960s theologian William Hamilton is only one who finds Ivan's protest unanswerable. Contrasting the characters of Ivan and Alyosha (Dostoevsky's "religious" hero), Hamilton comments that we are "unable to receive Alyosha" but "we can all receive Ivan with a terrible kind of delight. He is a true gift to us all, perhaps Dostoyevsky's supreme gift. Ivan's picture of himself we immediately recognize as a self-portrait; the God that is dead for him is dead for us."[3]

Nevertheless, the part of the novel in which Ivan's "rebellion" is presented is entitled "Pro et Contra," indicating that there is at least another side of the picture that must be taken into account. Certainly, what Dostoevsky offers is not a direct answer to Ivan, although the evidence of his letters is that he believed the novel as a whole did indeed provide such an answer. Yet since Bakhtin drew attention to the polyphonic nature of Dostoevsky's novels, readers have been alert to the fact that Dostoevsky's own views are typically hidden behind the complex and multisided interplay of other views set out in the novels. What is crucial to appraising these is that Dostoevsky refuses to separate the intellectual positions and lifeviews of his characters from their overall personal existence. To take up a position for or against God is not simply to make a metaphysical judgment. It is also to reveal something about oneself. However, we should immediately add that Dostoevsky is too good a novelist to have all the bad characters be atheists and all the good characters be Christians. Not only are key characters themselves split between belief and unbelief, sensuousness and holiness, and good and evil, but the entanglement of atheism and faith in the dynamics of human personality is itself a fundamental premise of Dostoevsky's account of human being. As he several times acknowledged, his own faith was the product of the "crucible of doubt" that was an ineluctable feature of nineteenth-century culture. In this regard, Dostoevsky's critical analysis of atheism is not simply a "Christian" response to the atheism that he encountered "out there" in his contemporary world. Rather, it is the record of a struggle with his own atheism "within." This essay, then, is offered not as the exposition of an exemplary Christian answer to atheism but as an exploration of what it meant for an existentially oriented thinker to struggle with the pros and contras of atheism and Christianity in the context of nineteenth-century Russia. But as the opening reference to Sartre indicates, the significance of Dostoevsky's struggle was not limited to his own time and place. In his own way, he sketched out some of the defining points and fundamental lines of demarcation that have remained more or less constantly in play ever since, and in this sense, his struggle and his response can be taken as exemplary beyond the limits of his own writings.

AN EXISTENTIAL APPROACH

At several points in this chapter I note instructive resonances between Dostoevsky's work and that of his slightly older Danish contemporary, Søren Kierkegaard. The first of these is that, like Kierkegaard (whose work he did not know), Dostoevsky thought that what is most important about us cannot be decided by objective factors alone. Understanding being human is a matter not of "what" human beings are but of "how" they are in their existence. However, unlike Kierkegaard (as he is conventionally understood), Dostoevsky did not see this solely as a matter for the individual subject but as something that gets worked out in the complex and therefore untidy processes of intersubjective life, inclusive of how we are in our family relationships, our preferential loves, and our relations to the wider community, from the neighborhood to the nation and even the international order.

Given the primacy of the subjective (or intersubjective), it is therefore entirely consistent that neither Dostoevsky nor his characters are really interested in the kind of proofs or disproofs of the existence of God that are the standard fare of philosophy of religion textbooks.[4] Those who want such things must look away now. Perhaps the nearest we get to a rationalistic argument is that offered by Smerdyakov, the illegitimate and unacknowledged Karamazov brother who lives as his father's servant. Smerdyakov is barely educated and is mockingly referred to by his father as "Balaam's ass," but he takes pleasure in pointing out the illogicalities of Scripture and dogma. Thus, his argument against the account of creation in Genesis 1 is that since God only created the sun, moon, and stars on the fourth day there could not have been any light on the first day.[5] Other characters too, including the depraved Karamazov père, mock the literalism of Scripture and popular belief. On this point (if only on this point), it seems they have the author on their side, since he too resists what we might call supernaturalist materialism, parodying its manifestations in the crazed monk Ferapont who sees little horned devils everywhere and slams doors on them so as to pinch their tails.[6] As the Devil himself says to Ivan Karamazov: "Proofs are no help to believing, especially material proofs. Thomas believed not because he saw Christ risen but because he wanted to believe before he saw."[7] It is for such reasons that not only the Devil but Dostoevsky himself seem committed to a broadly existentialist approach.

GOD AND IMMORTALITY

It is important to note at the outset that, for Dostoevsky, the question of God is inseparable from the question of personal immortality, that is, the question regarding human beings' ultimate destiny. Today, this conjunction is often overlooked, but it is of fundamental significance in Christian apologetics and in philosophical debates about the meaning of Christianity throughout the early modern and modern eras. When Kant links freedom, immortality, and God as three fundamental ideas of reason that cannot be demonstrated but only postulated (and that reason obliges us to postulate), he is not making a merely random connection but reflecting the logic of the debate in his time. Kierkegaard too makes this a defining element In his response to the Hegelian idealism. As he sees it, Hegelianism's inability to say anything about the ultimate destiny of the individual human subject exposes the deeply unsatisfactory character of its representation of Christianity.[8] At the same time, we can see that the reinterpretation of traditional Christian eschatology by a kind of realized eschatology in which the meaning of immortality is glossed in terms of a here-and-now participation in the cosmic whole is a typical mark of revisionist theologies, starting with Schleiermacher.[9] If Ivan's rebellion anticipates later protest atheism, then Dostoevsky's treatment of immortality goes right to the heart of the debates of his own time.

It is this conjunction of topics (God-immortality, atheism-extinction) that comes to expression in the climactic moment in *The Brothers Karamazov*, when the body of the saintly Elder Zosima starts to rot. In the context of the monastic culture in which Alyosha (the youngest Karamazov brother and a devoted follower of the Elder) participates, this seems powerful evidence that whatever Zosima's merits, they extend only to this life. Consequently, his mutation into a mere corpse falsifies the faith that he taught in life.

The view that even Christ was powerless against death similarly shatters the will to live of another Dostoievskian teenager, the nihilist Ippolit (in *The Idiot*). Like the eponymous idiot, Prince Myshkin, Ippolit is fascinated by Holbein's painting of the dead Christ, a painting that shows the corpse of the Savior without any religious or consolatory aura. "The question instinctively arises," he tells his listeners, that "if death is so awful and the laws of nature so mighty, how can they be overcome? How can they be overcome when even he did not conquer them, He who vanquished nature in his lifetime."[10] In such a picture, as he goes on to say, nature shows itself as "a huge machine of the most modern construction which, dull and insensible, has aimlessly clutched, crushed and swallowed up a great priceless Being, a Being worth all nature and its laws, worth the whole earth, which was created perhaps solely for the sake of the advent of that Being."[11] Ippolit is himself dying of tuberculosis and this leads him to conclude that, given the prospect of entire extinction, the pain of living is no longer worth enduring and he resolves on suicide.

Although this chapter largely keeps to the evidence of the novels, it is relevant to note that the question had a particular urgency for Dostoevsky himself, and not only in connection with the experience of facing imminent death after being sentenced to execution by firing squad. Perhaps even more significant are the reflections he jotted down on April 16, 1864, after the death of his first wife, a bereavement deeply colored by the preceding breakdown of their relationship, in which, whatever her faults, Dostoevsky knew himself to have behaved very badly. Such a situation understandably led him to reflect on whether they would ever see each other again, that is, whether, in the face of their failed relationship, there could be any hope for a future reconciliation. The prospect of a future heavenly union in Christ is, he writes, "the final goal of mankind," and he argues, "if at the attainment of the goal everything is extinguished and disappears," then the goal itself is "senseless." "Consequently," he concludes, "there is a future, heavenly life."[12] The argument, such as it is, seems broadly Kantian, and it may fall far short of persuasiveness. But while we shall say more about this passage in terms of the ultimate vision guiding Dostoevsky's thought, we note it for now simply as a marker regarding what, for him, was the necessary entanglement of the question of God with the question of immortality.

All that being said, Dostoevsky no more breaks the limits of the realist narrative world of his novels with regard to immortality than with regard to God. To the extent that we are allowed to glimpse a heavenly world opening up beyond this one, it is only revealed in dreams (like Alyosha's dream by the dead body of Zosima), in grotesque parodies (as in the story "Bobok," in which the narrator overhears the recently deceased talking in their coffins), or in avowed make-believe (as in the story "Christ's Christmas Tree"). The novels do not "show" the immortality that Dostoevsky believed would make sense of human life and that was integral to the meaning of faith in Christ. What they do show are the attitudes toward such a heavenly life on the part of their various dramatis personae and what believing, doubting, or disbelieving might mean.

BASIC TRUST

As I have noted, it is by no means the case that Dostoevsky straightforwardly aligns goodness with faith and badness with atheism. It is not that there is no correlation. There is a succession of characters, typically aristocrats, whose lack of faith, coupled with the lack of any need for productive work, brings about a state of boredom that can only be alleviated by vice and crime. Such are the figures of Prince Valkovsky (*The Insulted and the Injured*), Svidrigailov (*Crime and Punishment*), Versilov (*A Raw Youth*), and Stavrogin (*The Possessed*). However, the connection is not directly causal, and even among these there are indications of other impulses, such as rumors of Versilov's asceticism. On the opposite side we see characters of extreme moral depravity who, nevertheless, show at least the rudiments of faith. Perhaps the most striking example of this is the escaped convict Fedka in *The Possessed*. Fedka is an apparently remorseless killer, ready to kill for money. One of his victims is the simpleton Maria Lebyadkina, an entirely inoffensive character who even has something of the holy fool about her. Not only that, but he also desecrates an icon of the Mother of God, a sacrilege that, in the Orthodox milieu of the novel, is perhaps even more outrageous than homicide. However, explaining himself to Peter Verkhovensky, organizer of a circle of violent nihilists, Fedka claims that this doesn't indicate lack of faith:

> D'you see Pyotr Stepanovitch, I tell you truly that I have stripped the icons, but I only took out the pearls; and how do you know? Perhaps my own tear was transformed into a pearl in the furnace of the Most High to make up for my sufferings, seeing I am just that very orphan, having no daily refuge. Do you know from the books that once, in ancient times, a merchant with just such tearful sighs and prayers stole a pearl from the halo of the Mother of God, and afterwards, in the face of all the people, laid the whole price of it at her feet, and the Holy Mother sheltered him with her mantle before all the people.[13]

Fedka epitomizes an attitude that Dostoevsky encountered among the peasant convicts he got to know in prison, an attitude that, "beyond good and evil" and against all expectation, retains faith in divine mercy. It is an attitude reflected also in the way that local people referred to the convicts as "unfortunates," despite the evidence of their sometimes heinous crimes. Another example from the novels is the repulsive drunkard Marmeladov. Marmeladov's alcoholism has led to his loss of employment, the ruin of his family, and his daughter Sonya being sent to work the streets to support her mother and siblings. He is depicted as entirely the author of his own misfortunes. Yet Marmeladov, too, though no peasant, shares Fedka's hope in an economy of divine mercy beyond all moral calculation. When Christ comes again, he will not only call the righteous to himself; he will also call those, like him, who are "swine, made in the Image of the Beast and with his mark."[14] Moral degradation and faith, it seems, are not incompatible.

If faith can in this way coexist with moral and personal degradation, what difference, then, does it actually make?

Let us return to Ippolit. Ippolit's situation is pitiable. He is only seventeen or eighteen and dying of consumption. We have heard how he interprets Holbein's "Dead Christ" as epitomizing the ultimate triumph of death and how this leads him to regard suicide as the only real option. Before taking this step, however, he delivers a long speech setting out his "last testament," which he intends to finish with a public self-execution. But although he tries to present his position as a matter of rational deduction, he also confesses to "bad dreams." In one of these he becomes aware of a hideous scorpionlike monster in his room, which, when his dog tries to bite it, stings its tongue: "and I saw that the creature, though bitten in two, was still wriggling in her mouth, and was emitting from its crushed body on to the dog's tongue, a quantity of white fluid such as comes out of a squashed black beetles."[15] In another, the blind power that has destroyed Christ becomes "a huge and loathsome spider."[16] These are only two of the elements in Ippolit's lengthy testament that show how, beneath the façade of defiance, he is, in reality, desperately afraid—afraid not only of his impending death but also of a life that, as Heidegger (also a Dostoevsky reader) will put it, is thrown toward death.

So too in the case of Ivan Karamazov. In his "Rebellion," he batters Alyosha with a litany of cases of extreme cruelty to children, telling his devout brother that if this is what the world God has made is like, then no future harmony and no future forgiveness could possibly be worth the price demanded of life's innocent victims. It's not that he doesn't believe in God, he tells Alyosha, it's just that he "returns the ticket" (although in other scenes he acknowledges that, in his view, God does not exist nor is there an immortal life). At the same time, as he also tells Alyosha in the same conversation, he has an animal love of life that, he expects, will keep him going through the remainder of his youth. But when that animal desire fades, so will his own will to live. In other words, Ivan has no belief in the value of life, including his own life, over and above the physical instinct of survival. No less importantly, the progression of the novel shows that he is unwilling to accept the implications of his own hypothesis that if God doesn't exist, then everything is permitted, and for all his supposed love of life, he is unable to acknowledge his love for the beautiful Katerina Ivanovna. The cumulative pressure of the tension between his intellectual image of himself and the demands of life lead, in the end, to his complete breakdown.

A third case we might cite here is that of Anastasia Philippovna (*The*

Idiot). Anastasia had been sexually exploited by her custodian from childhood and, at the start of the novel, is about to be married off to avoid scandal. At the same time, another man, the violent Rogozhin, has become desperately infatuated with her and makes to steal her away from the designated husband and elope with her. Into this situation comes the novel's main character, the (almost) Christlike Prince Myshkin. He too is awestruck by her beauty, and he too offers her his hand; but in his case, what he offers is simple acceptance, based on his firm insight into her essential innocence—despite the circumstances that, in the novel, make her the epitome of a femme fatale. The resulting action sprawls across a multitude of chaotic relationships, but in the end it is impossible for Anastasia to accept the acceptance being offered by the Prince, and, jilting him at the altar, she goes with Rogozhin, knowing that in doing so she is going to her death. As femme fatale, she is a character who repeatedly scandalizes and terrifies many of those who come into contact with her. Yet what Dostoevsky lets us see is that, to borrow the title of another novel that deals with the sexual exploitation of children, she is one of those "insulted and injured" whose faith in the possibility of life offering anything good has been destroyed by the abuse they have suffered.[17] Unlike the male intellectuals, Ippolit and Ivan, Anastasia does not debate the existence of God, but her rejection of God is, in effect, to be inferred from her rejection of the forgiveness offered by the Prince.[18]

In these and many other Dostoievskian characters the root of atheism is not a set of intellectual beliefs about metaphysical states of affairs or historical facts but a psychological failure in the face of life and its demands. Here too we can see an instructive parallel to Kierkegaard, who, in *The Sickness unto Death*, distinguishes between what he calls the despair of defiance and the despair of weakness. The former is characterized as the will to be the self one chooses to be in despite of all circumstances, and the latter as the unwillingness to be the self that one is.[19] The despair of defiance maps fairly closely onto what, in his time, was often referred to as "Byronism" but would also be manifest in, for example, the atheism of Sartre and other modernist thinkers who regard human beings as capable of an unrestricted autonomy. Kierkegaard himself offers reasons for thinking that this kind of despair may ultimately be a mask for weakness. Behind the bravado, he suspects, is a fear of taking life on its own terms (which, of course, include cognitive limitations, moral fallibility, and mortality). Whatever Kierkegaard's view, however, each of Ippolit, Ivan, and Anastasia can be seen as illustrating just such a logic. Behind the acts and words of defiance, we see an incapacity to embrace their own lives in the concrete circumstances in which these are given them. In terms made popular by the psychologist Erik H. Erikson, it is a failure of "basic trust," a capacity that Erikson sees as the most basic stage of social trust established or failing to be established in the early stages of infancy. Erikson himself connects this to religion, stating, "Trust born of care is, in fact, the touchstone of the actuality of a given religion," and in his *Does God Exist?* Hans Küng has developed Erikson's argument as the basic element in a new apologetic.[20]

Now this may seem to move the criticism of atheism onto very unstable ground, as it seems to concede precisely what many atheists, including Freud, have argued, namely, that religious belief can be explained—and therefore explained away—in terms of childhood psychological development. However, what Dostoevsky's analyses invite us to consider is that the opposite might also be true—that it is not the believer who manifests a basic psychological malfunction but the unbeliever, the one incapable of a basic affirmation of life, in its entirety and as a whole. This, of course, says nothing and is not intended to say anything about the metaphysics of belief, but in a human and psychological perspective, it levels the playing field between religion and its critics. At the same time it also helps us to see the logic in the "faith" of a Fedka, because like the other Russian peasants whose faithful hearts are many times praised by Dostoevsky, what he manifests is just such a basic trust in life, recuperable from beneath the debris of all that has subsequently gone wrong.

GOD OR LIFE?

How does this struggle to achieve or to hold on to basic trust relate to the question of God? Even if we are persuaded by his examples that the atheists Dostoevsky depicts are afflicted by a deep psychological impairment and that this also contributes to shaping the particular form that their atheism takes, it may seem that the question of God is scarcely addressed. It is not just that there is neither metaphysics nor historical inquiry regarding the foundations of Christian faith to be found, but that what is being proposed is less a matter of "God" and more a matter of, quite simply "life." And if Dostoevsky's characters are "converted," then it seems that they are much more likely to find "life" than to find "God." Many readers of *Crime and Punishment* (though not all) are disappointed by the apparent sentimentality of the epilogue, in which the defiant Raskolnikov, who has wanted to raise himself "above all trembling creatures" and overstep the bounds of all moral and social norms, falls weeping at the feet of the Virgin-like figure of Sonya. Yet Dostoevsky himself does not describe this as a conversion to God, but succinctly comments that "instead of dialectics there was life."[21]

Is Dostoevsky himself, then, offering us a purely immanent faith, "a new religion of life," to borrow Don Cupitt's eloquent phrase?[22]

Certainly, it seems that Dostoevsky could not endorse any kind of belief that did not involve an affirmation of life. Like Ippolit, the Elder Zosima's brother Markel is a teenager, dying of consumption. Also like Ippolit, Markel is initially presented as a nihilist but, unlike him, undergoes a deathbed conversion. This conversion is strongly marked by a transformed attitude to the natural world. Looking out into the spring garden outside his window, he asks even the birds to forgive him. "There was so much of God's glory around me," he says, "birds, trees, meadows, sky, and I alone lived in shame, I alone dishonoured everything, and did not notice the beauty and glory of it all."[23] Later, Zosima himself starts to go down a path of worldly dissolution, until, as he sets out to fight a duel, he suddenly realizes the brutality of his behavior. "I stood as if dazed," he tells us, "and the sun was shining, the leaves were rejoicing, glistening, and the birds, the birds were praising God."[24] As a religious teacher he urges his fellow monks to "love all of God's creation, both the whole of it and every grain of sand. Love every leaf, every ray of God's light. Love animals, love plants, love each thing. If you love each thing, you will perceive the mystery of God in things."[25] Markel was right, he says, to ask forgiveness of the birds, "for all is like an ocean, all flows and connects; touch it in one place and it echoes at the other end of the world."[26] We are to ask God not for faith but for gladness—"Be glad as children, as birds in the sky."[27] And if our eyes were truly open, we would see that the interconnectedness of life extends beyond earth to other worlds and to the heavenly world itself, since "the roots of our thoughts and feelings are not here but in other worlds." This world is a kind of garden, planted by God with seeds from other worlds, and our life in the world "lives and grows only through its sense of being in touch with other mysterious worlds; if this sense is weakened or destroyed in you, that which has grown up in you dies. Then you become indifferent to life, and even come to hate it. So I think."[28] Zosima therefore urges his listeners to love the earth: "Love to throw yourself down on the earth and kiss it. Kiss the earth and love it, tirelessly, insatiably, love all men, love all things, seek this rapture and ecstasy, treasure it, for it is a gift from God, a great gift, and it is not given to many, but to those who are chosen."[29]

Intellectually, the view being developed here resonates with the doctrine of all-unity promoted by Dostoevsky's friend, the philosopher Vladimir Solovyov.[30] Consideration of this doctrine would take us away from our main theme, but it does allow us to clarify two points. The first is that (in this regard opposed to Kierkegaard), the question of immortality is not limited to the question of individual "survival" as a center of self-conscious existence. Instead, immortality is inseparable from the individual's continuing participation in the larger synthesis of all-unity. Dostoevsky's anguished question as to whether he will see his wife again is modulated into a question as to whether they will both have some part in this larger synthesis. In this regard, Dostoevsky himself would seem to come close to the theological revisionists.[31] The second is that it provides a framework for understanding the interconnection between our attitude to life and our attitude to God. Faith in God is not turning away from the world, as both critics of Christianity such as Nietzsche and many devout Christians themselves have supposed. Affirmation of life in the world may fall short of entire faith in God, but it is a necessary condition of such faith in its authentic rendition. However, if this provides a criterion by which to engage in the criticism of religion (and Dostoevsky himself uses it in this way, as in the depiction of Ferapont's life-denying asceticism), it also has implications for the understanding of atheism. The key point is not simply that atheism denies God but that it is itself untrue to life. In the case of Ivan himself this becomes apparent in that his own proclaimed love of life is not enough to enable him truly to confront the issues facing him in his immediate personal circumstances. Locked in a purely intellectual debate (largely with himself), he becomes progressively detached from reality, ending (as we have observed) with complete mental breakdown, illustrated by his hallucinatory conversation with the Devil.

If we take this point seriously, it offers an interesting way of relocating the debate between atheism and faith. For the question no longer concerns the possible existence of a divine being (or, as Tillich would say, Being Itself), but which of any given account of human existence offers the fullest affirmation of life—in all its complexity and contradictions. Nietzsche himself would see Dostoevsky's religiosity as symptomatic of its author's decadence, a religion of "pale criminals" such as Raskolnikov.[32] But if we follow Dostoevsky in reframing the question in terms of affirmation of life, the issue is better decided by the overall tendency of any given thinker's position. Dostoevsky undoubtedly presents examples of what we might call a "sickly" faith, but he also shows why they are incapable of giving expression to authentic Christian faith. In the end, the question is whether it is (let us say) Zarathustra or Alyosha who is most capable of embracing life in all its fulness, its terror and its beauty. However we decide the matter, it is then a secondary question as to what part their declared atheism or faith plays in producing that capability.

ATHEISM AS GOD SUBSTITUTE

A further important feature of Dostoevsky's approach to atheism is his view that many of the varieties of atheism on offer are, in effect, God substitutes and, as such, represent a kind of self-divinization of human beings. Again, this relates to important currents in modern atheism and to no less important elements of Christian and other religious critiques of atheisms perceived as engaging in self-divinization. In his *Religion and Philosophy in Germany*, Heinrich Heine was among the first to make this charge, directing his brilliant eloquence against both Romantic idealists (Fichte, Schelling, and Schlegel) and their materialist successors (Feuerbach and Marx).[33] Again, Kierkegaard made similar charges against the early Romantics and the Hegelians, extending the argument to bourgeois Christianity's sidelining of radical Christianity in favor of a pleasant comfortable life.[34]

In Dostoevsky's language, what we see here is an inversion of the Christian idea of the God-man (Jesus Christ as God Incarnate) and its replacement by the idea of the Man-God. The most explicit statement of such Prometheanism is in the programmatic doctrine of suicide expounded by the nihilist Kirillov on *The Possessed*. According to Kirillov, it is only the fear of death that has kept people in thrall to religion, and he therefore proposes to remove this fear by committing suicide. Crucially, he intends to do this for no reason other than his own will. That is to say, he does not seek death as the resolution or escape from some problem or affliction, and in this sense, his suicide is not at all pathological. On the contrary, it is the demonstration of his self-will and, as such, an act of direct defiance vis-à-vis God:

> "If God exists, all is His will and from His will I cannot escape. If not, it's all my will and I am bound to show self-will."
>
> "Self-will? But why are you bound?"
>
> "Because all will has become mine. Can it be that no one in the whole planet, after making an end of God and believing in his own will, will dare to express his self-will on the most vital point? It's like a beggar inheriting a fortune and being afraid of it and not daring to approach the bag of gold, thinking himself too weak to own it. I want to manifest my self-will. I may be the only one, but I'll do it."[35]

Kirillov's defiance is eloquent, but in the light of the role of life or all-unity in the God-relationship, the error of atheism is not simply that of hubris vis-à-vis God. To be sure, not only Kirillov but Raskolnikov (*Crime and Punishment*) declares himself to be engaged in transgressing the moral limits imposed by religion and society in a kind of proto-Nietzschean manner. Nevertheless, the deeper problem is that atheism actually imposes limits on human possibilities that also foreshorten what we might expect from life. Consequently, the failure of the various God substitutes that atheism has to offer is that they aggrandize one aspect of life in such a way as to occlude or incapacitate other aspects that are essential to the overall holistic development of human beings. Kirillov claims that he rejoices in all aspects of life, even the movements of a spider's legs—but he cannot accept that life exceeds the scope of his own will.

The key "God substitutes" identified by Dostoevsky are socialist and nonsocialist varieties of materialism, the church, idealism, and the nation. I therefore briefly consider these as they appear and are criticized in the major fiction. Before doing so, however, we should note that while the first is likely to take an explicitly atheistic form, the others may be rhetorically presented as religious and even Christian. However, to the extent that they do in fact function as God substitutes or expressions of the will to power of the Man-God, Dostoevsky allows us to see that they may really prove to be covert forms of atheism.

Clearly, Dostoevsky regards the radical revolutionary nihilism espoused by the terrorists in *The Possessed* and by Raskolnikov as the ultimate expression of modern materialism. Yet it would be a mistake to see Dostoevsky solely as a critic of the political left. Although the utopian socialist Chernyshevsky is often cited in the secondary literature as the prime target of *Notes from Underground*, Dostoevsky's attack extends far beyond Chernyshevsky.[36] The kind of rational materialist egoism that is ridiculed in the *Notes* is, in Marxist terms, very much at the core of the kind of capitalist ideology associated with phenomena such as the Great Exhibition. Materialism of this kind starts from what it takes to be scientifically established account of the laws of nature that are taken as the basis for developing social policy on a strictly utilitarian basis. According to this approach, human beings are necessarily motivated by what serves their rational self-interest, and this being so, these interests can themselves be "calculated and tabulated."[37] Governance becomes a matter of algorithms.[38] In the underground man's view, however, this makes human life the equivalent of the ant heap, because social relationships are reduced to mere functionality and the human being is essentially no different from a piano key.[39] The supreme symbol of this development is, precisely, the Great Exhibition's Crystal Palace, a glass-and-steel environment that Chernyshevsky—with very different aims—had taken as an exemplary structure in which to house his own future socialist utopia.

All of this, however, leaves out what the underground man takes to be fundamentally characteristic of human beings, namely, their freedom. Economic self-interest is not the highest or exclusive motive of human beings, and in a world governed by economic rationality, we cannot rule out that a person "would even risk his cakes and would deliberately desire the most fatal rubbish, the most uneconomical absurdity, simply to introduce into all this positive good sense his fatal fantastic element. It is just his fantastic dreams, his vulgar folly that he will desire to retain, simply in order to prove to himself—as though that were so necessary—that men still are men and not the keys of a piano, which the laws of nature threaten to control so completely that soon one will be able to desire nothing but by the calendar."[40] Quite simply, economic determinism omits what, according to the underground man, actually matters most to human beings. On his view, the Crystal Palace is in effect no better than a glorified henhouse, a functional arrangement that serves the satisfaction of material needs (e.g., providing shelter from the rain).[41] Such needs exist and must be met, but they are not everything. An ideology that makes them the measure of all that human beings are and can be therefore foreshortens and limits our view of human being. Importantly, this is not just a matter of theoretical positions, since this is an ideology to be applied in social, economic, and political practice, with consequent effects on human experience and life.

A second manifestation of the Man-God (and perhaps the most obvious and best-known in all of Dostoevsky's authorship) is the church itself. This is the burden of Ivan's "poem" of the Grand Inquisitor.[42] Ivan imagines Christ as returning to earth at the height of the Spanish Inquisition. He is arrested and imprisoned by the Grand Inquisitor, who explains to him that "we," that is, the church, have "corrected" his work. Christ's estimate of human beings, the Inquisitor tells him at great length, was too high. He supposed that they were capable of freely turning to God without the inducements of earthly bread and without the guidance of authoritative teachers. "Miracle, mystery, and authority" are what human beings crave—not the freedom in which Christ believed. It is this that the church offers, taking from the masses the freedom of belief and conscience that they find so unendurable. In a moment of frankness, the Inquisitor tells Christ that "we have gone over to *him*" (meaning the Devil). In these terms, the church is itself the preeminent and historically most successful version of the Man-God, "the self-divinization of the human race," as Kierkegaard had put it.

Of course, Dostoevsky frames this story as, quite specifically, applying to the Roman Catholic Church, which, like many other Russian authors, he sees as having been corrupted by worldly values in a quite distinctive way. As Prince Myshkin says, Roman Catholicism has essentially the same materialist outlook as socialism and is, indeed, the historical source of socialism. However, its religious and even Christian aura makes it, in effect, even worse than socialism.[43] Nevertheless, it is not difficult to extend the criticism to other forms of historical Christianity, and there is evidence that even the censors who read the manuscript prior to publication considered that it could be turned against Orthodoxy itself. Dostoevsky is undoubtedly critical of much contemporary church practice—the priest who comes to conduct Marmeladov's funeral, for example, seems interested only in collecting his fee, and Zosima is candid about the clergy's neglect of their duties. The superstition of much popular belief is also portrayed at various points in the novels, as well as the mere formality of much churchgoing. Nevertheless, Dostoevsky seems to have remained convinced that, especially among the peasants, the Russian heart retained an intimate bond with Christ that was somehow resistant to corruption.

Turning next to what Dmitri Karamazov calls "Schillerism," we may say that compared with socialist and capitalist materialism, the Schiller-inspired cult of the good, the true, and the beautiful might seem to have a certain spiritual pathos and, as such, to blend rather easily with a religious view of life. "Goodness," "truth," and "beauty" are, after all, integrated as transcendentals within Thomistic theism. Nevertheless, in the particular form in which they appear in the nineteenth century, they seem to Dostoevsky to bring about a foreshortening of human possibilities no less than what happens in materialism. Precisely because they are ideals abstracted from life, they are ultimately unable to move life or to engage it. It offers an aesthetic justification of life that runs up against the same limits that Kierkegaard had earlier seen as inherent in the aestheticism of his time.

An example of the existential consequences of such aesthetic idealism is the figure of Stepan Trofimovitch Verkhovensky in *The Possessed*. The novel is set in the late 1860s or early 1870s, and Stepan Trofimovitch is described as living the self-invented myth of an internal exile, excluded from intellectual life since the 1840s on account of his liberal views. At the fête that presages the grotesque and violent climax of the novel, Stepan Trofimovitch is given the opportunity to deliver what amounts to his confession of faith: "I maintain," he declares, "that Shakespeare and Raphael are more precious than the emancipation of the serfs, more precious than Nationalism, more precious than Socialism, more precious than the young generation, more precious than chemistry, more precious than almost all humanity because they are the fruit of all humanity and perhaps the highest fruit that can be."[44]

Stepan Trofimovitch's affirmation of the transcendental value of beauty precipitates a near riot. Yet across the course of the novel as a whole, we are enabled to see that not only is his aestheticism incapable of resisting the force of contemporary nihilism, but the difference between his aestheticism and the nihilists' materialism is at times paper thin. With regard to the former, he is shown to be an entirely ineffectual man who is constantly vacillating, incapable of making decisions, living out a fictitious self-image that he uses to sponge off a patroness who believes him to be a genuinely great intellectual figure. There seems ultimately to be nothing to him apart from a fragile web of fabrications.

In narrative terms, it is telling that Stepan Trofimovitch is the father of Peter, leader of the nihilists, and we are enabled to see that his neglectful behavior toward his son played a major role in the latter's sociopathic tendencies. He is not only the ideological forebear of the 1860s nihilists; he is also their literal progenitor. To drive the lesson home, Dostoevsky tells us that he had once been the owner of Fedka, the escaped convict, whom he had sold into the army to pay a gambling debt, thus inaugurating Fedka's descent into a life of crime. At the very beginning of the novel we are told that he was also the author of a dramatic poem in the last scene of which "we are suddenly shown the Tower of Babel, and certain athletes at last finish building it with a song of new hope, and when at length they complete the topmost pinnacle, the lord (of Olympus, let us say) takes flight in a comic fashion, and man, grasping the situation and seizing his place, at once begins a new life with new insights into things."[45] No matter how fancifully dressed up in the mystificatory language of mythology, and however ineffectual, this can be read as a fairly explicit statement of the program of the Man-God that is no less radical in its theological implications than Kirillov's explicit defiance.

Yet there are seeds of redemption in idealism that are perhaps lacking in materialism. If the choice is between "Raphael and petroleum," as Stepan Trofimovitch declares, do we not sense that, like him, Dostoevsky too would choose Raphael?[46] As if indicating the redemptive possibilities of the idealist position, Stepan Trofimovitch does attain a kind of salvation at the end of the novel, and although the narrator intimates that perhaps his reception of the last rites had as much to do with an aesthetic sense of occasion as with genuine faith, it is he who offers the interpretation of the Gadarene swine that provides the novel with its title.

The relations between idealism and faith are also explored by Dmitri Karamazov, who, introducing himself to Alyosha, begins by citing Schiller's "Ode to Joy." Yet where Schiller's words exhort us to faithfulness to the earth as the necessary condition of ascent to universal joy, Dmitri (whose very name invokes the earth-goddess Demeter) fears that if he gives himself to the earth as the poet urges, he will simply descend into his own animal depths. "Beauty!" he exclaims. "I can't endure the thought that a man of lofty mind and heart begins with the ideal of the Madonna and ends with the ideal of Sodom. . . . Believe me, that for the immense mass of mankind beauty is found in Sodom."[47] Yet despite his manifold personal flaws (his violence, his drunkenness, his sensuality), Dmitri's love of the earth does, in the end, enable him to find, if not the Madonna, then something of the joy to which Schiller points. If beauty is not conceived as an ideal separated from life but as a power of life and therefore to be found in life, then indeed it may, as another Dostoevsky character says, "save the world." But "beauty" in abstraction from life is an ideal that cannot be more than an impotent substitute for faith (and the same, we might guess, would go for "truth" and "goodness").

A similar pattern emerges in a fourth version of human self-divinization, namely, nationalism. Here, arguably, Dostoevsky's own views are especially hard to disentangle from the novels. We know from his *Diary of a Writer* that he propounded fiercely nationalist views, seeing Russia as the divinely appointed guardian of Orthodoxy and as such destined to retake Constantinople on behalf of Orthodox Christendom. He hailed the Russian volunteers who went to fight for their fellow Slavs in Bulgaria as cleansing the nation from its peacetime inertia. In short, he believed in Russia. But just how far did such belief extend?

In *The Possessed* we encounter the idea that Russia is a uniquely "God-bearing" nation, that is to say, that Russia is a kind of historical matrix from which a new incarnation or a further deepening and extension of Christ's original incarnation is to come. This is a view forcibly expressed by Shatov, often said to be among Dostoevsky's fictional characters that bear the closest resemblance to their author. "Do you know who are the only 'god-bearing' people on earth, destined to regenerate and save the world in the name of a new God and to whom are given the keys of life and of the new world?," Shatov asks Stavrogin rhetorically. However, as the conversation proceeds, it is made clear that this was originally Stavrogin's own idea and that at the time when he first propounded it he was already a convinced atheist. Nevertheless, it seems that Shatov has now taken it and incorporated it into his own creed. Nations, he tells Stavrogin, are the products of an "unknown and inexplicable force," "the force of the persistent assertion of one's own existence, and a denial of death. It's the spirit of life, as the Scriptures call it, 'the river of living water,' the drying up of which is threatened in the Apocalypse. It's the aesthetic principle, as the philosophers call it, the ethical principle with which they identify it, 'the seeking for God' as I call it more simply."[48] This "God," however, is "the synthetic principle of the whole people, taken from its beginning to its end." Rejecting Stavrogin's objection that he is reducing God to an attribute of nationality he protests that, "on the contrary, I raise the people to God . . . The people is the body of God."[49] Yet pushed further by Stavrogin, and stammering that he believes in Russia, in "her Orthodoxy," in the body of Christ and in a new Advent in Russia, he cannot quite affirm that he believes in God, only that he "will believe."[50]

On this basis of the—admittedly difficult—chapter, it would seem that Dostoevsky exposes the idea of the people as the body of God as yet another form of self-divinization and therefore implicitly atheistic. It may represent an aspiration toward faith, as in Shatov's "I will believe," but it is not faith. Even if Dostoevsky himself is more tempted by this idea than by any of materialism, idealism, and Catholicism, it seems that he has identified its fatal flaw. In *The Brothers Karamazov*, the Elder Zosima, usually seen as the supreme representative of Dostoevskian religiosity, also affirms the special religious destiny of Russia. However, there are significant differences. Observing the threat of modern materialism, Zosima declares his belief that, as opposed to the educated classes, the Russian people have retained their natural affinity with Christ. "The salvation of Russia comes from the people," he states.[51] Yet it is not the people who save themselves or raise themselves to God. Rather, "God will save Russia as he has saved her any times. Salvation will come from the people, from their faith and their meekness."[52] It is in her humility that Russia is great, precisely because humility is the human form of the incarnate Christ and it is for the sake of this humility—rather than the self-assertion of the God-bearing nation—that God will save Russia.

In this connection, we may discern in the love of nation (specifically for Dostoevsky, love of Russia and her people) a pattern not unlike that which we found in the case of beauty. In a merely aesthetic view of life, beauty may be absolutized and reified, abstracted from the world and from the vivifying stream of life and on this basis serve as a kind of God substitute. Yet beauty may also be a means of awakening the individual to a life beyond that of the ego—beauty may save the world. And if the ideal of beauty can lead to Sodom, it also has the power to draw us toward the Madonna. So too in the case of the nation, which Shatov tellingly identifies it with the aesthetic idea. Although this can be a form of utopian human self-assertion, it can also become a privileged locus of divine action if it is grounded in the humble common life of the people. By way of contrast, it is hard to envisage Dostoevsky seeing any possibilities of good in the algorithms of economic materialism or in the hierarchical life of the Catholic Church. The ideologies of the ant heap and the Grand Inquisitor seem beyond redemption. Beauty and love of nation, however, have an intrinsic tendency to exceed all calculation and may, under optimal conditions, become media of divine salvation. In these cases, the line between atheism and the kind of affirmation of life that opens the path toward the great synthesis of all-unity can become blurred and, just maybe, an initially atheistic position can evolve into a position of faith—a movement we see most clearly marked in the "Schillerian" Dmitri.[53]

CONCLUSION

Dostoevsky is a novelist, and all the possibilities sketched in this chapter have been drawn from literary texts that are open to widely divergent interpretations. Just about every claim I have made is contestable. This is acknowledged. Furthermore, interpretation is not only challenged by the fact that Dostoevsky's characters are complex and developing like many fictional characters. Many also indulge in the strategic deception of others and are prone to self-deception. At the same time, our estimation of their identity is based on their self-presentation in the context of the novels, a self-presentation that has the character of performance and is determined as such not only by their need for self-expression but also by their reaction to the actual or anticipated views of others—what Bakhtin called "double-voiced discourse."

The story "The Dream of a Ridiculous Man" locates the first manifestation of the Fall as learning to lie.[54] In the fallen world of Dostoevsky's novels, it is therefore no surprise that lying is a pervasive feature of and a habit that, despite his patriotism, Dostoevsky seems to regard as a distinctively Russian weakness. *The Idiot* is an eminent example of how mendacity and self-deception play a more than incidental role in the whole dynamic of the novel. The initial stages of the plot are set in motion by Anastasia's abuser contriving an arranged marriage to conceal his own abusive relationship with her and by the pretense that Ganya will marry her for love rather than for a handsome payout. In this situation, what is most distinctive about the Prince is precisely his naïve honesty, saying what he thinks as he thinks and without pretense. When asked over a polite haut-bourgeois breakfast what he thinks of Aglaya, one of the four daughters of the family who are present, he blurts out that she is so beautiful one is afraid to look at her— though not as beautiful as Anastasia Philippovna, a candor that initially amuses and then shocks his listeners.[55] As it unfolds, the novel presents us with a whole cast of liars: Lebedev, who seems to lie purely for the sake of it; the retired and near-senile General Ivolgin, whose long and rambling reminiscences are repeatedly shown to be entirely fictitious; and the nihilist Burdovsky, who, under the influence of his friends, claims to have been disinherited in favor of Prince Myshkin; we have also seen how Ippolit's atheistic defiance is itself based upon profound self-deception.[56] This, however, means that we too as readers, both in *The Idiot* and throughout the novels, are having constantly to sift lies and truth. *De omnibus dubitandum est*—and our assessment of the real views and real motives of the actors must reckon both with their deceptions of others and their self-deceptions.

That, probably, is the beginning of a new chapter. At the same time it presents us with a paradox that extends to many aspects of Dostoevsky's fictional world, including the question of atheism. Quite apart from the fact that everything in the novels is, by definition, fiction, the primary access we have to the characters is through what they say about one another and about themselves, whether in conversation or inner dialogue. Given the pervasive atmosphere of mendacity, this means that readers are constantly challenged as to just who to trust and how much to trust them. Who really believes in God? Who is a true atheist? Who remains caught in the crucible of doubt, simultaneously crippled by weakness and defiance? And just how much should we trust what any of these characters (or their real-life incarnations) tell us about their belief or unbelief?

Dostoevsky's self-limitation as a realist writer means that we rarely, if ever, encounter a pure type of belief or a pure type of atheism but, instead, a succession of characters struggling confusedly between the two. If that was a true reflection of his time, does the same apply to ours? Has the question got any easier? Has science—or, perhaps more importantly, rational economics (the ubiquitous market forces and the algorithms that ensure their effective functioning)—secured its final triumph over the fantasies of freedom and responsibility? Perhaps the fact that we continue to read Dostoevsky suggests not—but this also suggests that neither can the hope of salvation entirely free itself from the counter-possibility of a radical atheism. If we are not interested in the struggle, then Dostoevsky probably has nothing much to tell us.

NOTES

1. Jean-Paul Sartre, *Existentialisme est un humanisme* (Paris: Nagel, 1970), 36.
2. I choose my words carefully. Whether Dostoevsky succeeded in creating a persuasive Christian novel is a whole other question. Whatever his authorial intentions, it is likewise open to debate as to just how orthodox (or indeed, Orthodox) the novel's religious vision actually is.
3. William Hamilton, "Banished from the Land of Unity" in, *Radical Theology and the Death of God*, ed. Thomas J. J. Altizer and William Hamilton (Harmondsworth, UK: Pelican, 1966), 94.
4. Many philosophers of religion return the favor by simply ignoring him. John Hick's *Evil and the God of Love* mentions Dostoevsky in only one footnote in the section "Some Residual Problems": John Hick, *Evil and the God of Love* (London: Fontana, 1968), 386. A notable exception is Stewart R. Sutherland, *Atheism and the Rejection of God: Contemporary Philosophy and the Brothers Karamazov* (Oxford, UK: Basil Blackwell, 1977).
5. F. M. Dostoevsky, *The Brothers Karamazov*, trans. Constance Garnett (London: Heinemann, 1955), 124.
6. Dostoevsky, 170.

ATHEISM AND THE AFFIRMATION OF LIFE • 195

7. Dostoevsky, 674.
8. Again, it is striking that Kierkegaard too makes this a defining element in his response to the Hegelian idealism that he saw as implicitly atheistic. See esp. Søren Kierkegaard, *Concluding Unscientific Postscript*, trans. H. V. and E. H. Hong (Princeton, NJ: Princeton University Press, 1991), 171–77.
9. See my article "Death," in *The Oxford Handbook of Theology and Modern European Thought*, ed. Nicholas Adams, George Pattison, and Graham Ward (Oxford: Oxford University Press, 2013), 193–212.
10. F. M. Dostoevsky, *The Idiot*, trans. Constance Garnett (New York: Macmillan, 1951), 400.
11. Dostoevsky, 400.
12. Cited in Steven Cassedy, *Dostoevsky's Religion* (Stanford, CA: Stanford University Press, 2005), 116.
13. F. M. Dostoevsky, *The Possessed*, trans. Constance Garnett (London: Heinemann, 1946), 509.
14. F. M. Dostoevsky, *Crime and Punishment*, trans. Constance Garnett (London: Heinemann, 1929), 21.
15. Dostoevsky, *Idiot*, 383.
16. Dostoevsky, 401.
17. Nelly, the child at the center of the action of *The Insulted and the Injured*, is likewise unable to forgive her violators and, despite the efforts of her rescuers, dies unreconciled.
18. Another female character in whom an analogous dynamic is played out is the handicapped adolescent girl, Liza, from *The Brothers Karamazov*. In her case the background is not sexual abuse but physical illness.
19. See Søren Kierkegaard, *The Sickness unto Death*, trans. H. V. and E. H. Hong (Princeton, NJ: Princeton University Press, 1980), 49–74.
20. See Erik H. Erikson, *Childhood and Society* (1950; Harmondsworth, UK: Penguin, 1965), 239–43. The quote given is at 242. For Küng, see Hans Küng, *Does God Exist?*, trans. Edward Quinn (London: Collins, 1980), esp. II.E, 427–78.
21. Dostoevsky, *Crime and Punishment*, 492 (translation amended). For a reading of Dostoevsky that brings this aspect of his work to the fore, see Predrag Cicovacki, *Dostoevsky and the Affirmation of Life* (Brunswick NJ: Transaction, 2012).
22. Which, as the evolution of Cupitt's own thought makes clear, is predicated on the death of any objective divine being.
23. Dostoevsky, *Brothers Karamazov*, 288.
24. Dostoevsky, 298.
25. Dostoevsky, 319.
26. Dostoevsky, 319.
27. Dostoevsky, 320.
28. Dostoevsky, 320.
29. Dostoevsky, 322.
30. First developed in his highly influential lectures on divine humanity (Godmanhood). See Vladimir Solovyov, *Lectures on Divine Humanity*, trans. Boris Jakim (New York: Lindisfarne, 1995).
31. See my contribution "Death," in *The Oxford Handbook of Theology and Modern European Thought*, ed. Nicholas Adams, George Pattison, and Graham Ward (Oxford: Oxford University Press, 2013), 193–212.

32. The section "Of the Pale Criminal" (*Vom bleichen Verbrecher*) in *Thus Spoke Zarathustra* may not itself be directly related to Nietzsche's reading of Dostoevsky. Although Nietzsche was polemically responsive to Dostoevsky in several of his works, he appreciated the Russian author's psychological acumen. See Paolo Stellino, *Nietzsche and Dostoevsky: On the Verge of Nihilism* (Bern: Peter Lang, 2015).
33. For discussion, see George Pattison, "'Man-God' and "God-Manhood,'" in *Theosis/Deification: Christian Doctrines of Divinizaton East and West*, ed. Rob Faesen and John Arblaster (Leuven, Belgium: Peeters, 2018), 174–77.
34. This is the view developed especially forcefully in Kierkegaard's attack on the established "People's Church" at the very end of his life. The bourgeois-Biedermeier version of Christianity is, of course, much less dramatic than Dostoevsky's Grand Inquisitor, but Kierkegaard's point seems to be essentially the same as Dostoevsky's.
35. Dostoevsky, *Possessed*, 561.
36. Nikolai Gavrilovich Chernyshevsky (1828–1889) was a Russian utopian thinker strongly influenced by Feuerbach; his novel *What Is to Be Done?* depicts a socialist utopia in which men and women live in open relationships in communes housed in steel and glass "phalansteries," applying science to cultivate even the remotest regions. This proved one of the most influential books on the Russian Left in the nineteenth century, and Lenin would later take the title for one of his own works.
37. F. M. Dostoevsky "Notes from Underground" in *White Nights and Other Stories*, trans. Constance Garnett (London: Heinemann, 1950), 73.
38. Dostoevsky, 68. Dostoevsky uses the word "logarithm."
39. Dostoevsky, 73.
40. Dostoevsky, 73.
41. Dostoevsky, 77.
42. Dostoevsky, *Brothers Karamazov*, 253–72.
43. Dostoevsky, *Idiot*, 532–34. Interestingly, we learn that similar ideas have been expressed by Stavrogin, thus making them the common conviction of both the most saintly and the most nihilistic of Dostoevsky's characters.
44. Dostoevsky, *Possessed*, 439.
45. Dostoevsky, 4.
46. Dostoevsky, 439. Dostoevsky's wife presented him with a photographic copy of the Sistine Madonna that he had seen in Dresden and particularly loved. He had it hung on his study wall.
47. Dostoevsky, *Brothers Karamazov*, 106.
48. Dostoevsky, *Possessed*, 226.
49. Dostoevsky, 227.
50. Dostoevsky, 229.
51. Dostoevsky, *Brothers Karamazov*, 327.
52. Dostoevsky, 328.
53. Readers of this chapter are, I suspect, more likely to see "beauty" than "nation" as a privileged site of religious life. Both the history of the twentieth century and the nationalisms of our own time have made many, especially those working in the academy, skeptical of exaggerated claims on behalf of any one nation. This suspicion is well grounded—but we err if we too easily dismiss the kinds of attachments that the concrete forms of common life and narratives of shared history and culture can engender. Minimally, this needs to be understood—and the percep-

tion that members of the academy may have tended to equate nationalism with fascism without further reflection may itself have contributed to the resurgence of sometimes violent nationalisms today. However, we can also say to Dostoevsky that, like many contemporary nationalists, he might benefit from reflecting further on the distinctions between nation, political society, and state (a distinction made by Jacques Maritain).

54. F. M. Dostoevsky, "The Dream of a Ridiculous Man," in *An Honest Thief and Other Stories*, trans. Constance Garnett (London: Heinemann, 1950), 321.
55. Dostoevsky, *Idiot*, 73.
56. *The Brothers Karamazov* similarly features a procession of lies, from the buffoonery of Fyodor Karamazov, through Ivan's self-deception, through to the court case against Dmitri, in which neither prosecution nor defense seems to be concerned with the truth at all, but only its rhetorical effect.

REFERENCES

Cassedy, Steven. *Dostoevsky's Religion*. Stanford, CA: Stanford University Press, 2005.
Cicovacki, Predrag. *Dostoevsky and the Affirmation of Life*. New Brunswick, NJ: Transaction Books, 2012.
Erikson, Erik H. *Childhood and Society*. 1950. Harmondsworth, UK: Penguin, 1965.
Hamilton, William. "Banished from the Land of Unity." In *Radical Theology and the Death of God*, edited by Thomas J. J. Altizer and William Hamilton. Harmondsworth, UK: Pelican, 1966.
Dostoevsky, F. M. *The Brothers Karamazov*. Translated by Constance Garnett. London: Heinemann, 1955.
———. *Crime and Punishment*. Translated by Constance Garnett (London: Heinemann, 1929.
———. "The Dream of a Ridiculous Man." In *An Honest Thief and Other Stories*, translated by Constance Garnett. London: Heinemann, 1950.
———. *The Idiot*. Translated by Constance Garnett. New York: Macmillan, 1951.
———. "Notes from Underground." In *White Nights and Other Stories*, translated by Constance Garnett. London: Heinemann, 1950.
———. *The Possessed*. Translated by Constance Garnett. London: Heinemann, 1946.
Hick, John. *Evil and the God of Love*. London: Fontana, 1968.
Kierkegaard, Søren. *Concluding Unscientific Postscript*. Translated by H. V. and E. H. Hong. Princeton, NJ: Princeton University Press, 1991.
———. *The Sickness unto Death*. Translated by H. V. and E. H. Hong. Princeton, NJ: Princeton University Press, 1980.
Küng, Hans. *Does God Exist?* Translated by Edward Quinn. London: Collins, 1980.
Pattison, George. "Death." In *The Oxford Handbook of Theology and Modern European Thought*, edited by Nicholas Adams, George Pattison, and Graham Ward, 193–212. Oxford: Oxford University Press, 2013.
———. "Man-God and 'God-Manhood.'" In *Theosis/Deification. Christian Doc-*

trines of Divinization East and West, edited by Rob Faesen and John Arblaster. Leuven, Belgium: Peeters, 2018, 171–90.

Sartre, Jean-Paul. *Existentialisme est un humanisme.* Paris: Nagel, 1970.

Solovyov, Vladimir. *Lectures on Divine Humanity.* Translated by Boris Jakim. New York: Lindisfarne, 1995.

Stellino, Paolo. *Nietzsche and Dostoevsky. On the Verge of Nihilism.* Bern: Peter Lang, 2015.

Sutherland, Stewart R. *Atheism and the Rejection of God: Contemporary Philosophy and the Brothers Karamazov.* Oxford, UK: Basil Blackwell, 1977.

AFTERWORD

The Drama of Atheism

Constance M. Furey

The most challenging course I took in college had a one word title: Alienation. I had no idea what I was getting into. Little guidance was provided on the first day—or any day thereafter. The professor's few introductory words included the announcement that one of our primary texts was out of print. Only one copy of *The Drama of Atheist Humanism*, by Henri de Lubac, would be available.[1] We would find it in the reserve room at the library, available for two-hour checkouts. This complicated our daily schedules but increased our motivation to read, and it had the unexpected benefit of giving us reason to make conversation—"How far did you get? What time are you checking it back in?"—the kind of incidental conversation that felt impossible in the seminar room, given the difficulty of the course and the formality of the professor. *The Drama of Atheist Humanism* was not long. It was hard to pigeonhole, though less difficult than many of our other texts, including Hannah Arendt's *Totalitarianism*, filled as it was with biblical images and summaries of Feuerbach, Hegel, Marx, Nietzsche, and many other names equally unknown and often hard to pronounce. I was captivated.

Everyday atheism is of no particular significance, de Lubac says at the outset. The atheism that creates real drama represents a "living force" capable of "replacing what it destroys." De Lubac was not himself an atheist. On the contrary. He was a French Jesuit, a faithful Catholic, and an architect of Vatican II. He wrote in opposition to atheism, insisting on the first page that the atheisms he would survey had one thing in common: the annihilation of the human person. Yet the book was as sympathetic as it was critical, as curious as it was certain, as generous in naming and describing atheist humanisms as it was eloquent in denouncing them. Here was a religious person making a case for a rejection of religion, a believer explaining the reasons God needed to be killed off, or exposed as an illusion.

I don't remember atheism being debated in the small mostly Christian towns where I grew up in the 1970s and 1980s, but a curious teen could readily see that many believers were immoral, and many good people, unbelievers. Evil was unknown, but tragic deaths were not, and Holocaust memoirs read compulsively during boring classes, or movies like *The Killing Fields,* offered searing depictions of human brutality. Like Ivan Karamazov, I could not imagine believing in a god who allowed systematic and casual cruelty, and like Nietzsche, I thought the absence of god might create more abundant life. This does not mean I had read Dostoevsky, or any philosophers. My convictions were inchoate, energized more by adolescent righteousness than knowledge or study. And I had never encountered a believer like de Lubac. "It is not the purpose of faith in God to install us comfortably in our earthly life that we may go to sleep in it," he wrote. Many of the Christian students I have taught in the past twenty years would find that statement of faith as surprising as I did. "On the contrary, faith disturbs us and continually upsets the too beautiful balance of our mental conceptions and our social structures" (ix): the intrigue unfolded from there, page after page, fulfilling the promise of *The Drama*'s title.

I would not—do not—read Lubac's book the same way now. It is easy to be distracted by his Christian exclusivism and tempting to just assess his work historically, as an expression of a twentieth-century Catholic thought. Yet this book still has the power to thrill, making atheism central to a drama I did not encounter again until participating in the conference that gave rise to *this* book, the one you read on your screen or hold open in your hands.

The conversations at that 2018 conference, organized by David Newheiser, were intense and unpredictable. Guided by Newheiser's call to consider atheism anew, participants were entirely uninterested in rehearsing or reenacting the polemics of the New Atheists and their opponents. Theologians, intellectual historians, cultural critics, and literary scholars collectively refused narrow definitions of belief, tired arguments about normative versus descriptive claims, and simplistic metaphysical arguments. We read and thought about Nietzsche and Dante and Einstein, Hume and Dostoevsky and Eagleton. We were, as Newheiser says in his introduction, uninterested in denying or defending a literalist supernaturalism, united in our interest in atheism's diversity, and intrigued by the possibility that new studies of atheism might unravel the single thread linking religion to belief.

These generative conversations echo throughout this volume's eight essays. Full of unexpected arguments, each offers its own dramatic account while collectively confirming that atheism's multifaceted drama has often been overshadowed by the huckster out front, luring passersby with a simple cry, "God! Alive or Dead? True or False?" The volume's refusal to assume a simple opposition between atheism and theology is especially powerful, as is its attention to atheism's affect. We encounter both, for example, in Devin Singh's opening declaration that "protest atheism" is the "true kernel" of Christian theology and call to Christians to "tarry in the reality of absence" of Christ. Singh's normative conclusion denies the difference between atheism and theism, focusing instead on the political implications of this tarrying: rather than hailing Christ as king of kings, Christians must realize that "all kings are dead and gone and that we have kept their myths alive too long."

Denys Turner similarly emphasizes the affective implications of belief and nonbelief alike in his essay about the atheism of nominalism and Nietzsche. The profoundly serious German gadfly may be the "first truly consistent nominalist," Turner concludes, for in denying any and all essentialism, Nietzsche "grasp[s] fully, and joyously, nominalism's atheist implications." What Turner reveals in Nietzsche, Susannah Ticciati identifies as the crux of any debate about atheism or theism: What feelings and actions does a given belief inspire? What kind of life does the believer or unbeliever live? Indeed, as she puts it with bold simplicity, there should be no anxiety about maintaining the distinction between theist and atheist. Rather than worry about countering atheism, the question for Christians is how the claim that God exists might be "uttered wisely"—with a wisdom forged through the crucible of folly.

The value of Tacciati's insistence that debates about atheism should focus on lifeworld and attitudes is confirmed in Andre Willis's "Atheism and Community" and Mary-Jane Rubenstein's "Atheism and Pantheism." Surveying Hume and Rorty, Willis demonstrates that both believed that atheism is premised on a commitment to inquiry as a communal activity. And Rubenstein's assessment of Einstein's controversial denials and avowals of faith likewise concludes with a ringing endorsement of a life-affirming conviction: "real" pantheism, she argues, would shed determinism and reason and instead assume "the complex perspectivalism of the universe itself."

Is pantheism's perspectivalism akin to embracing fiction's capacity to let us live the lives of others? Henning Tegtmeyer's essay on apophaticism and atheism cautions those eager to celebrate the denial of positive truth claims or the fluidities enhanced by fiction. However attractive it might be to seek some distance from metaphysical assertions, he argues, apophaticism and fictionalism alike have the potential to weaken or dilute all convictions. Here again, affect and cognition are revealed to be inseparable, even as the bracing force of Tegtmeyer's conclusion is countered by the power of literature surveyed Vittorio Montemaggi's chapter on Dante and George Pattison's on Dostoevsky. In what does the difference between believing and not believing in God consist? For Dante, to deny God is to denounce love. Conversely, relating to God is inextricable from encountering other human beings. Both require the process of exploration that *The Divine Comedy* depicts, which explains—as Montemaggi concludes—why Dante rightly chose "to do theology in and through a literary text, a narrative poem telling the story of such a journey." So too with Dostoevsky, characterized by Pattison as one who understands that that the root of atheism is not a metaphysical argument but a "psychological failure."

Like many contemporary philosophers, Dostoevsky responded to this failure by offering a "religion of life" predicated on the rejection of any metaphysics that posits the otherness of a divine being. In these concluding two examples, a premodern epic poem and a modern novelist's creations, literature presents itself as a crucial interlocuter in the discussion staged in the preceding essays, about atheism and its implications. What should we make of their arresting insights and conclusions? Rather than pursuing the fruitless project of defining atheism, or debating the relative virtues of atheism and theism, all of the essays in this volume are animated by these vital questions. Where do we find a religion of life? What convictions, commitments, genres, arguments, sources, and forms of solace and challenge hold out the promise of more and better life?

Any reader compelled by these questions will be enlivened by the work of these contributors and the sources they illuminate. What they offer, I believe, is what I first experienced in reading de Lubac, as a naïve undergraduate. I now recognize as a hope inflected with negativity, to borrow a phrase from David Newheiser's *Hope in a Secular Age:* a commitment to thoughtful life and living thought that holds "affirmation and negation together in tension," as Newheiser says, in "an ethical practice of openness to the unexpected."[2] What better place to find this hope, the holding of affirmation and negation together, than in an volume devoted to open inquiry and unexpected conclusions about atheism, a topic that for too long, and in too many venues, has been drained of real drama.

NOTES

1. Henri de Lubac, *The Drama of Atheist Humanism*, trans. Edith Riley (New York: World Publishing Co., 1969).
2. David Newheiser, *Hope in a Secular Age: Deconstruction, Negative Theology, and the Future of Faith* (Cambridge: Cambridge University Press, 2019), 144, 155, 156.

ACKNOWLEDGMENTS

David Newheiser

As a kid growing up in suburban America, I experienced atheism as a source of distant fascination. It was only as an undergraduate that I encountered actual, honest-to-God atheists—first in the college dining hall and then in my coursework. Something within me was moved by the integrity and insight of Nietzsche, Feuerbach, Camus, and Derrida. During my graduate work, these atheists provided the lens that brought the arcane formulas of medieval Christian thought into focus. Even now, I find that I cannot make sense of religious traditions without their help, and I cannot understand atheism without taking religion seriously.

This instinct led me to organize the conference from which this collection originates. As Constance Furey describes in her afterword, it was an extraordinary experience. Over the course of four beautiful days, we formed an impromptu community devoted to the knotty relationship between religion and its critics. I am grateful to each of the authors, but particular thanks are due to the other participants in the conference for their commitment to a conversation that has enriched every page: Nicholas Adams, Alda Balthrop-Lewis, Leora Batnitsky, Kathi Beier, Ryan Coyne, Rachel Davies, Fiona Ellis, Stephan van Erp, Christiaan Jacobs-Vandegeer, Noreen Khawaja, and Charles Lockwood.

The conference was part of a project on atheism that I led from 2016 to 2019. I am grateful to the Institute for Religion and Critical Inquiry at Australian Catholic University for supporting the project, and particularly to the institute's directors, James McLaren and Peter Howard. Special thanks are due to the administrative staff who supported the project: Kerry Barnes, Claudio Betti, Angela Marino, Emily Moore, Linda Tracey, and David Dawson Vasquez. I am also grateful to the project's other members, whose companionship has been a gift: Rachel Davies, Stephan van Erp, Robyn Horner, Christiaan Jacobs-Vandegeer, Charles Lockwood, Henning Tegtmeyer, and Denys Turner.

Although work on this collection began before the pandemic arrived, we completed the manuscript in the shadow of COVID-19. The experience has underlined what was already clear: each of us, even the "able bodied," depends upon others for support. I cannot name each person who has supported each author in this collection, but I acknowledge their labor. In a year in which my own abilities were temporarily altered, my work on the introduction benefited from the help of Alda Balthrop-Lewis, Leora Batnitsky, Stephen Bush, Fiona Ellis, and Kathryn Tanner. I am grateful to the anonymous readers for two very helpful reports. Thanks to Kate Mertes for preparing the index, to Katherine Faydash for copyediting the text, and to Kyle Wagner (our editor at the press) for his patience during a time when the world was unsettled.

LIST OF CONTRIBUTORS

CONSTANCE M. FUREY is Professor of Religious Studies at Indiana University, where she is also cofounder of the Center for Religion and the Human. A specialist in Renaissance and Reformation Christianity, she has written articles on topics including utopia and friendship, discernment and folly, exemplarity and invective, and current trends in the study of religion and critique. Her books include *Poetic Relations: Faith and Intimacy in the English Reformation* (Chicago, 2016) and *Devotion: Three Inquiries in Religion, Literature, and Political Imagination* (Chicago, 2021).

VITTORIO MONTEMAGGI is Reader in Religion, Literature and the Arts in the Department of Theology and Religious Studies at King's College London and Director of the Von Hügel Institute for Critical Catholic Inquiry at St Edmund's College, Cambridge. He is also an adjunct professor at the London Global Gateway of the University of Notre Dame and affiliate of Notre Dame's Center for Italian Studies. His publications include *Reading Dante's* Commedia *as Theology: Divinity Realized in Human Encounter* (2016); *Dante, Mercy, and the Beauty of the Human Person* (coedited with L. J. DeLorenzo, 2017); and *Dante's* Commedia: *Theology as Poetry* (coedited with M. Treherne, 2010).

DAVID NEWHEISER is a Senior Research Fellow in the Institute for Religion and Critical Inquiry at Australian Catholic University and an affiliate of the university's Gender and Women's History Research Centre. His research explores the role of religious traditions in debates over ethics, politics, and culture. He is the author of *Hope in a Secular Age* (2019), and he is codirector of an interdisciplinary collaboration on the ritual dimensions of contemporary art. His current book project considers the link between premodern miracles and democratic imagination.

GEORGE PATTISON is retired scholar and Anglican priest. He is Honorary Professional Research Fellow in the School of Critical Studies, at the University of Glasgow. He has taught in the universities of Cambridge, Aarhus, Copenhagen, Oxford, and Glasgow and has published extensively in the area of European religious thought in the nineteenth and twentieth centuries, with particular emphasis on German idealism and its critics. His most recent work is a three part "philosophy of Christian life," comprising *A Phenomenology of the Devout Life* (2018), *A Rhetorics of the Word* (2019), and *A Metaphysics of Love* (2021), all published by Oxford University Press. He is also coeditor of *The Oxford Handbook of Russian Religious Thought* (2019).

MARY-JANE RUBENSTEIN is Professor of Religion and Science in Society at Wesleyan University. She is the author of *Astrotopia: The Dangerous Religion of the Corporate Space Race* (Chicago, 2022), *Pantheologies: Gods, Worlds, Monsters* (Columbia, 2018), *Worlds without End: The Many Lives of the Multiverse* (Columbia, 2014), and *Strange Wonder: The Closure of Metaphysics and the Opening of Awe* (Columbia, 2009). She is also coeditor with Catherine Keller of *Entangled Worlds: Religion, Science, and New Materialisms* (Fordham, 2017) and coauthor with Thomas A. Carlson and Mark C. Taylor of *Image: Three Inquiries in Technology and Imagination* (Chicago, 2021).

DEVIN SINGH is Associate Professor of Religion at Dartmouth College and faculty associate in Dartmouth's Consortium of Studies in Race, Migration, and Sexuality. He teaches courses on modern religious thought in the West, social ethics, philosophy of religion, and the relations among religion, economics, and politics. Singh is the author of *Divine Currency: The Theological Power of Money in the West* (2018) and *Economy and Modern Christian Thought* (2022), coeditor of *Reimagining Leadership on the Commons* (2021), and author of articles in *Journal of Religious Ethics*, *Harvard Theological Review*, *Scottish Journal of Theology*, *Implicit Religion*, *Political Theology*, *Religions*, and *Telos*.

HENNING TEGTMEYER obtained a PhD in philosophy in 2004 and a habilitation in 2012 (both at the University of Leipzig). He was Visiting Professor at the Johannes Gutenberg University Mainz from 2010 to 2012 and at the Freie Universität Berlin from 2012 to 2013. Since 2013, he has been Associate Professor of Metaphysics and Philosophy of Religion at KU Leuven. In 2022, he was Honorary Professor of Philosophy at Durham University. Selected publications include *Formbezug und Weltbezug. Die Deutungsoffenheit der Kunst* (mentis, 2006;

de Gruyter, 2008); *Sinnkritisches Philosophieren* (de Gruyter, 2013), coedited with Sebastian Rödl; and *Gott, Geist, Vernunft. Prinzipien und Probleme der Natürlichen Theologie* (Mohr Siebeck, 2013).

SUSANNAH TICCIATI is Professor of Christian Theology at King's College London. She is author of *Reading Augustine: On Signs, Christ, Truth and the Interpretation of Scripture* (T&T Clark, 2022), *A New Apophaticism: Augustine and the Redemption of Signs* (Brill, 2013), and *Job and the Disruption of Identity: Reading beyond Barth* (T&T Clark, 2005).

DENYS TURNER, formerly Horace Tracy Pitkin Professor at Yale University and Norris-Hulse Professor at Cambridge University, is now at last retired from teaching, his first love. He has written a few books, *The Darkness of God*, *Julian of Norwich*, *Theologian*, *Thomas Aquinas, a Portrait*, being among them, and forthcoming with Cambridge, *Dante the Theologian*. Otherwise he happily gardens and cooks with his wife, Courtney Palmbush, historian and novelist.

ANDRE C. WILLIS is Associate Professor of Religious Studies at Brown University. He is a philosopher of religion whose work focuses on Enlightenment reflections on religion, African American religious thought, critical theory, and democratic citizenship as it relates to "religious" notions of hope, recognition, and belonging. Willis earned a BA at Yale in philosophy and his MA and PhD at Harvard in the Committee on the Study of Religion. He is the author of *Towards a Humean True Religion* (2015) and is currently working on a manuscript about African American religion and politics that is tentatively titled *Afro-theisms and Post-democracy*. He has published articles in international journals such as *Hume Studies*, *Journal of Scottish Philosophy*, *Political Theology*, *Critical Philosophy of Race*, and *Radical America*.

INDEX

abandonment, ascension as, 129–34, 137, 144
absent God. *See* political theology and the absent God
accusation, atheism as, 5–6
Adams, Nicholas, 96, 97, 172n24
Agamben, Giorgio, 134–39, 143
agnosticism, 118–20, 123n4, 125n39
Alice's Adventures in Wonderland (Carroll), 65, 79
American Pragmatists, 42, 59n1
analogy, Aquinas's doctrine of, 98–99
angels, Aquinas on, 81n8
Anglophone philosophy, atheism in, 1, 4, 12n8
Anselm of Canterbury, 121
Antichrist, 143
antisemitic attacks on Einstein, 21–22, 26–27
apophatic theology, 10, 105–23, 201–2; in Dante's *Comedy*, 156; defined, 107–8; fictionalism, 111, 121–22, 125nn47–48; fideism and, 117–18, 121, 124n34; generalized apophatics, 111, 112–15; invocationalism, 111, 118–20, 122; linguistic and nonlinguistic strategies of separation from ordinary discourse, 111; metaphysical aspirations of, 122–23; New Atheists and, 86, 89, 90, 98; ontotheology and, 106–7, 123; political theology and, Peterson on, 141–42; potential collapse into atheism of, 102n31, 109–10; premodern concepts of, 6, 14n32; problems and dilemmas raised by, 107–10; sacramentalism, 111–12, 115–18, 121, 122; scripturalism, 111, 120–21, 125n44; strategies for avoiding dilemmas of, 110–12

Aquinas, Thomas, 71, 72, 81n8, 82n18, 82n20, 98–99, 134, 189
Arendt, Hannah, 199
Aristotle, 110, 123n9, 135
Asad, Talal, 8–9
ascension: as/and abandonment, 129–34, 137, 144, 146; in Dante's *Comedy*, 162
assemblage, concept of, 8, 14n41
atheism, 1–12; academic study of, 1; as accusation, 5–6; affective resonance and drama of, 11, 199–202; in Anglophone philosophy, 1, 4, 12n8; belief, atheism equated with, 1–5; Christianity and atheism, focus on relationship between, 9, 15n47 (*see also* Christianity); debates between theists and atheists, 41, 60n5; diversity and variety of, 1–2, 3, 11–12; engagement with ethics and metaphysics, 10 (*see also* apophatic theology; truth and transformation); in European philosophy, 12n8; God, meaning(s) of, 107, 213n4; historical development of, concept of, 5–6; as hypothesis, 1, 2–3; as identity, 6–8; influential exemplars of variety in, 9–10 (*see also* Einstein, Albert; Nietzsche, Friedrich; Rorty, Richard, and David Hume); literature and, 10 (*see also* Dante Alighieri, *Comedy*; Dostoevsky, Fyodor); methodological approach to, 8–9; modernity and, 6–8; multiple motivations for, 8; overlapping with theism, 41–42,

209

atheism (*continued*)
43, 56–59; politics and, 10, 129–47, 201 (*see also* political theology and the absent God); relationship to religion/theistic belief, 1; theoretical versus practical, 5; white male focus of most discussion of, 13n21
Atheism (Baggini), 88
Augustine of Hippo, 134, 135

Baggini, Julian, 88
Bakhtin, Mikhail, 176, 193
Bakunin, Mikhail, 8
Balthrop-Lewis, Alda, 171n5
Barth, Karl, 121
Bataille, Georges, 150n46
Bayle, Pierre, 19
Beatrice, in Dante's *Comedy*, 156, 159–61, 171n2, 171n12
Beattie, Tina, 86, 88, 90
belief, atheism, and theism, 1–3, 9
Berkeley, George, 42
Berlant, Lauren, 15n42
binary versus triadic truth claims, 96–97
"Bobok" (Dostoevsky), 179
Bohr, Niels, 21, 29–32
Bonner, Hypatia, 8
Born, Hedwig, 31
Born, Max, 31
Boscovich, Robert John, 76, 82n21
Breaking the Spell (Dennett), 2, 86–87
Brothers Karamazaov, The (Dostoevsky), 175–79, 181, 184, 185, 188–91, 192, 195n18, 197n56, 200
Buddhism, 49–51, 57, 61n17, 138
Bullivant, Stephan, 4
Byronism, 182

Calvin, John, and Calvinism, 5, 145–46
cannibalism, 5
Caputo, John, 112, 114, 115
Catholics and Catholicism: belief, definition of religion as, 9; de Lubac and, 200; Dostoevsky on, 188, 192; on Einstein, 21–23, 24, 25, 26; final vocabulary, Rorty on, 58; Protestants, atheistic accusations against, 5; sacramentalism in, 111, 116
Cattoi, Thomas, 138
Cavalcante dei Cavalcanti, in Dante's *Comedy*, 171n2
Chalcedonian Definition, 97
Chernyshevsky, Nikolai Gavrilovich, 187, 196n36

Cheyne, George, 46
Chicago Daily Tribune, 25
Christianity: as atheism, in Roman antiquity, 5; atheistic kernel at heart of, 129–30; atheists focusing on, 3–4; focus on relationship between atheism and, 9, 15n47; heterodoxy, atheism as, 6; literalism and its alternatives, 4, 12n13; modern scientific objectivity and, 6–7; Nietzsche, as explicit target of, 79; Protestants and Catholics, atheistic accusations of, 5. *See also* apophatic theology; Catholics and Catholicism; Dante Alighieri, *Comedy*; Dostoevsky, Fyodor; Eucharist; Orthodox tradition; political theology and the absent God; Protestants and Protestantism; truth and transformation
"Christ's Christmas Tree" (Dostoevsky), 179
church, (lack of) presence of Christ in, 145
Cohen, Hyman, 26
Comedy (Dante). *See* Dante Alighieri, *Comedy*
common life, Hume's conception of, 48, 53, 57
common sense, Rorty on, 50–51
complementarity, Bohr's concept of, 30
conceptualism, of Ockham, 69–71
Constantine (Roman emperor), 140
contingency: conceptualism and, 71; nominalism and, 66–67; Rorty and Hume on, 44–48, 53, 66–67
Contingency, Irony, and Solidarity (Rorty), 43, 44, 49, 53
Copernicus, Nicholas, 76
Coyne, Ryan, 27
Crime and Punishment (Dostoevsky), 180, 183, 185, 186–87
Critique of Pure Reason (Kant), 105
Crystal Palace, Great Exhibition (1851), 187, 188
Cupitt, Don, 183, 195n22
Cutler, Sir John, 82n15

Dante Alighieri, *Comedy*, 10, 155–70, 200, 202; on abandonment of hope and journey through hell, 156, 163–67; apophaticism of, 156; atheism in, 155–58, 169–70, 171n5; Christ, belief in, 157–58; on divine absence, 147–48n9; heretics in *Inferno*, as atheists, 156; hope as underlying energy of, 156, 158–63, 171n12, 172n15; love in, 156, 157–58, 163; Pauline stumbling block and, 103n48; pride in, 161, 169,

170, 171–72nn14–15, 171n12; provisionality of hell in, 172n18; sin and atheism in, 157, 166–67, 171n5; sin and beatitude in, 172n22; spiritual journey of Dante in, 167–70, 172n23
Darwin, Charles, 24
Daston, Lorraine, 14n34
Dawkins, Richard, 2, 3, 76, 79, 87, 88, 90, 98, 100
"Dead Christ" (Holbein), 178, 181
debates between theists and atheists, 41, 60n5
de Botton, Alain, 87–88
de Lubac, Henri, 199–200, 202
Dennett, Daniel, 2, 76, 79, 86–87, 88, 90, 99, 103n36
Derrida, Jacques, 12n8
Descartes, René, 66, 73–75, 82n20
Dewey, John, 42, 59n1
d'Holbach, Paul-Henri, 6
dialectical materialism, 106
Dialogues Concerning Natural Religion (Hume), 43, 60n5
Diary of a Writer (Dostoevsky), 191
Diderot, Denis, 6
Diogenes, 5
diversity. *See* race/gender
divine revelation: sacramentalism and, 116; scripturalism and, 120–21
Dix, Morgan, 20
Does God Exist? (Küng), 183
Dostoevsky, Fyodor, 10, 175–94, 202; on atheism as God substitute, 185–92; on basic trust, 179–83; death of first wife, 179, 185; on divine absence, 144; existential approach of, 175, 177; God/life in, 183–85; Heidegger and, 181; Kierkegaard compared, 177, 178, 182, 184, 186, 188, 189, 195n8, 196n34; mendacity and self-deception of characters of, 193–94, 197n56; Orthodox tradition and, 180, 188–89, 191, 194n2; on personal immortality, 178–79; on pros and contras of atheism and Christianity, 175–76; Russian nationalism of, 191–92, 196–97n53; Russian nihilism and, 178, 180, 184, 186, 187, 189–90, 193, 196n43. *See also specific works*
Douglass, Frederick, 8
drama of atheism, 11, 199–202
Drama of Atheist Humanism, The (de Lubac), 199–200
"Dream of a Ridiculous Man, The" (Dostoevsky), 193

Eagleton, Terry, 79, 85, 86, 88–89, 90–91, 200
Eckhart, Meister, 106, 123
Einstein, Albert, 9–10, 19–33, 200, 201; antisemitism of attacks on, 21–22, 26–27; atheism, denial of, 35n37, 35nn37–38; classical theism, commonalities with, 29–30, 32; on free will and deterministic cosmos, 27–28, 31–32; Hitler, alleged excusing of behavior of, 26–27; lecture on religion and science, 24–27; mismatching of theology and cosmology of, 29–30, 32, 37n52; *New York Times Magazine* article on religion and science, 23–24; pantheism's equation with atheism and, 19–21; perspectival pantheism and, 32–33, 201; public outcry over theories and comments of, 21–27; on quantum disturbances, 30–31; on rationality and mystery of universe, 24, 27–28, 101n1; relativity, theory of, 21–23, 28–30, 36–37n50, 36nn47–48; Spinoza's God, on adherence to, 22–23, 27–28, 35n28, 37n52
Eliot, George, 76
Emerson, Ralph Waldo, 20, 59n1
empty throne, Christian iconography of, 137–39, 149n26
End of Faith, The (Harris), 2, 102n10
Enquiry Concerning Human Understanding (Hume), 52, 54–55
Enquiry Concerning the Principles of Morals (Hume), 47, 59
Epicurus, 5
Erikson, Erik H., 182–83
Essays Moral, Political and Literary (Hume), 41
essentialism, 70–72
ethics, atheism, and religion. *See* truth and transformation
Eucharist: abandonment and presence in, 132; in apophatic theology and sacramentalism, 116–17
European philosophy, atheism in, 12n8
Eusebius of Caesarea, 140
Existence of God, The (Swinburne), 4

Farinata degli Uberti, in Dante's *Comedy*, 171n2
feminist perspective on New Atheists, 86
Fergusson, David, 86, 88, 89
Feuerbach, Ludwig, 7–8, 14n39, 105, 186, 196n36, 199
Fichte, Johann Gottlieb, 186

fictionalism, 111, 121–22, 125nn47–48
fideism, 117–18, 121, 124n34
final vocabulary, Rorty on, 49–51, 58, 59
1 Corinthians. *See* truth and transformation
Flew, Anthony, 4
folly and wisdom, 1 Corinthians 1:18–25 on, 91–94, 95, 96, 100
Foster, Kenelm, 157
Foucault, Michel, 15n44
Fowler, Dean, 37n52
Frankenberry, Nancy, 21
Freedom essay of Schelling, 123n8
Freehof, Solomon B., 24
free will, Einstein on, 27–28, 31
Frege, Gottlob, 124n10, 220
Freud, Sigmund, 44, 46, 105, 183
fundamentalism: Einstein, attacks on, 26–27; New Atheist identification of religion with, 2–4
Furey, Constance M., 11, 199, 205

Garasse, François, 5
Gautier, Théophile, 5
Geach, Peter, 67–68, 81n3
gender. *See* race/gender
generalized apophatics, 111, 112–15
generalized nominalism, 114
glory and glorification, 134–37
Gnosticism, 135
God: Dostoevsky on atheism as substitute for, 185–92; meaning(s) of, 107, 213n4
God and Philosophy (Flew), 4
God Delusion, The (Dawkins), 2, 3, 87
God Is Not Great (Hitchens), 2
Goldstein, Herbert S., 22–23
Great Exhibition (1851), 187
Greek antiquity, atheism in, 5
Gregory of Nazianzus, 137, 140

Hamilton, William, 175–76
Harris, Sam, 2, 87, 88, 102n10, 102n15
Hart, David Bentley, 85–86, 89, 90, 91
Hegel, Georg Wilhelm Friedrich, 42, 61n18, 186, 195n8, 199
Heidegger, Martin, 42, 61n18, 105–7, 123n2, 124n20, 181
Heine, Heinrich, 186
heterodoxy, atheism as, 6, 156
hetoimasia, 138
Hick, John, 194n4
history, Hume's approach to, 45–48, 53, 55
History of England (Hume), 46–47
Hitchens, Christopher, 2

Hitler, Adolf, 26–27
Hobbes, Thomas: essentialism rejected by, 70, 71; Hume influenced by, 55; Nietzsche and, 78–81; nominalistic logic of, 68, 69, 70, 79, 81n4
Holbein, Hans, "Dead Christ," 178, 181
Holy Spirit, theorizations about, 131, 132, 133
Hope in a Secular Age (Newheiser), 202
hope in Dante's *Comedy*. *See* Dante Alighieri, *Comedy*
Hume, David, 10, 11, 66–67, 71–76, 82n18, 105, 200, 201. *See also* Rorty, Richard, and David Hume; *and specific works*
Humpty-Dumpty, in *Alice in Wonderland*, 65, 67, 69
hypothesis, atheism as, 1, 2–3

identity, atheism as, 6–8
Idiot, The (Dostoevsky), 178–79, 181–82, 184, 193
India, atheism in, 15n47
Insulted and the Injured, The (Dostoevsky), 180, 195n17
Investiture Controversy, 132
invocationalism, 111, 118–20, 122
Ironic Hume, The (Price), 51–52
irony, of Rorty and Hume, 48–53, 57, 60n13, 61n18
Islam: belief, definition of religion as, 9; Harris on extremism in, 87, 102n10; political theology of Christianity compared, 131; scripturalism in, 120

James, St., in Dante's *Comedy*, 156, 158–61
James, William, 11–12, 59n1, 82n19
Jammer, Max, 25
Jews and Judaism: antisemitic attacks on Einstein, 21–22, 26–27; Christian displacement and supersession of, 144, 149–50n38; as Christian *katechon*, 143, 144; on Einstein, 22–23, 24, 25–26; political theology of Christianity compared, 131; sacramentalism in, 111; scripturalism in, 120
Justin Martyr, 5

Kant, Immanuel, 23, 56, 105, 178, 179
kataphatic theology, 105–6, 108, 110, 111, 112, 115, 116, 120, 122–23
katechon, 143, 144, 145
Kenny, Anthony, 118, 119, 125n39
Kepler, Johannes, 23

Kierkegaard, Søren, 177, 178, 182, 184, 186, 188, 189, 195n8, 196n34
Killing Fields, The (film), 200
Küng, Hans, 183

la Faye, Jacques de, 19
Laplace, Pierre-Simon, 75
LeDrew, Stephen, 14n40
Lefort, Claude, 147n4
"Letter to a Physician" (Hume), 46
liberal irony, 48–53, 57, 60n13, 61n18
literature, atheism, and theism, 10. *See also* Dante Alighieri, *Comedy*; Dostoevsky, Fyodor
Livingston, Donald W., 48, 57, 58, 59, 60n12
Locke, John, 42
love in Dante's *Comedy*, 156, 157–58, 163
Luther, Martin, 5–6, 135

Marion, Jean-Luc, 115–19, 124n20, 124n22, 124n26, 124n28, 124n34
Marx, Karl, and Marxism, 8, 80, 85, 186, 187, 199
materialistic atomism, 76
Mawson, Tim, 120
medieval concept of *scientia* and *religio*, 7
metaphysics, atheism, and religion, 105–7. *See also* apophatic theology
Misak, Cheryl, 61n16
moderate skepticism, of Hume, 52–53, 75
modernity and atheism, 6–8
Moltmann, Jürgen, 141, 144, 149n33
"Monotheism as a Political Problem" (Peterson), 139–43
Montemaggi, Vittorio, 10, 103–4n48, 147–48n9, 155, 202, 205
moral relativism, 34n17

names and naming, 65, 67–69
Nancy, Jean-Luc, 12n8
Natural History of Religion (Hume), 46–47, 55
Nazis, 23, 26–27
negative theology. *See* apophatic theology
Neurath, Otto, 67
New Atheists, 1, 2–3, 14n40, 85–91, 100, 200. *See also* specific New Atheists by name
Newheiser, David, 1, 60n3, 170, 200, 202, 205–6
Newton, Isaac, and Newtonian physics, 21, 23, 28–29, 75
New York Times, 25, 35n25
New York Times Magazine, 23–24
Nicholas of Cusa, 106, 123

Nietzsche, Friedrich: Arendt on, 199; Dostoevsky and, 185, 196n32; drama of atheism and, 11, 200; Einstein and, 23, 27; on faith as turning away from world, 185, 200; fictionalism and, 125n48; identified as atheist, 8; metaphysics and natural theology, rejection of, 105–6, 123n2; Rorty influenced by, 42, 44, 45, 46, 61n18
Nietzsche and nominalism, 10, 65–81, 201; Christianity as explicit target of, 79; conceptualism of Ockham and, 69–71; defining and describing nominalism, 65–69; Hobbes and, 78–81; Hume and, 66–67, 71–76
nihilism, Russian, and Dostoevsky, 178, 180, 184, 186, 187, 189–90, 193, 196n43
nominalism: generalized, 114; Nietzsche and (*see* Nietzsche and nominalism)
North American liberal society, Rorty's promotion of, 53, 54
"Notes from Underground" (Dostoevsky), 187–88
Novalis, 19

Ockham. *See* William of Ockham
O'Connell, Cardinal William Henry, 21–23
ontotheology, 105–7, 123
Oppy, Graham, 14n39
Orthodox tradition: Dostoevsky and, 180, 188–89, 191, 194n2; sacramentalism and apophatic theology in, 111
Oxford Handbook of Atheism, The (2013), 4

paganism, 13n25, 135, 140
pantheism: Einstein on adherence to Spinoza's God, 19, 22–23, 24, 25, 27, 31, 35n38, 37n52; equated with atheism, 19–21, 23; perspectival, 32–33, 201; of Spinoza, 19, 23, 106
paradoxical theology, 108–9
parousia, 129, 138–39, 143, 145
Pattison, George, 10, 123n5, 161–62, 170, 175, 202, 206
Paul (apostle), 96, 99, 104n48, 130. *See also under* truth and transformation: folly and wisdom, 1 Corinthians 1:18–25 on; relationship between, in context of 1 Corinthians 1
Pelletier, Jenny, 81n5
Pentecost, 133
"People's Church," Kierkegaard's attack on, 196n34
Peter Lombard, *Sentences*, 158–59

Peterson, Erik, 137, 139–43, 149n33
Phillips, D. Z., 125n37
Phillipson, Nicholas, 46
Philosophical Melancholy and Delirium (Livingston), 48
Pierce, C. S., 59n1, 61n16
Pius XI (pope), 23
Plantinga, Alvin, 4
Plato, 71, 72, 81n9, 106, 115
Plotinus, 106, 108, 123
political theology and the absent God, 10, 129–47, 201; ascension and/as abandonment, 129–34, 137, 144, 146; Christian tradition, atheistic kernel at heart of, 129–30; church, (lack of) presence of Christ in, 145; comparison of Christianity, Islam, and Judaism, 131; divine transcendence and impossibility of political theology, 139–42; empty throne, Christian iconography of, 137–39, 149n26; glory, anxieties masked by, 134–37; Holy Spirit, theorizations about, 131, 132, 133; *katechon*, 143, 144, 145; parousia, delay of, 129, 138–39, 143, 145; protest atheism and problem of theodicy, 144–47, 201; return of Christ, dealing with absence of, 143–44; Trinity/trinitarianism and, 134–35, 137, 140–41, 143
polytheism, 5, 33, 41, 46–47, 123n4
Possessed, The (Dostoevsky), 180, 186, 187, 189–92
poverty and the poor, 145, 150n42
practical versus theoretical atheism, 5
Pragmatism as Romantic Polytheism (Rorty), 41
prayer, invocationalism, and apophatic theology, 111, 118–20, 125n37
predication, two-name theory of, 67–68
Price, John Vladimir, 51–52
pride in Dante's *Comedy*, 161, 169, 170, 171–72nn14–15, 171n12
process metaphysics, 106
Prometheanism, 186
Proslogion (Anselm), 121
Protestant Reformation, 6, 132, 145
Protestants and Protestantism: absence of Christ underlined by, 145–46; belief, definition of religion as, 9; Catholics, atheistic accusations against, 5; on Einstein, 24; final vocabulary, Rorty on, 58; modern scientific method, turn to, 6, 7; scripturalism in, 120
protest atheism, 144–47, 201

Proust, Marcel, 51, 61n18
Pseudo-Dionysius the Areopagite, 14n32, 106, 109, 116

quantum disturbances, Einstein on, 30–31

race/gender: antisemitic attacks on Einstein, 21–22, 26–27; atheism, white male focus of most discussion of, 13n21; Hollywood, Cardinal O'Connell's denunciation of, 22; New Atheists, feminist perspective on, 86; North American liberal society, Rorty's promotion of, 53, 54; pantheism, feminized nonanthropomorphism of, 20; "single permanent reality," as Western notion, 61n17
Ramsey, Michael, 44
Raw Youth, A (Dostoevsky), 180
redescription, 47
Reformation, 6, 132
relativism, moral, 34n17
relativity, Einstein's theory of, 21–23, 28–30, 36–37n50, 36nn47–48
religion. *See also* literature, atheism, and theism
Religion and Philosophy (Heine), 186
Religion for Atheists (de Botton), 87–88
religion/theism: academic study of, 8; belief, equated with, 1–3, 9; debates between theists and atheists, 41, 60n5; decline in religious identification, 1; diversity of, discounted by New Atheists, 2–3; Einstein's article on development of, 23–24; fundamentalism, equated by atheists with, 2–4; modern concept of, 8; overlapping with atheism, 41–42, 43, 56–59; relationship to atheism, 1. *See also* apophatic theology; science and religion; truth and transformation; *and specific types*
Roman antiquity, atheism in, 5
Romantics and Romanticism, 186
Rorty, Richard, and David Hume, 10, 41–59, 201; American Pragmatism and, 42, 59n1; contingency of Rorty and Hume's approach to history and common life, 44–48, 53, 55–56, 57, 66–67; distinctions between, 56–57; final vocabulary, Rorty on, 49–51, 58, 59; liberal irony of Rorty and Humean moderate skepticism, 48–53, 57, 60n13, 61n18, 75; overlapping of theism/atheism and, 41–42, 43, 56–59; redescription, 47; resemblances between, 42–44; solidarity of Rorty and Hume's

sympathy, 53–56, 61n23; strong poet, Rorty on, 45–46, 47, 56, 57; true and false philosophers, Hume on, 46–48, 56–59, 60n12, 62n29
Rubenstein, Mary-Jane, 10, 19, 101n1, 201, 206
Russell, Bertrand, 3–4
Russian nihilism, and Dostoevsky, 178, 180, 184, 186, 187, 189–90, 193, 196n43
Ryrie, Alec, 7

sacramentalism, 111–12, 115–18, 121, 122
Sade, Marquis de, 8
Sagan, Carl, 31–32
Sanchez, Michelle Chaplin, 150n44
Sansom, Dennis, 60n13
Sartre, Jean-Paul, 175, 176
Satanism, 125n40
Schacht, Richard, 125n48
Schelling, Friedrich, 123n8, 186
Schiller, Friedrich, and Schillerism, 189–90, 192
Schlegel, Friedrich, 186
Schleiermacher, Friedrich, 23, 178
Schmitt, Carl, 133, 143
Schneider, H. J., 125n47
Schopenhauer, Arthur, 20–21, 23, 34n7, 106, 123n2
Schwartz, Regina, 170
science and religion: Einstein's article and lecture on, 23–27; equation of statements about the world in, 4; medieval concept of *scientia* and *religio*, 7; modern conception of, 6–7; New Atheists on, 2, 3; objectivity of, 14n34; ultimate foundations, ghost of, 76
scientific atheism, 144
scientism, 86
scripturalism and apophatic theology, 111, 120–21, 125n44
secularism and secularization, 1, 8
Sentences (Lombard), 158–59
Shaftesbury, Lord, 60n5
Sheen, Fulton John, 26
Shelley, Percy, 8
Sickness unto Death, The (Kierkegaard), 182
Siebert, Donald, 47
silence, apophatic, 115, 156
sin and atheism in Dante's *Comedy*, 157, 166–67, 171n5
sin and beatitude in Dante's *Comedy*, 172n22
Singh, Devin, 10, 21, 129, 201, 206
skepticism: in ancient philosophy, 113; moderate skepticism, of Hume, 52–53, 75

Socrates, accused of atheism, 5
solidarity, Rorty on, 53–56, 61n23
Solovyov, V. S., 184
sorites paradox, 113
Spinoza, Baruch: Einstein on adherence to God of, 19, 22–23, 24, 25, 27, 31, 35n38, 37n52; pantheism of, 19, 23, 106
Stanton, Elizabeth Cady, 8
Stent, Gunther, 32
Stout, Jeffrey, 59n1
strong poet, Rorty on, 45–46, 47, 56, 57
stumbling block (σκάνδαλον), 1 Corinthians 1:18–25 on, 94–96
Swinburne, Algernon Charles, 82n28
Swinburne, Richard, 4
sympathy, Hume on, 53–56

Tegtmeyer, Henning, 10, 102n31, 103n46, 105, 201–2, 206–7
Tertullian, 140
Thate, Michael J., 148n14
theism. *See* religion/theism
theodicy, problem of, 144–47, 200
Theophilus of Antioch, 5, 13n25
theoretical versus practical atheism, 5
Third Theological Oration (Gregory of Nazianzus), 140
Thomas Aquinas. *See* Aquinas, Thomas
Thoreau, Henry David, 20
Thus Spake Zarathustra (Nietzsche), 185, 196n32
Ticciati, Susannah, 10, 85, 170, 201, 207
Tillich, Paul, 185
Toland, John, 19, 33n1
Tonstad, Linn Marie, 148n12
Totalitarianism (Arendt), 199
transcendentalism, 20
Treatise of Human Nature, A (Hume), 48, 52, 54–55, 61n25
triadic versus binary truth claims, 96–97
Trinity/trinitarianism, 134–35, 137, 140–41, 143
true and false philosophers, Hume on, 46–48, 56–59, 60n12, 62n29
Trump, Donald, 24–25
truth and transformation, 10, 85–101; apophatic theology, impatience of New Atheists with, 86, 89, 90, 98; binary versus triadic truth claims, 96–97; folly and wisdom, 1 Corinthians 1:18–25 on, 91–94, 95, 96, 100; for versus between atheist and theist, 102n31, 103n36, 103n46; Montemaggi and, 103–4n48; New Atheists'

truth and transformation (*continued*)
  failure to account for relationship between, 85–91, 100; relationship between, in context of 1 Corinthians 1, 97–100; shared centrality of truth and effect to atheist/theist argumentation, 86–89; Tegtmeyer and, 102n31, 103n46; theological interlocutors replicating structural separation of, 88–91, 100; Turner and, 86, 89–90, 91, 94, 99, 103n46
Tsing, Anna, 14–15n41
Turner, Denys, 10, 65, 86, 89–90, 91, 94, 99, 103n46, 164–65, 170, 201, 207

Varieties of Religious Experience, The (James), 11
Viereck, George Sylvester, 34n15
Virgil: in Dante's *Comedy*, 156, 164, 169, 172n18; Hume citing, 44, 60n8
Viveiros de Castro, Eduardo, 33

Walberg, Tim, 24–25
Warranted Christian Belief (Plantinga), 4
Washington Post, 25
West, Cornel, 59n1
What Is to Be Done? (Chernyshevsky), 196n36
Whitman, Walt, 20
"Why I Am Not a Christian" (Russell), 3–4
William of Ockham, 66, 69–71, 75, 81n3, 81n5, 81n9
Williams, Michael, 52, 57
Williams, Rowan, 171
Willis, Andre C., 10, 41, 201, 207
Wittgenstein, Ludwig, 44, 46, 118, 125n37
Wright, Phyllis, 27